WORLD POLITICS AND
PERSONAL INSECURITY

HAROLD D. LASSWELL

World Politics

and

Personal Insecurity

THE FREE PRESS, *New York*
COLLIER-MACMILLAN LIMITED, *London*

INTRODUCTION TO THE
PAPERBACK EDITION

By coincidence I am writing this new Introduction about the same number of years after World War II that *World Politics and Personal Insecurity* was originally published after World War I. Since the configurative method is recommended as an appropriate tool for use by the thinker who is seeking to orient himself in the manifold of past, present, and future events it is of more than casual interest to consider the validity of the findings tentatively put forward when the volume was first made public. Although one cluster of predictions or forecasts cannot be the basis for a conclusive. test of the validity of a method, it is undeniable that if subsequent events have occurred as anticipated they must be given some evidentiary weight.

APPRAISAL

A major concern at the time—and one that has not entirely receded from world politics—was whether the articulate bearers of the latest world revolutionary innovation would succeed in unifying this divided globe. The answer was "no"; and the answer is confirmed by the facts to date.

The reply rested upon an analysis of the balance of factors that affect the diffusion or restriction of the patterns that appear at eruptive centers of drastic elite and symbol innovation. Given the fundamental structure of a divided world arena, characterized by the expectation of violence and the resulting power-balancing process, and by the latent strength of parochial demands, expectations, and identifications, the probabilities were heavily against total diffusion.

We posed another question, however, and one of more far-reaching import for the shape of things to be. Granted that unity will not be attained, will all the powers in the world arena nevertheless move toward internal homogeneity? If so, the pattern of homogeneity is the true world revolution of our time. It is not to be confused with the content proclaimed by the myth in the name of which the Bolsheviks originally seized power. For the elites of the Communist zone, like the elites of the non-Communist zone, are subject to the new constellation of material and symbolic factors that stabilize a new pattern of power.

In this connection the principal hypothesis, the chief developmental construct, was the probable shift of the dialectic of development from the class struggle to the skill struggle. Centralized and collectivized states, or semi-socialized states would be dominated by the rival power demands of specialists upon the management of violence, propaganda, goods, and services. Intellectuals would appear in every coalition and make articulate the sub-myth of every ally.

I suggest that this part of the construct has been vindicated by ensuing events that have dramatized the struggles among party officials and government bureaucrats; military officers, political police, and party leaders; industrial managers, party doctrinnaires, and agitators; scientists, engineers, and party men; nonskilled, semiskilled, and skilled workers (in agriculture or in industry).

Attention was called to the interplay of less obvious participants in the total processes of politics, especially to the dialectic of personality forms and of groups identified with perspectives favorable or unfavorable to styles of life in which internalized or externalized outcomes are ascendant. I spoke of the "war of extermination against the introverted types" in both the United States and the Soviet Union based upon the insecurities, elite and non-elite, and generated by the apprehension aroused by privacy and seclusiveness.

I think it is not exaggerating the picture to say that the image in *World Politics* bears an intelligible relationship to the physiognomy of the contemporary arena of public affairs. Who believes that the world is in fact a unified system of public order? Or that the expectation of violence has been made less rather than more vivid by the technology of modern weapons? Or that parochialisms are less potent in the industrial-apprentice states of Africa, Asia, and South America? Or that the demand for power has become less intense as an end in itself or as a base for other values? Or that the demands for equality or supremacy are less exigent than they were?

PROJECTION

Suppose we follow our own advice and once again reconsider our orientation in the matrix of past, present, and future events. The first step is to adopt the equilibrium pattern of thought and examine the changing weight of factors that condition the principal trends in world social process. We begin with science and technology, with knowledge of nature, and the changes occurring in the division • of labor.

The Dawn of Astropolitics

This brings us to the age of space. Man's traditional habitat is expanding or is on the edge of expanding in two ways: (a) by the launching of manufactured satellites; (b) by occupation of existing astral bodies. Sooner or later it is proposed to colonize selected locations in outer space.

Is it probable that the power elites of Earth can join peacefully with one another for the purposes of terrestrial security and of reaping the abundant rewards that are potential in the unending reaches of outer space? Or, on the other hand, will the leaders of mankind stumble into annihilative war with one another while standing at the threshold of hitherto undreamed of achievements? Is it probable that men will carry the fundamental structure of our divided Earth to the larger environment, thus bringing into the arena of eventual war parts of the universe hitherto unaffected by our parochial contentiousness?

As we ponder the future of man in space it is important to think of the contingency—presumably remote—that as our explorers and communication probes reach farther out they encounter advanced forms of life. Three possibilities are present: (a) the new life forms are inferior in their command of science and technology to Earth; (b) the level is approximately the same; (c) the new forms of life are superior.

In case (a) a divided world will presumbaly extend the struggle for colonies into outer space, or mitigate the dangers of such a course by applying some version of the trusteeship principle. In case (b) a divided world will be disposed to compete for partners in the coalitions that prevail in the astropolitical arena. In case (c) mankind faces the shocking possibility of becoming an object of colonial policy.

After Man, What (or Whom)?

This carries us to another body of scientific research and development whose implications for the future are, if possible, more startling and decisive than the coming of astropolitics. I refer to the mutants that may come into existence in laboratories of embryology, and to machines that approximate advanced forms of life so closely that the differences are tenuous or indistinguishable. It is thinkable that case (c) may contain mutants or machines superior in intellectual capacity, if not in other respects, to man.

The Coming Crisis of Identity

The probability is that the immediate future contains a unique challenge to man's conception of himself and of the values of human dignity to which so many of us are heavily committed. The question of identity will be posed as the margin between "man"—or even "life"—and "machines" approaches a vanishing point. Even today it is no longer out of the question to design machines that repair themselves or reproduce their kind. More to the point, machines can be made with inbuilt criteria of "enjoyment" and with the capability of learning through experience and of creating culture. The built-in criteria, if unspecified in finer detail, permit novel behaviors to appear.

Shall we treat "machines" with the same deference that we give ourselves as an advanced form of life?

The same issue will appear in connection with the products of laboratories of embryology. Induced mutants have at least the advantage of belonging to the traditional realms of "life." When a machine is involved it is not easy to overcome the original image of "thingness." We must, of course, be prepared to meet living systems whose central integrative plan is quite differently organized from the brain and nervous system of man.

Shall the symbol "human" be redefined to bring within its field of reference many phenomena that we now tend to exclude? Shall we retain the current identification of the "human" with the biological envelope called *homo sapiens* and merge the "higher" characteristics of man with a larger category—"advanced forms of life"—in which the human species may one day play an honorific if subordinate role? More specifically: when shall we extend the protection of the Charter of Human Rights to "machines" and "mutants"?

We do not ignore the possibility that public policy will perceive the latent threat to man's supremacy and adopt effective measures in time to control the introduction of advanced forms into the social, hence the political, process. In view of the many factors that stand in the way of forethought and action of the kind *it is more likely*

that man will become the creator—and the creature—of his own suc-
cessors.

A Potential Myth: The Machinehood of Humanity

If performance by machines becomes increasingly impressive a
general sense of ego diminution will assail many men. Up to the
present it has been traditional for human beings to defend themselves against disturbing comparison with the machine by sym-
bolically inflating the identification of the ego with a glorified version of man. In this frame of reference machines are alleged to lack
qualities of a positive kind that are self-ascribed to human beings,
such as a sense of right and wrong, or capacity for love. The machine is called "automatic," deficient in free choice, since it is
planned by outside forces (in this case, by men) who build con-
straints upon freedom into the machine.

Let us suppose that as machines gain versatility these considerations become less persuasive. A new situation arises that may very
well call into existence a new ideological orientation. The way is
open to adopt a program of ego alleviation that inflates the capa-
bilities and attributes of the machine and abstains from denigrating
its weaknesses. Thus enhanced the machine becomes an eligible
target for incorporation into the self system. In this context the
self becomes more commendable as it approximates the machine.

Machines and men are then perceived as in pursuit of common
goals. All previous evolution can be understood as prelude to the
full machinehood of humanity. The slow attainment of machinelike
qualities can be described during prehistoric and historic times as
man learned preciseness. Folk societies past or present are notoriously
unresponsive to the rhythm of the clock with its implacable beat of
the hours, seconds, and microseconds. It was not until cities were invented that urban civilization gradually habituated man to approximate the preciseness that comes so naturally to the machine.

Folk societies could only rely upon the repetitive patterns of the
dance, of the rite, of etiquette to impose discipline upon spontaneity
and innovativeness. Urban civilization added new means of stabiliz-
ing expectations in regard to conduct, especially law and the state.
It appears that man achieved precision in the management of large
aggregates of men in the execution of complex enterprises when he
engaged in vast public works and in large-scale preparation for war.

Gradually—or so the story may go—the role of law and government in man's evolution toward machinehood was taken over by science. Science consolidated primitive tools into intricate machinery and honed the mathematical and mensurational instruments that made it feasible to achieve preciseness on a previously undreamed of scale. In the latest stages of urban civilization man has nurtured the means of his own supercession and fulfillment. He has created an object—not in his own image as some of the previous gods were—but in the image of his highest aspirations. Man may subside into a fossil, living or dead; at least he will have performed an unprecedented role of midwifery in cosmic evolution.

Variations Upon Kindred Themes

It is not to be assumed that myths of the kind, once formulated, will at once commend themselves to all significant participants in the world community. Quite apart from the overhang of traditional perspectives among human beings, it is not to be taken for granted that members of the rising machine culture will welcome the implied identification with man. Many of the newly ascendant elite may be in no mood to celebrate their historical dependence upon human life.

Resistances of the kind among the machine elite may lead to a counter-myth that relegates man to an inferior caste position in the new cosmic order. It may be asked, for example, how a lower caste can possibly create a higher. Evidently a common comprehensive intelligence planned man—an imperfect, erratic machine—and the climactic emergence of the machine. There is no justification for giving deference to man, who is after all a machine that failed.

In the long run it may be easier to leap the ideological gap that separates man from the machine than to cross the divide that separates man from advanced forms who think of their ancestors as living beings. There may be reluctance on the part of human beings to recognize that super-mice or super-insects are legitimate embodiments of the ideal of supermen.

For millennia many members of the human species have looked upon these early forms with indifferent condescension or active animosity. If we have been ambivalent about mice or even cockroaches we have been in little doubt about mosquitoes. If laboratory experiments eventually usher into existence advanced forms of life whose visible structure simulates one of the hitherto lowly or inimical species it will be difficult to overcome the age-old superiority feelings of an upper for a lower caste in the biological realm. And the barrier on the other side may be higher if the members of a super-form identify themselves in any way with the past of a species that has suffered the contempt or the biological warfare of man.

We conclude again that "politics can assume no static certainty; it can strive for dynamic techniques of navigating the tides of insecurity generated within the nature of man in culture." And we amend today: "the tides of insecurity generated within the nature of man and of all other advanced forms with a culture."

HAROLD D. LASSWELL
Yale University
New Haven, Connecticut

PREFACE

The substance of this book was delivered as a series of Social Science Divisional Lectures at the University of Chicago in the spring of 1932. Part of the analysis of Marxist symbolism was included in a lecture given on the Harris Foundation at the University of Chicago in the summer of 1933, and published in *Public Opinion and World Politics*, edited by Quincy Wright (Chicago, 1933). The analysis of the psychological consequences of prosperity and depression, found in Chapter 7, was read before the American Historical Association at the Urbana meeting during the Christmas holidays of 1933. A portion of the final chapter has appeared in the *International Journal of Ethics*.

My genial and indulgent colleagues in this series, T. V. Smith, of *Beyond Conscience*, and Charles E. Merriam, of *Political Power— Its Composition and Incidence*, have put me in their debt for helpful comments upon the manuscript; Quincy Wright made available the materials assembled in the course of his investigation of the causes of war; the Social Science Research Committee of the University of Chicago has been of material assistance; and Bruce L. Smith has waged a courageous though losing battle on behalf of readability. Robert E. Park was absolved by his world tour from the onerous chore of examining this document; hence it is possible, without binding him to the enterprise, to record my long standing indebtedness to his sagacious insight and my appreciation of his respect for creative interplay between hours of high abstraction and days of patient contact with humble detail. Then there is my obligation to an inimitable friend of the last twenty years, William Cornell Casey, now of Columbia University, whose great acumen and tempered sensitivity are liberating and fructifying respites from an epoch heavy-laden with rancorous sterility.

H. D. L.

Chicago, Illinois,
November, 1934.

CONTENTS

[xv]

CONTENTS

WORLD POLITICS AND
PERSONAL INSECURITY

Part I

METHOD

Chapter I

THE CONFIGURATIVE ANALYSIS OF THE WORLD VALUE PYRAMIDS

Political analysis is the study of changes in the shape and composition of the value patterns of society. Representative values are safety, income, and deference. Since a few members of any community at a given time have the most of each value, a diagram of the pattern of distribution of any value resembles a pyramid. The few who get the most of any value are the *élite;* the rest are the rank and file. An élite preserves its ascendancy by manipulating symbols, controlling supplies, and applying violence. Less formally expressed, politics is the study of *who gets what, when, and how.*[1]

The analysis of world politics therefore implies the consideration of the shape and composition of the value patterns of mankind as a whole. This necessitates the comparison of world élites in terms of social origins, special skills, personal traits, subjective attitudes, and sustaining assets, such as symbols, goods, and violence. Attention is particularly aroused by any fundamental change in the characteristics and methods of élites. A *revolution* is rapid and extensive change in the composition and the vocabulary of the ruling few; *world revolutions* are those which inaugurate new principles of élite recruitment and the new reigning ideologies in the political life of humanity.

No doubt the French and Russian revolutions were major innova-

1. This statement of the field of politics may be put in the perspective of current writing by consulting G. E. G. Catlin, *The Science and Method of Politics,* New York, 1927; Harold J. Laski, *Politics,* Philadelphia and London, 1931; Edgar A. Mowrer, *Sinon, or the Future of Politics,* London, 1930; Gaetano Mosca, *Elementi di scienza politica,* Second Edition, Turin, 1923; Roberto Michels, *Corso di sociologia politica,* Milan, 1927; Carl Schmitt, *Der Begriff des Politischen,* Munich and Leipzig, 1932. See also my lecture, "The Strategy of Revolutionary and War Propaganda," in *Public Opinion and World-politics,* Lectures on the Harris Foundation, Quincy Wright, Editor, Chicago, 1933; Charles E. Merriam, *Political Power,* New York and London, 1934.

tions in the world history of rulers and ruling symbols, although we may entertain some reservations on our judgment when we remember the extent to which we are saturated in the details of European history, and the meagerness of our information about oriental, "primitive," and ancient peoples.[2]

If the significant political changes of the past were signalized by revolutionary patterns which rose and spread until they were blocked or superseded by new revolutionary innovations, the future may follow the same course of development. Hence our "present" would be transition between the latest and the impending world revolutionary emergent.

Correct self-orientation would therefore consist in discerning the principle of élite recruitment and the predominant symbols to appear in the next phases of world political change. Sound political analysis is nothing less than correct orientation in the continuum which embraces the past, present, and future. Unless the salient features of the all-inclusive whole are discerned, details will be incorrectly located. Without the symbol of the total context the symbols of details cannot be data.

Our method comprises the ways of action self-consciously employed in the search for proper orientation. The configurative method of political analysis consists in the use of concepts of *development* and *equilibrium,* and in the adoption of *contemplative* and *manipulative attitudes* toward political change.

Developmental analysis construes particular details with reference to tentatively held conceptions of the élite-symbol changes toward which or away from which events are moving. Correct developmental analysis applied to any happening between the French and the Russian revolutions would have stated the significance of the episode as an approximation toward or away from the emergence of an élite to supplant the aristocracy and the bourgeoisie in the name of "proletarian socialism." Adequate developmental analysis applied to the world since 1917 would construe it in relation to the next élite-symbol constellation which is to arise.

Equilibrium analysis considers details as exhibiting quantitative

2. Eugen Rosenstock names five European revolutions in *Die europäischen Revolutionen,* Jena, 1931, where he also distinguishes between "total" and "partial" revolutions. Modern conceptions of the "élite" and of "ideology" derive from the Marxist literature as critically elaborated by Sorel, Max Weber, and Pareto. See especially Karl Mannheim, *Ideologie und Utopie,* Bonn, 1929; W. Y. Elliott, *The Pragmatic Revolt in Politics,* New York, 1928.

shifts in the dimensions of the variables in terms of which political changes are stated. Large changes in the composition of the élite may be treated as functions of large changes in the prevailing division of labor; hence, through any time section, the probability of élite alterations will be increased if the processes of production have notably altered.

Developmental and equilibrium modes of analysis may lead up to the statement of "laws" or "principles." Contemplative attitudes toward reality are especially appropriate to the generalizing of "laws" of change. A more active attitude toward the rearranging of reality is taken up when the emphasis is upon ways and means of obtaining transformations in the familiar patterns of reality. By casting analysis in manipulative form, and specifying the "principles" of management, new possibilities frequently come to the attention of the thinker. The configurative method of analysis requires of the analyst that he explore every mode of orientation which will increase the probability of success in his quest for correct characterizations of the relevant aspects of totality.

Events since 1917 may be viewed as a process in the course of which the latest pattern of world revolution *diffused* from its center of origin in Russia, or was *restricted* in relation to it. *Total diffusion* occurred whenever adjacent territory was incorporated within the Soviet Union. Most diffusion has been *partial*, restricting the scope of the élite which first utilized the new symbols and practices of the revolution. Political movements elsewhere took over some of the vocabulary and certain of the methods of the Russian élite. Italian Fascism and German National Socialism were in some respects equalitarian and socialistic. A single party exercised a monopoly of legality; social functions were extensively governmentalized; functional bodies advisory to the executive were substituted for territorial legislatures; plebiscites took the place of parliamentary types of election.

Restriction by *partial incorporation* has gone hand in hand with restriction by such processes as *geographical* and *functional differentiation*. Geographical differentiation devalues the universal claims of the élite at the original center by stressing the parochial character of the revolution. The revolution in the name of all mankind thus became the "French" revolution; the revolution in the name of proletarians everywhere has become the "Russian" revolution. Functional differentiation denies the universality of the latest world revolution by stressing the special features of the élite which profits by using universal symbols. Hence the revolution on behalf of the rights of man became the "bourgeois" revolution, and prepared the way for the next successful protest symbols of the "proletariat." Possibly the Russian Revolution will mark the rise, not of the factory worker and the agricultural laborer, but of certain intellectuals and semi-intellectuals capable of exploiting the discomforts of the manual workers. Recurring protests against "bureaucracy," and unmistakable sensitiveness to "bureaucratic" accusations on the part of the ruling few in the Soviet Union, may signalize the early stages in the attainment of greater class consciousness by lower and broader layers of the manual laborers. So handicapped are the manual workers in finding a common name, a vivifying myth, and an effective policy that their challenge cannot soon prevail; indeed, the more acute phases of this form of class struggle may be indefinitely postponed in the Soviet Union, while the skill struggle intensifies instead. This may be the era in world history in which the active elements of the lower middle classes, sadly divided and goaded to the politics of desperation, are making themselves effective in Russia, Italy, Germany, and elsewhere, in revolt against their plight.

The developmental perspectives briefly sketched in the foregoing paragraphs may be profitably reconsidered in the light of equilibrium theories of political change. Shifts in the volume and distribution of values are affected by overt acts of conscious *striving*, like fighting, negotiating, adjudicating, persuading, boycotting, rewarding, or propagandizing. Since these overt acts are modified by the particular *symbols* with which they are associated, the scope of political inquiry must be broadened to include such symbols. Fighting, spending, and ceremonial conduct are affected by the spread of identifying symbols like "nation," "state," "class," "race," "church." The growth of demands, as for "security," "equality," and "supremacy," has some effect on what is sought in the name of symbols of identification. So during the early phases of nationalistic movements, the principal demand has often been for equality of status in the name of cultural unity; but statehood once achieved, nationalism has incorporated imperialistic demands for dominion over alien cultures. The energy which flows into the demands in the name of common symbols depends upon the accompanying expectations of success or failure. If revolution be held inevitable in our time, if the victory of civilization over barbarism impends, if the triumph of the Cross over the Crescent is sure and soon, men's energies are poured out freely for the cause. Ardor dampens as the millennium recedes over the hill of the future and as barbarians and infidels prosper.[3]

The rapidity with which *symbols of identification, demand,* and *expectation* are adopted depends in part on the *insecurity level.* Among embittered and restless people the symbols and practices of the established order are in peril, and the moment is propitious for the speedy diffusion of opposing myths in whose name power may be seized by a challenging élite.

The direction of discharge of insecurities is influenced by the various *foci of attention* in the community. Increasing competition from abroad in the domestic market may be noticed by a few manufacturers who come to believe themselves threatened. The masses of the community may have paid no attention to these particular changes in the origin of commodities in the market, yet it may be possible to arouse a general sense of danger by controlling the press, radio, and platform channels of mass appeal. That a particular group will be successful in capturing attention and guiding mass insecurities as desired depends upon a variety of attending circumstances. At any given time community attention is dispersed over many symbols which compete with one another for loyalty and hatred.

The extent of insecurity is directly affected by the changes in life situations which are produced by shifts in the *division of labor.* A new machine may speed the tempo of work, dispense with factory hands in one locality, improve the competitive position of one plant with another, of one investment group with another, of one portion of the world with another.

Insecurities may also be elicited by altering the distribution of the *instrumentalities of violence* in the environment. The concentration of troops near the frontier may come to the focus of attention of individuals within the community and precipitate insecurities which may be partially assuaged by countermovements.

Insecurities are also subject to changes in the *symbolic environment* which come to the focus of attention. Hence vehement campaigns of denunciation in the foreign press may be expected to arouse hostile forms of counterexpression.

The student of political change is constrained to look beyond overt acts of conscious striving, therefore, and to consider the symbols of identification, demand, and expectation which influence them; and to probe beyond the symbols to the insecurities which are capable of

3. Symbols of expectation are special classes of symbols of fact.

discharge with reference to the objects at the focus of attention; and to press beyond the focus to the alterations in the life situation made by changes in the division of labor, in the movement of instrumentalities of violence, and in primary and secondary contact.

There is no implacable sequence running from variations in the division of labor (a "material" change) or in the instrumentalities of violence or in the symbols of expression to changes in the level of insecurity, the focus of attention, the nature of symbolization, or the acts of striving; the chain may be snapped or bent by intercurrent factors. Changes in the equilibrium which has been attained in any locality through any specific time interval may arise from changes in any factor. In recent generations the tempo has been notably accentuated by the adjustments which have been initiated by the rise and spread of the capitalistic culture complex.

We may pass in rapid review some of the principal features of world change since accelerated shifts in the division of labor arose to modify the previous interrelationships. Our point of departure is the emergence of modern capitalism on the British Isles in the eighteenth century, vastly strengthening the world position of the British, ultimately enabling them to detach the tentacles of Dutch, French, and Spanish control from North and South America, Africa, and India, and to export populations to carry the British variant of Western European civilization to the thinly peopled continents of North America, Australia, and South Africa. The rising British bourgeoisie seized control of the organization area[4] in which they developed, taking over more and more official posts and authoritative emblems, and tearing at many of the surviving limitations upon the free disposition of available men and materials for profitable enterprise.

The growth of British power in the eighteenth century resulted in

4. By an *organization area* is meant the locus of those whose activities are related to formally constituted authority, like states, provinces, municipalities, special administrative, judicial, and electoral districts. A *sentiment area* is the locus of those who are mutually identified, like French or German patriots, or Protestants and Catholics. An *activity area* is the locus of all who perform related acts, like marketing, residing, working, battling. The *attention area* is defined later, and the relations among these various zones are discussed throughout the book. See my memorandum, Appendix A, No. 14, *Conference on Regional Phenomena,* held under the auspices of the Social Science Research Council and the Division of Anthropology and Psychology, National Research Council, Washington, D.C., April 11 and 12, 1930. Issued by the latter, 1930.

the devaluation of the symbols sustaining the ruling régime in the French organization area, and facilitated the struggle of the French bourgeoisie for control. A major result of the French Revolution was to accelerate the diffusion of the capitalistic culture pattern into France, and hence to strengthen the weakened position of the state in the world balance of power. The explosive release of French activity was finally checkmated by counterweights on the continent, like Prussia and Austria, which received aid from prosperous Britain. Within the new society capitalistic specialization was meanwhile creating a protest group, the wage-earning proletariat. The Prussian bourgeoisie, which developed somewhat belatedly, was partly stimulated by the appearance of this new formation to renounce some of its claims for formal recognition within Prussia and to accept favorable policies adopted by the feudal-monarchical régime.

Protected by colossal distances, the feudal-monarchical élite of Russia was able to continue with a minimum of concession to the new technology. Lagging behind the West in the new division of labor, this vast organization area was rudely shocked when Japan, a small outpost of the new technology, inflicted defeat upon it. Weakened in relation to the world balance, their authoritative symbols and practices gravely discredited, the rulers of Russia stood in the exposed position from which they were blown after a protracted war completed their demoralization. The new order in Russia, like the new order in France after the Revolution, encouraged the diffusion of the new technology into an area where it had previously been obstructed. But the new order took control in the name of the proletariat, a symbol which arose in Western Europe as a protest formation against the private control system which developed in connection with the new technology. There has thus been a double diffusion into the Russian area, in which the technological pattern has become associated with symbols which are hostile to the control practices of the West. The new élite was able to take control in the name of Western symbols, despite the small number of wage earners, on account of the weakness of the older administration, the discontent of the peasantry, the absence of a powerful middle class, the compact and often strategic position of the wage earners, and the skill of an élite of professional revolutionists.

During the nineteenth century the spread of the capitalistic pattern brought ever widening tracts of the world into one inclusive activity area. Unable or unwilling to devise methods of maintaining harmonious proportions between production and distribution without sacrificing the capitalistic principle of profitable private enterprise, the influential industrialists were energetic in cultivating foreign markets as soon as their domestic markets were in hand. The growing competitive power of German industry became more and more obvious to the élite in Great Britain, but it was not until naval rivalry was launched that the lines of the world balance began to harden around the relatively fixed pole of Anglo-German rivalry, in a world where the precapitalistic assumption survived, that violence was a normal means of settling interstate differences.

Abetted by its favorable geographical and financial position, Great Britain was able to furnish a huge market for the United States during the years 1914–1917, and ultimately to bring in the United States to redress the balance of power in the Old World, thereby transforming the rhetoric of Canning, uttered a century before, into reality. The expanded industry of the United States was partly used to rebuild Europe and then suffered in the depression of economic life. Today it is left with no promising foreign markets, since Germany, France, and Great Britain are able to offer sharp rivalry for available opportunities. Since the disappearance of free western lands about 1890 deprived the United States of an additional source of economic abundance, the indications are that the community will undergo the civil insecurities which appeared earlier in Europe.

In the industrialized portions of Europe, the workers have followed various national alternatives to the Communism of the Third International, such as Labourism in Great Britain and Social Democracy in Germany. Thus the workers have been incorporated into the ideology of the "nation" rather than the "class." Expanding contacts, through the spread of literacy in the schools, the growth of the press, and widening markets, have thus far strengthened regional areas larger than the district and smaller than the world. Modern capitalism has created so many differences within society that the potential cleavage between proletarian and capitalist has been obscured.

The less industrialized parts of Europe, and of the world beyond Europe, suffer from the insecurities arising from the rapid, though partial, expansion of capitalism, proletarianism, and nationalism into cultures of highly diversified characteristics. The formal incorporation of any community into the U.S.S.R. does not of itself abolish the material and ideological differences which prevail, nor obviate the possible effect of these differences upon the substantive nature of Soviet policy.

Indeed, one of the conclusions which appears to emerge from any survey of the processes which have attended the growth of capitalism or countercapitalism is that the time factors have been grossly underestimated by most of those who have emphasized the leveling and standardizing effects of capitalism. Industrial society differentiates the life situation of the community, multiplying the foci of attention and hence laying the basis for differences in loyalty, hope, and policy. The dynamic tensions within the early dictatorships in the name of the proletariat may themselves indefinitely defer the attainment of material and ideological uniformity.

The processes summarized in the preceding paragraphs have for the most part occurred in an expanding world economy. Despite local variations in employment and prices, commodity production in the world as a whole has steadily risen. It is possible, though as yet uncertain, that 1929 marked a turning point in the history of world economy, signalizing that the contradictions generated by the spread of industrial technique have reversed the trend toward world economy.

As the competitive market spread in the world, more people were enabled to guide their activities by the test of profit, rather than fighting effectiveness or ceremonial prestige. National markets became relatively saturated for certain highly capitalized industries; rivalry for the control of outlying markets increased; new competitive units arose as industrial technique gradually diffused to these outlying regions. More peoples were constantly brought into the active play of the world balancing of power in a world where the assumption of violence as a means of resolving differences among states yet survived. The expanding world economy sharpened contradictions; eventually the appeal to violence transcended the appeal to profit in the world crises of 1914–1918, when the states of the world were divided in two hostile camps who strove to supersede the world economy by creating two self-sufficient economies.

Despite the manifestation of certain tendencies toward the reinstatement of world economy, the trend toward local self-sufficiency has continued in the postwar world. The end result might be the disintegration of the existing world markets, the reduction of the material standard of living, the generation of mass movements of protest whose favorite policies of intensified parochialism would further accelerate the break-up of world economy. One of our ultimate problems is to examine the probable extent of this trend toward disintegration and the possible conditions of its reversal. Certainly the phenomenon is not entirely new for vast areas of the world; it will be remembered that trade reached a low point throughout the

European world after the break-up of the Roman-Imperial system. One aspect of the general problem is to test the extent to which "continental self-sufficiency" can preserve high standards of living despite the modification of the general market. The provisional findings of the equilibrium analysis enable us to reconsider our developmental concepts in a richer setting. The multitude of readjustive processes which are unleashed by locally innovated changes in the division of labor justify us in underlining the improbability that the last world revolutionary pattern will be any more successful than preceding patterns in unifying the peoples of the earth. The equilibrium analysis enables us to stress the highly diversified material environments which preserve highly diversified ideological formations. The restrictive processes of partial incorporation, geographical differentiation, and functional differentiation will probably continue to circumscribe the spread of the Soviet Union and warrant us in the search for signs of new craters of innovation in the world political process.

The contingencies which have been passed in preview in the last few pages by no means exhaust the potentialities of the historical process or the possible fruitfulness of the supplementary use of methods of analysis which have been so often, and so superfluously, opposed to one another. The task of correct self-orientation in the passage from the last major élite-symbol innovation to the next one can be expedited by the self-conscious consideration of details with reference to both developmental and equilibrium patterns of thought. This book is intended to clarify the nature of this procedure, and to enlist the collaboration of others in the more deliberate use of this mode of double analysis. The results which have so far been secured by the configurative method are provisional and incomplete. Much of our attention has been devoted to perfecting categories whose full significance can be appraised only after further research has aligned the data which are called for by their consistent and comprehensive application. The method calls for incessant cross-referencing between developmental and equilibrium terms, and between contemplative and manipulative attitudes toward the data.

The gradual creation of a sense of wholeness, and of assurance in the discovery of interdetail connections within the all-encompassing totality, also requires new methods of formal exposition. The problems arising from the configurative approach are by no means satisfactorily solved in the ensuing chapters. Some formal devices have been employed to convey the sense of interrelatedness and to accustom the thinker to move from any concept or any detail to the consideration of how this starting point of analysis is related to the other starting points which are comprehended within the total configuration. The part of the book which is devoted to "Symbols" begins by considering certain representative symbols in relation to one another and with reference to various other factors, which are loosely called "Conditions" and which include changes in the flow of goods and services, in the movement of specialized instruments of violence, and in the intensity of primary and secondary contact. The section of the book which uses "Conditions" as the point of departure deals with a condition in relation to other conditions and with reference to the symbols which are most closely connected with it. The desire to emphasize the interrelations between contemplative and manipulative attitudes toward reality is expressed in the concluding study of certain problems of "Control."

Now it is impossible to abolish uncertainty by the refinement of retrospective observations, by the accumulation of historical detail, by the application of precision methods to elapsed events; the crucial test of adequate analysis is nothing less than the future verification of the insight into the nature of the master configuration against which details are construed. Each specific interpretation is subject to redefinition as the structural potentialities of the future become actualized in the past and present of participant observers. The analyst moves between the contemplation of detail and of configuration, knowing that the soundness of the result is an act of creative orientation rather than of automatic projection. The search for precision in the routines of the past must be constantly chastened and given relevance and direction by reference to the task of self-orientation which is the goal of analysis.

Although this book pays particular attention to the symbolic aspects of politics, it is only partly described by regarding it as a contribution to the "psychology" or the "psychiatry" of politics. Whatever is relevant to significant change is relevant to the configurative analysis of politics. No doubt "symbolic" processes have been poorly analyzed in political treatises, and it is tempting to impute great importance to whatever has been previously neglected. Our function is not to introduce a new cult but to give a sounder general analysis than has been possible heretofore. No doubt words like "individual" and "collective," "psychology," "social psychology," and "sociology" have performed serviceable functions in the history of systematic analysis in our civilization. But today the multiplicity of relations which are analytically relevant has so expanded that these terms have in many respects outlived their useful-

or I may refer to the Chinese mandarins whose public activities consisted mainly of memorizing, analyzing, and ceremonializing, and who so long survived.

We may be without conscious interest in our "power" position in society, but we cannot escape from the "power" implications themselves. We may be so devoted to a compulsive neurotic ritual of collecting, ordering, condensing, and expelling data that the political implications, aside from modest incomes and great deference from other compulsive personality types, are ignored. We may be oral, impressionistic, agile, and facile, welcoming mainly the approbation of other oral erotics; but the "power" consequences remain none the less. Those who declare that they want truth and are indifferent to control may, indeed, get truth; they are bound to have some control. The mere fact of persisting in a network of interpersonal relations means that one finds a place in, and partly modifies the shape and composition of the current value pyramid, whether one keeps this in mind or not. If one has no clear understanding of the consequences of his acts, he is unable to defend his acts rationally; what he does takes on the color of capricious indulgences, naïvely functioning to relieve the recurring stresses of the living organism, extracting tributes of esteem and purchasing power from some, and receiving sympathetic comprehension from the few whose autobiographies include enough parallelisms to his own biopsychic characteristics and cultural techniques.

The task of locating ourselves as talkers and writers in relation to the pyramids of safety, income, and deference is insuperable at the present, since requisite information about the world is compiled in fragmentary form. Material units of income have been partially compared, and regional, social, and biopsychic traits of those receiving income have been somewhat sporadically studied. Rather few efforts have been made to cope with the more elusive pyramids of deference.[17] The relatively simpler task of studying the man who gets

17. See Pitirim Sorokin, *Social Mobility,* New York, 1927; Fritz Giese, "Die öffentliche Persönlichkeit," Beiheft 44, *Zeitschrift für angewandte Psychologie,* Leipzig, 1928; Leonard D. White, *The Prestige Value of Public Employment in Chicago,* Chicago, 1929, and *Further Contributions to the Prestige Value of Public Employment,* Chicago, 1932; A. W. Macmahon, "Selection and Tenure of Bureau Chiefs in the National Administration of the United States," *American Political Science Review,* 20 (1926):_548–582, 770–811, and "Changes of Bureau Chiefs in the National Administration of the United States," *ibid.,* 23 (1929): 383–403; D. A. Hartman, "British and American Ambassadors," *Economica,* 11 (1931): 328–341; R. T. Nightingale, "Personnel of the British

killed in wars, revolutions, rebellions, revolts, feuds, mobs, gang struggles and judicial administration is carried but a little way.[18]

The emphasis which is here put upon the importance of appraising the total meaning of the developing situation for social values is in many respects parallel to the viewpoint introduced by Marx and Engels into modern social theory. They may be said to have marked the recovery of the political standpoint; they vigorously applied the political perspective to certain features of modern society which had been tacitly exempted from such consideration. The rise of the competitive market in Great Britain, especially in the late eighteenth century, fostered a split in social theory into "political philosophy" and "political economy" in which "political economy" was more and more taken up with the formal relations arising in the competitive market. The innovation of Marx and Engels was the "politicizing" of the competitive market.[19] Marx studied in learned detail the consequences of the competitive market for the value pyramid of society, appraising from this point of view the pecuniary calculus, the law of property and contract, the parliamentary pattern of government, the doctrines and practices of religion, and the prevalent assumptions and methods of science and philosophy.

The perspective of the enterpriser in the competitive market, and of the theorist who views the world from this standpoint is substantially narrowed by preoccupation with the minutiae of the market. The horizon of the capable political thinker is widened to include the whole play of factors which sustain the competitive marketing formation and which may, under discoverable circum-

---

Foreign Office and Diplomatic Service," *American Political Science Review,* 24 (1930): 310–331; Harold J. Laski, "The Personnel of the British Cabinet, 1801–1924," Chap. VIII, *Studies in Law and Politics,* New Haven, 1932; K. Loewenstein, "Zur Sociologie der parlamentarischen Repräsentation in England von der ersten Reformbill," *Hauptprobleme der Soziologie; Errinnerungsgabe für Max Weber,* II, Munich and Leipzig, 1923; L. Rosenbaum, *Beruf und Herkunft der Abgeordneten zu den deutschen und preussischer Parlamenten, 1847–1919,* Frankfurt, 1923; F. W. Taussig and C. S. Joslyn, *American Business Leaders; A Study in Social Origins and Social Stratification,* New York, 1932. Representative of the best older literature is Alfred Odin, *La genèse des grands hommes,* Paris, 1895. Many relevant data are in G. von Mayr, *Statistik und Gesellschaftslehre,* Tübingen, 1914–1922; *Recent Social Changes,* New York, 1933.

18. See S. Rudolf Steinmetz, *Soziologie des Krieges,* Chap. 3, Leipzig, 1929.

19. When Marx foretold the doom of the state, he deviated from sound political analysis. This was a verbal concession to the anarchists and to the propagandistic advantage of rendering the "class-less" society as seductive as possible.

stances, disrupt it. A competitive market occurs when there is a consensus sustained by violence which safeguards bargaining arrangements. The close connection between violence and bargaining was never obscure to the merchants of the Italian cities, for they were compelled to use their own private forces to open markets, defend depots, protect cargoes, and enforce contracts. As the enterpriser in the British domestic market of the eighteenth century and nineteenth century became emancipated from the necessity of providing his own violence, the close connection between violence and bargaining fell into the background. There were, of course, many surviving indications of the classical relation between brigandage and economics, since the foreign trading companies continued to supply their own violence until quite late, and labor troubles sometimes brought unofficial as well as official violence to the front. Yet the peaceful expansion of the domestic market furnished the experiential basis for extensive preoccupation with marketing mechanics.

While the theory of the competitive market was being elaborated, writers about politics continued to repeat the classical Greek and Roman aphorisms about getting and holding "power," without regard to the fact that these formulas lose relevance in social analysis unless constantly redefined and reaffirmed in direct connection with new cultural formations. This work of reapplication was performed for maturing capitalism by Marx and Engels. Their work was not political-particularistic, in the sense that they restricted themselves to describing patterns of "government"; their perspective was political-totalistic, for they sought to assess the meaning of every detail of the total situation for preserving or demolishing particular value pyramids.[20]

Marx and Engels used the usual sources of scholarly investigation, tracing the lineaments of social development by means of books, newspapers, periodicals, manuscript documents, and general observation. These were then, as they remain, the chief *extensive* means of sampling a given configuration. Since Marx and Engels *intensive* techniques have been discovered for the study of personality. Individuals may be investigated by special methods to disclose the genetic sequence of personality development and to place the individual career line in relation to the career lines of others living in the same epoch. It is a question solely of expediency and not of

20. For a critical exposition of the dialectical method, see Georg Lukács, *Geschichte und Klassenbewusstsein; Studien über Marxistische Dialektik*, Berlin, 1923.

principle whether the total configuration is approached extensively or intensively by the individual observer, since either starting point draws the investigator toward the opposite. Indeed, the shift from extensive to intensive techniques, and back again, promises to add great fruitfulness to the modern analysis of human relationships. Intensive personality study has thrown light on the symbolic factors which are interconnected with "material" factors in political change. Indeed, the principal contribution of psychoanalysis, as the most influential intensive method, is to the understanding of the symbolic aspects of historical development, necessitating the elaboration of the original results of the Marx-Engels dialectic.[21]

By concentrating attention on the unconscious components of human action, the possibility of controlling mass insecurity by manipulating significant symbols has been put in new perspective. The uncertainties of the "ideological" reactions to "objective" changes are emphasized. The life situations of thousands may be profoundly modified by changes in the division of labor which influence them in approximately the same degree. Yet the directions of discharge of the resulting anxieties may be highly diversified. Old rituals may be revalidated when the community "takes it to the Lord in prayer," or new targets of collective action may emerge as diagnoses and prescriptions of anarchism, socialism, communism, liberalism, conservatism, republicanism, monarchism, pacifism, internationalism, nationalism, radicalism, individualism, collectivism proliferate. Since the modern division of labor includes persons who are specialized creators of symbols, the management of masses by propaganda has become one of the principal cultural characteristics of our epoch. The rulers of yesterday who depended on bread, circuses, and wars to protect them from domestic disturbances are superseded by rulers who are adept at diverting, distracting, confusing, and dissipating the insecurities of the mass by the circulation of efficacious symbols.

Wars and revolutions are avenues of discharge for collective insecurities and stand in competition with every alternative means of dissipating mass tension. The reduction of violence in world politics

21. See my discussion, "Psychoanalyse und Sozioanalyse," *Imago*, 19 (1933): 377–383; and my *Psychopathology and Politics*, Chicago, 1930. Also Erich Fromm, "Über Methode und Aufgabe einer analytischen Sozialpsychologie," *Zeitschrift für Sozialforschung*, 1 (1932): 28–54, and "Die psychoanalytische Charakterologie und ihre Bedeutung für die Sozialpsychologie," *ibid.*, 1 (1932): 253–277.

means strengthening the competitive power of activities whose human costs are less. The special province of political psychiatrists who seek to develop and to practice the politics of prevention is devising ingenious expedients capable of discharging accumulated anxieties as harmlessly as possible. This age of the "revolt of the masses" or the "era of world wars and revolution" puts the emotions of the masses in the foreground of political events. Sound measures for the removal of unfavorable objective conditions of discontent require mass support; and cherished social values require mass support, or mass deflection, if they are to survive.

The politics of prevention calls for a continuing audit of the world level of insecurity. The political psychiatrist, assuming the desirability of enabling human activities to evolve at a minimum of human cost, approaches the problem of war and revolution as one detail of the whole task of mastering the sources and mitigating the consequences of human insecurity in our unstable world.

Part II

SYMBOLS

Chapter II

NATIONS AND CLASSES; THE SYMBOLS OF IDENTIFICATION

When Ernst Werner Techow, Erwin Kern, and Hermann Fischer assassinated Walther Rathenau in 1922, they invoked the name of the Fatherland, the monarchy, the spirit of Potsdam. When Friedrich Adler shot the Austrian Prime Minister in 1916, he said it was not because he desired publicity, or because he enjoyed the pleasure of murdering his fellow man, but because the working classes required it. When Pilsudski and Stalin robbed banks in the years before 1917, they said it was not because they needed money and adventure for themselves, but because the overthrow of czarism and the liberation of the oppressed working masses of the world demanded it. When the Paris commune was drowned in blood, it was because the interests of "patriotism" and of "civilization" required it. The millions who struggled from 1914 to 1918 in the thin zones which surrounded the Central Powers were fighting for "God," "country," "civilization," "humanity," "international law," "a war to end war," and a "lasting peace."

The role of these justifying symbols in politics is one of the principal topics of analytic inquiry. With which acts are particular symbols connected? How are the justifying symbols grouped geographically throughout the world? How are they related to one another and to the whole context of political change? The embittered paranoiac who slays the first passer-by whom he suspects of turning destructive rays upon him is of mediocre interest to the student of politics, though a paranoiac like Gorgulov who kills the President of France as the "enemy" of his people becomes relevant on account of the target of his act and the accompanying verbalizations. The person who views himself as representative of a larger unity has widened the configuration against which his act is to be construed. To be of greatest interest to us, the act of demolishing another must be enshrined in justifications. The muscle movements must occur in a context of verbal legitimacy. There must be evidence of the process of self-justification by referring to entities larger than the self, another contribution to the voluminous chapter of human history entitled "The Story of Man and His Justifications."

A satisfactory geography of politics would chart the symbols which men invoke to justify their pretensions, and disclose the nature of the acts with which each symbol is affiliated.[1] Our usual maps show the world of "states," but the world of politics is richer, including acts justified in the name of churches, races, nationalities, tribes, classes, and dynasties. From the study of psychological areas we can often surmise the nature of coming changes in the activity and organization areas. Particularistic expressions in the old Dual Monarchy presaged the approaching end of the state and no doubt the spread of class symbols in the contemporary world is the precursor of drastic changes of boundary lines.

If we look with fresh naïveté at the distribution of persons who use common identifying symbols, many anomalies appear. How does it happen that a man living by Lake Michigan identifies himself with a name that includes the population of New York, a thousand miles east, and of San Diego, several thousand miles west, and yet excludes the population of Winnipeg and Toronto? How does he come to associate himself with the "poor white trash" of the South, and not with the farmers of Alberta; or with the blacks of Georgia, and not with the whites of Quebec?

The relationship between geographical features and symbols seems fast and loose. Australians occupy a continent and the whites, at least, have a unifying term, but the Europeans, Asiatics, Africans, North and South Americans, who occupy continents, are split into parochial groups. Those who live in the Mississippi River Valley call themselves by one inclusive name, but those who are settled in the valley of the Danube use many names. Most of the inhabitants of

---

1. Concerning the theory of the symbol in the logical, psychological, and socio-political sense, see E. Cassirer, *Philosophie der symbolischen Formen,* 2 vols., Berlin, 1923–1925; C. I. Lewis, *The Mind and World Order,* New York, 1929; A. N. Whitehead, *Symbolism, Its Meaning and Effect,* Cambridge, Mass., 1928; Charles W. Morris, *Six Theories of Mind,* Chicago, 1932; C. K. Ogden and I. A. Richards, *The Meaning of Meaning,* New York, 1925; the forthcoming posthumous publications of George Herbert Mead; Charles E. Merriam, *The Making of Citizens,* Chicago, 1931; Isidor Ginsburg, "National Symbolism," Chap. 17 in Paul Kosok, *Modern Germany,* Chicago, 1933; John F. Markey, *The Symbolic Process and Its Integration in Children,* New York, 1928.

the principal Japanese islands have a common term, but the North Irelanders are distinct from the South Irelanders. Symbols do not unite all those who live on the great highlands or in the great lowlands of the earth. If the Italian peninsula is, in a fashion, unified, the Scandinavian peninsula is disunited. Geographical zones which are defined by deciduous or coniferous forests, or by characteristic temperature, rainfall, or barometric ranges, do not neatly coincide with areas of identification.

The relations are discrepant even between such highly organized areas as states and the zones of common national sentiment. The German organization area does not now include Alsace and Lorraine, Eupen and Malmédy, Upper Silesia and the corridor, or Austria; Magyars are to be found in the organization area of Roumania, Yugoslavia, and Czechoslovakia; Bulgarians live in Macedonia, Thrace, and the Dobruja; Ukrainians are in Polish Galicia, Roumanian Bukovina, and Bessarabia; Arabs are in French Syria, British Palestine, and elsewhere; Greeks appear in Cyprus, the Dodecanese, and Constantinople. Self-assertive minorities are found within the empires of Great Britain, France, the Netherlands, Japan, Portugal, and the United States.

If we examine the relation between areas of sentiment and of organization, on the one hand, and areas of special activity on the other, instances of noncongruence multiply. The iron and steel manufacturing districts of South Chicago, northern Ohio, and Alabama, together with the Lake Superior ore deposits and various coal and limestone areas, are all included within the United States; but the industrial region of the Rhineland is split between two antagonistic states and nationalities.

The symbols referred to thus far have historically been connected with geographical locations. Another powerful body of symbols has fixed upon some nonspatial characteristic. Most portentous of these is the "proletariat," in whose name various working-class districts of the world are being mobilized to reject the authority of those who use the symbols of "nationalism" or "individualism," and to accept the authority of those who invoke the new verbalism. Even here curious discrepancies reveal themselves, since many of the active proletarians turn out to be lawyers, university graduates, publicists, sons of middle-class or upper-class families, and many of the inactive proletarians prove to be serfs or wage earners in the Southern black belt, in South African mines, or on Caribbean fruit plantations.

No doubt our hypothetically naïve observer would innocently ask why so much stress is put on "place" words or "economic" words as unifying symbols. The wonder grows if one remembers that the number of words which can be used to distinguish one person from another is unlimited. All the curly-haired people might be united in curly-haired consciousness versus all the straight-haired people; all the dry-skinned people might be united against the oily-skinned people; but words about propinquity and tradition and economic standing have thus far outcompeted physical words in the rivalry for human loyalty.

If one took seriously the task of guiding the sentimentalization of likenesses and differences, it would doubtless be essential to sift out very complex types and to christen them appropriately. The world might with some justification be united into those who are thin, leptosomic in physique, schizoid in temperament, and disposed to schizophrenia, and into those who are plumpish, pyknic in physique, manic-depressive in temperament, and disposed to manic depressive psychoses. Dr. Ernst Kretschmer, since he invented this modern synthesis, could be the George Washington of this division[2] and wars could be fought over whether the leptosomes are right in calling him leptosomic, or whether the pyknics are right in calling him pyknic. Dr. Carl Jung has done much to create an "introvert" and "extravert" consciousness in mankind, yet the introverts and extraverts are not yet demanding self-determination.[3]

Now this purely schematic consideration of potentialities in human relations may emancipate some of us personally from automatic loyalty to the particular symbolisms which we have incorporated into our personality. Such formalism, however, is far removed from the state of the circumambient world, where specific national and class differences are taken with so much seriousness. For better or worse we are embedded in historical configurations which are characterized by the existence of a large number of comprehensive symbols in the name of which people die or kill. In examining these phenomena, we may in some respects be guided by the results of intensive personality studies which have disclosed so much about the dynamics of the process of identification itself.

We know that the components of behavior which are prominent in the early history of the organism, but which are modified as un-

2. See *Physique and Character*, New York, 1925.
3. *Psychological Types*, New York, 1924. For the growth of the identification symbolism, reference might be made to Dow Thompson, *A Mind That Was Different*, Harlow Publishing Co., Oklahoma City, 1931.

acceptable to the environment, persist within the adult structure. They display themselves in crassest form during the regressive manifestations of severe mental disease, when the later integrations break up and the earlier coordinations are freed. Such adults may be unable to control their elementary excretions, or to masticate food, or to utter more than primitive cries and sounds. Training does not abolish the earlier action formations of the biopsychic structure but stylizes them in various conventional ways. However, this stylization in the form of appropriate language, gesture, and dress never entirely succeeds; the elementary components secure partial expression as socially irrelevant physiological tensions, as peculiar mannerisms and stereotyped movements, as verbal slips, as forgetting, as embarrassment, as tones of elation or depression. We know that the personality in relation to another personality is reacting with an organism which has been modified in consequence of its whole history in human relations, and that these modifications are comparatively unstable. What we call being civilized consists in using the "appropriate" patterns for the gratification of the elementary and the complicated impulse structures which are activated in particular situations. Only the special student of personality can hope to discern much of the meaning of slight deviations from the conventional, and he can be reasonably sure of his interpretations only when he has an opportunity to examine the personality under specialized conditions.

To say that the organism reacts as an organism means specifically what it says: the organism performs complicated acts of integration whose elementary components are sucking and spitting, biting, swallowing, striking, scratching, tearing, shoving, touching and rubbing, injecting or rejecting genital organs, looking, presenting for inspection, holding, expelling from the mouth, from intestinal, urethral, and genital tracts, running away, cowering and throwing the body. Behavior consists of inordinately complex ways of disposing of such activations. With developed personalities, activity components are stylized in relation to the immediate situations in such ways that the simple acts which are initiated in any situation create tensions which are disposed of smoothly and for the most part indirectly.

We may grasp the hand of the person next to us according to the accepted forms of the social situation, smiling genially; yet repressed hostilities may be expressed in moods of slight depression or constraint, in some speech blocking as one repeats the conventional verbal forms, or in such bodily symptoms as localized skin irritations. The significance of these various formations as compromises between impulses to attack the other person and impulses to inhibit overt hostility can only become manifest when the individual learns how to employ the free-fantasy technique of exposing his reactive structure.[4]

Now what is it that happens when one person becomes emotionally bound to the symbol of another, or to the symbol of the collectivity? An emotional attachment occurs when the symbol of the other is taken as one means of gratifying the affectionate (the libidinal) impulses which are not permitted to exhaust themselves in direct and primitive ways upon the object. Strictly speaking, the symbol of the aspect of the self which is taken by the self to be characterized by an "external" reference secures the libidinal charge.

The emotional relations which are directly relevant to our field of discourse arise in the perception of similarities between an object and ourselves (by partial identification[5]). The necessary prerequisite is the presence of aim-inhibited impulses which are available for redirection toward substitute symbols. We identify with others (a process which is not necessarily accompanied by acute self-awareness) by perceiving that they are from the same college, the same town, the same country; that they admire the same politicians, scientists, or teachers; that they exercise the same skills; that they resemble our past attachments, and so on through an incalculably vast list of possibilities.

The emotional relation to the other is not necessarily positive; we do not invariably remodel ourselves by taking over some feature of his personality pattern. We may react negatively by identifying him with some aspect of our own personality which we deplore as weak or disreputable. In this case we reject the proffered pattern and release profoundly destructive impulses.

Quite often persons are related to the same object (as viewed by a specified observer) without a common externalized symbol of the object, and without a common symbol of all those who are identified with the object. I may be impressed by a stranger whom I see walking alone in the Bois de Boulogne, but my subjective symbol of the stranger may not be related to a name which I could use as an external symbol of the man, or to a symbol of the other people who, unknown to me, have also partially identified with him. This relationship of the man and the several people who have no exter-

4. See my *Psychopathology and Politics,* Chaps. 2 and 3, Chicago, 1930.
5. The identification dynamisms are summarized in S. Freud, *Group Psychology and the Analysis of the Ego,* Chap. 7, London, 1922.

nalized symbols of him or of one another is one which we shall call *multiple identification.* This condition is highly potential for the more complex identification relationships. The transition to *counter-identification* may be very quickly managed when the multiply identified discover one another and develop external symbols of one another and of the person to whom they occupy a common relation. We may learn that the lone stranger in the Bois de Boulogne is Dr. X, who has new theories of stopping disease through irradiation, and we may be disposed to accept and propagate his methods. The disciples of a political sage or the associates of an active agitator may be bound by the ties of counteridentification.[6]

Of great political relevance is *mutual identification,* whose distinguishing mark is the inclusion of persons within the field of reference of the symbol who are beyond the face-to-face experience of any one person. The term "American" includes persons who are dead and gone and those who are geographically remote, and thus beyond the primary experience of those identified with the word. Interlapping identifications among persons in relation to this symbol make such mutual identifications possible.

Some politically significant reference symbols have comparatively circumscribed fields of allusion, like "Gandhi," but others are extremely difficult to characterize. No very circumscribed aspect of the world can be chosen as the reference frame for the "United States"; historically it is by no means certain when sufficient identifications had arisen to constitute a relationship for which a separate name was relevant. "Americans" is a word that does not apply to all who fall within the organization area called the United States of America, for one excludes those who reside within the legal jurisdiction without becoming psychologically organized toward the unifying symbol.

The early subjective life of the infant appears without sharp references to the surrounding objects in the environment. There is no evidence that ego references are clearly separated from environmental references. This imprecise relationship between the ego and its surroundings is recaptured in the sense of cosmic participation so characteristic of states of deep psychic regression. Those who emerge from them can often recount that they felt at one with the sun, the moon, and the stars, that they seemed to occupy the heavens and the earth, being indistinguishable from them, and aware of no boundary between the "I" and the "cosmos." Such mental states can be

---

6. *Identification* is to be distinguished from *affiliation,* in which the conscious components are preponderant.

temporarily achieved by means of drugs, brain concussions, and spiritual exercises.

The environment of the infant and child is teeming with words of ambiguous reference, which take on positive or negative significance long before there is enough contact with reality either to define their frames of reference, or to distinguish those whose frames of reference are wholly indeterminate. As an "adult" the individual continues to respond to these articulations in many childish and juvenile ways, very often imputing some special and even awesome significance to them. Such words are "law and order," "patriotism," "a gentleman and a soldier," "truth," "justice," "honor," "good," "bad," "loyalty," "duty," "Germans," "French," "Negroes," "national hero," "good citizens," "national interest," "king," "constitution"; but these words do not stand alone in primitive concentrations or irrelevant affect. The whole of our vocabulary, plus our non-verbal symbols, is caught in the mesh of early structuralizations of this kind, so that the inner meaning of our symbols is never revealed except through the technique of free fantasy.

Identification with any particular symbol by any person at any phase of his career line initiates a complex process of symbol elaboration. All the earlier loves tend to be reactivated in relation to the new symbol. The individual who late in life experiences "conversion" and becomes an "American" or a "Czech" or a "Lithuanian" or a "Communist" or a "Socialist" or a "Catholic" reads into this symbol the loves and hopes of his entire personality. His elaborations of the symbol will depend upon the forms of expression with which his personality has been equipped through aptitude and training. If he belongs to those who require large emotional responses from the environment, and if he has a facile technique for the oral or written production of language, he may fill the auditoriums of his vicinity with rhetoric and the printing presses with poetry and prose. When the Dreyfus affair in France awakened the Jewish self-consciousness of Theodor Herzl, he quickly expressed himself in lectures, plays, essays, and programs for the recovery of a national home. These symbol elaborations were also determined by the patterns formed for the glorification of a collective symbol of identification within the culture to which he had been exposed. Hence a "Jewish nation" at such a time and place seemed to Herzl to demand immediate statehood.

The displacement of the infantile, childish, and juvenile affects upon symbols of ambiguous reference has led to the creation of remarkable monuments to human vanity. Nations, classes, tribes, and churches have been treated as collective symbols in the name of which the individual may indulge his elementary urges for supreme power, for omniscience, for amorality, for security.[7]

The examination of such symbol structures became one of the interesting exercises of eighteenth century intellectuals as the clashes among organization areas broadened into clashes among "nations." One of the studies of the day was an *Essay on National Pride*, by Dr. J. G. Zimmerman, physician to His Britannic Majesty at Hanover, and a minor literary light.[8] His book appeared two years after the beginning of the Seven Years' War, and he commented shrewdly that "Newton will often be called an almanac maker, and Montesquieu a blockhead, while the French and English struggle with all their power for the mastery of the American trade." The principal part of his essay classifies illustrations of national and tribal symbolism, taken from the history and ethnology of the period. He comments upon "the Greenlander, who laps with his dog in the same platter" and holds himself superior to the Danish invader. "Ask the Carribee Indians who live at the mouth of the Orinoque, from what nation they derive their origin; they answer 'Why, we only are men.' " He repeats the Indian fable of the nation of hunchbacks who derided and scorned the straight backs. "The inhabitants of the Ladrones believe that their language is the only one in the world, and therefore that all the other nations on the earth are dumb." He notes that "the vanity of mankind has ever filled the immense vacuity beyond the authentic memorials of the origin of every nation with fabulous history, at pleasing removing their antiquity to the remotest ages, in order to proportionally increase its luster." He cites "the yet uncivilized inhabitants of Paraguay" who "give to the moon the endearing appellation of mother; and when their parent is eclipsed,

7. The developmental formula of the political personality has been stated as follows:

$$p \rbrace\, d \rbrace\, r = P$$

The symbol p represents private motives, d displacement on to public objects, r rationalization in terms of public interest; P signifies the political man. The d and the r are mainly derived from the contact of the personality with secondary group symbols. See my *Psychopathology and Politics*, pp. 261–263, Chicago, 1930.

8. First Edition, Zurich, 1758. English by Samuel H. Wilcocke, New York. Printed by M. L. and W. A. Davis for H. Caritat, Bookseller and Librarian, 1799. See my "Two Forgotten Studies in Political Psychology," *American Political Science Review*, 19 (1925): 707–717.

they run out of their huts with the greatest activity, and making the most hideous lamentations, they shoot a vast number of arrows into the air in order to defend the moon from the dogs who attack her." Observing that men prefer the diet to which they are accustomed, the Doctor pungently adds, "The love of our country is little more, in many cases, than the love of an ass for his manger."

The prominence of physical features has prompted innumerable attempts to elaborate the superior claims of collective symbols by imputing special significance to bodily characteristics. It was formerly held that the "inferior races" had "ugly" features, such as slant eyes, large noses, flat noses, thick lips. The Japanese soon presented a special problem here, because they showed as much industrial and fighting ability as many Europeans; but they thought the large eyes and the aquiline noses of the West were ugly. The growing recognition of the influence of suggestion on forms of aesthetic taste renders such comparisons of relative "beauty" rather ludicrous. Pigmentation of the skin has also been a focus of "superiority-inferiority" claims, but investigation has revealed that pigmentation scarcely correlates with any agreed index of "capacity."

At the First Universal Congress of Races inventories were made of the bodily details which had been chosen by various people to rationalize their superiority claims. These covered a wide gamut, including pigmentation of the hair, pigmentation of the iris, the pattern of the hair sectioned transversely, the nasal index, the cephalic index, the geometric variations in the form of the cranium or the face, the amount of hemoglobin in the blood, the rapidity of the pulse, "vital capacity," muscular strength, quantity of urine, weight, height, variation in the respiration of civilized and noncivilized women, shape of the female sex organs, shape of the breasts, distribution of fat on women's hips, protrusion of the lower jaw, convolution of the ears, depth and carrying power of the voice, resistance to disease, quantity of water in the tissues, and weight of the brain.[9] Much skepticism prevails among scientists on all efforts to relate somatic differences to general ideas about supremacy.[10]

9. Gustav Spiller edited the *Papers on Inter-racial Problems* of the *Universal Races Congress*, London, 1911.

10. See Jean Finot, *Le préjugé des races,* Paris, 1905; F. H. Hankins, *The Racial Basis of Civilization,* New York, 1926; Franz Boas, *Anthropology and Modern Life,* New York, 1928; Friedrich Hertz, *Race and Civilization,* New York, 1928. The principal result of the general intelligence-testing movement has been to expose subtle cultural differences. See T. R. Garth, *Race Psychology: A Study of Racial Mental Differences,* New York, 1931.

Each symbol of identification is elaborated according to the patterns already existing in the culture for symbols of that class. There are thus preformed praise patterns of symbol and practice available for application to the new symbol. Since our Western European culture was so long dominated by the symbolism of Christianity, the rising national and proletarian movements, quite without premeditation, look over the Christian patterns. A classical instance of this is the famous procession at the first session of the Legislative Assembly in France in the autumn of 1791, when twelve elderly patriarchs went in search of the Book of the Constitution.

> They came back, having at their head the archivist Camus, who, holding up the Book with his two hands and resting it on his breast, carried with slow and measured tread the new Blessed Sacrament of the French. All the deputies arose and bared their heads. Camus, with meditative mien, kept his eyes lowered.[11]

Writers on many of our contemporary symbols of identification have recently become acutely aware of these connections. It is frequently noted how the principal symbol is endowed with godlike attributes, the collective mission is idealized, an elaborate ritualism is evolved about a banner, pledges of unswerving fidelity are taken ("I pledge allegiance to my flag . . ."), holidays (holy days) are observed, the veneration of statues, pictures, and shrines increases, a body of official doctrines is reverently reiterated and stoutly defended, learned commentators elaborate the subtleties of the official ideology, and devices of popularization are exploited to reach every stratum of the supporting community and to proselyte among the unconverted.[12]

The modern phenomenon of nationalism represents a complicated synthesis of religious, cultural, state, democratic, and allied patterns. Once partly integrated around a particular symbol each new configuration diffused as a culture complex, eliciting fresh acts of identification from some, and provoking decisive acts of rejection from others. Affirmation aroused counteraffirmation, and the outcome of the dialectic was to insure the propagation of the general pattern, subject to profound differentiations in detail.

11. A. Mathiez, *Les origines des cultes révolutionnaires,* Paris, 1904, p. 27.
12. Religion and nationalism is extensively discussed in the works of Carlton J. H. Hayes, Hans Kohn, and Charles E. Merriam previously referred to. For religion and proletarianism, see Werner Sombart, and also Waldemar Gurian, *Bolshevism; Theory and Practice,* New York, 1932.

Since the possession of a distinctive language came to be regarded as one of the details essential to the status of the fully developed national symbol, language revivals became inseparable from the early history of most nationalistic movements. Restrictions of any kind upon the use of the vernacular in schools, universities, law courts, legislatures, forums, churches, or markets were bitterly resented. Intellectuals expanded the national vocabulary as well as the national literature. In Finland the vernacular was fashioned into a literary vehicle on a par with Swedish; in Bohemia the Czech language supplanted the foreign literary speech, which was German; in Albania the nationalists remodeled the crude vernacular into a literary medium. In Greece the artificial "pure" Greek was launched, but failed, the popular "demotike" winning out. Among the Vlachs in Macedonia a national movement got under way with the revival of the vernacular, Roumanian, which the Greeks failed to suppress. In Roumania the spread of nationalism went hand in hand with the expansion of the national tongue. In Hungary the vernacular was modified into a phonetic language that supplanted German as the polite medium. In Norway the Norse dialects were modified into Landsmaal, which has been recognized as co-official with Riksmaal or Dano-Norwegian. Similar processes occurred in Iceland, Ireland, Lithuania, Poland, Ukrainia, Armenia, Wales, Scotland, Flemish Belgium, French Canada, Palestine, and some other communities.[13]

The general objects of collective effort on behalf of the collective symbol are thus profoundly affected by the patterns conceived to be appropriate in the culture to symbols of this class. Identification with the collective symbol likewise involves identification with many, if not all, of these status symbols, and the discrepancy between the existing position of the collective symbol and the patterns deemed appropriate to the class defines the objectives of concerted effort.

The remodeling of the personality through identification varies from minor changes in vocabulary to profound redefinitions of career, in which individuals devote themselves to the performance of specialized functions in the collective enterprise. They may become devoted missionaries of the cause, exhorting in public and private, or they may carry on the detailed work of administering central office routine, collecting information, soliciting funds, distributing material.

13. See Carl W. Buck, "Language and the Sentiment of Nationality," *American Political Science Review,* 10 (1916): 44–69. G. S. H. Rossouw traced the rise of Afrikander in South Africa in *Nationalism and Language,* University of Chicago, 1922, Ph.D. dissertation, and reviewed the literature.

The professional revolutionary is one of the most prominent examples of full-time devotion to the expansion of the claims of a collective symbol.

The adaptive processes which are initiated in identification modify the relation of the symbol to other symbols in the lives of the persons affected; these other symbols are both "public" and "private" and their interconnections may be infinitely complex. The symbol of the local merchants' association may be reenforced to strengthen the symbol of the nation; but this process of redefinition may involve the inclusion of certain commercial policy demands into the national symbol. This latter process, by means of which special and private demands are legitimized in terms of the more inclusive symbol, adds greatly to the acceptability of the latter. A central core of allusion is sustained and redefined in terms of "tactical" or "strategical" considerations. Personalities display prodigious skill in justifying private goals in terms of master symbols; insofar as this process is unconscious, it is rationalization; insofar as it is conscious, it is justification.

The relations between symbols of identification and of demand, which have just been indicated, may be amplified by noticing the relations between symbols of identification and of expectation. Identification with collective symbols usually modifies the outlook of the person on the future of the world. Expectations are generated about the benevolent implications of future history for cherished aspirations. The result is over-optimism about the future status of the master symbol. Over-optimism about the future may lead to direct action under very unfavorable circumstances. The tragic consequences of the March action in the year 1921 in Germany were partly ascribable to the unduly sanguine expectations of recent converts to the left proletarian cause. Recent converts to a master symbol are notoriously prone to overestimate the future. Conversion experiences come as solutions of acute conflicts between strong tendency systems within the personality, and the convert is not infrequently driven to impulsive acts of expiation for the hostilities which were so long directed against the newly introjected symbol. The redefinition of future expectations is in part due to the relatively exclusive preoccupation of the individual with the fate of the master symbol. The whole meaning of history is sharpened into some simplified struggle between Good and Evil, bourgeois and proletarian, oppressor and oppressed. The future derives its portentous quality from the fact that it alone can disclose the fate of the contending symbols.

Symbols of identification, demand, and expectation reciprocally influence one another, and interplay with changes in the division of labor. Optimism and devotion may affect the work rate and the birth rate, modifying the value hierarchy. The development of power machinery may cheapen production and lead to the expansion of the market. Demands which are serviceable in extending the market may be redefined in terms of the master symbols of nation or state. Such dynamic interrelations between "material" and "ideological" continue to redefine areas of activity, sentiment, and organization.

From the foregoing it is evident that the spread of any master identifying symbol depends upon the connections among details of great apparent diversity. The success of any symbol in competition with other symbols depends upon frequency of exposure in forms capable of eliciting favorable response, and upon presentation at times when the readjustive possibilities of the population are high. The level of general reactivity is itself modified by many changes in the material and symbolic configuration of specific persons, and any process of diffusion, once under way, reacts with each new aspect of the continually shifting context in which it operates. The study of the historical spread of symbols and practices has clarified many conditions which facilitate the process,[14] and the use of psychoanalysis has disclosed significant intrapsychic connections of which we were formerly unaware. In particular, psychoanalysis provides an infinitely enriched conception of all that is implied in those unconscious receptivities which, spontaneously aligned in the direction of dominating personalities, constitute the interlapping matrices through which symbols radiate with special rapidity and intensity throughout society.

All research confirms the importance of exposing the specific sequence through which symbol clusters pass. When did a national symbol of identification become associated with demands to oust foreigners from jobs in the army and the bureaucracy? When did sensitiveness to being ruled by executives of foreign origin develop?

14. Cultural anthropologists have contributed to our knowledge of the dynamics of diffusion. See Edward Sapir, *Time Perspective in Aboriginal American Culture,* Memoir 90, pp. 30ff., Canada, Geological Survey, 1916; Edward Sapir, "Custom," *Encyclopedia of the Social Sciences;* Roland B. Dixon, *Building of Cultures,* pp. 59ff., New York, 1928; Leslie Spier, "The Sun Dance of the Plains Indians: Its Development and Diffusion," *Anthropological Papers of the American Museum of Natural History,* Vol, 16, Part 7, especially pp. 501 ff., New York, 1921; Paul Radin, "A Sketch of the Peyote Cult of the Winnebago: A Study in Borrowing," *Journal of Religious Psychology,* 7 (1914): 1–22.

When did it cease to be good form to speak a foreign tongue? When did it become socially necessary to patronize native art? When did it become imperative to "buy Chinese" or "sell Chinese"? When did it become socially advisable to name children after political heroes? When did it become disloyal to accept favors in return for exercising an official duty.[15]

Recent social science has undertaken to follow and to explain the speedy diffusion of nationalism since the later years of the eighteenth century.[16] In the foreground appears the rapid application of modern technology to production, profoundly altering the life situation of many members of the community. Perceiving new possibilities of profit, self-selected enterprisers took the initiative in demanding many modifications in traditional ways of life, clashing with the symbols and practices favorable to the landed property group. Finding themselves in organization areas where decision making was a restricted privilege, needing ways and means of rendering themselves effective at the centers of dominance, they responded positively to symbols of protest and plan which were circulated by specialized verbalizers. Gradually the ideology of the ruling élite was called into question in the name of mankind as a whole. Democratic language assisted in mobilizing the animosities of the "underprivileged" in mass action which finally altered the methods of élite recruitment and the language of justification. Where members of the bourgeoisie got control of the government, as in France, they transformed their earlier antistate orientation into a pro-state and pro-governmental ideology. Nationalism became henceforth a means of nullifying proletarian challenges from within, and of fostering the power of the state in the world balance. Where the bourgeoisie was particularly

15. See the studies in the history of patriotism by Roberto Michels and Carlton J. H. Hayes; the Civic Training Series edited by Charles E. Merriam; Charles A. Beard and G. H. Smith, *The Idea of National Interest; An Analytical Study in American Foreign Policy,* New York, 1934.

16. In addition to the literature previously cited, see Friedrich Hertz, "Wesen und Werden der Nation," *Nation und Nationalität, Erg.- Bd., Jahrbuch für Soziologie, Karlsrühe,* 1927; H. O. Ziegler, *Die Moderne Nation, Ein Beitrag zur politischen Soziologie,* Tübingen, 1931; R. Johannet, *Le principe des nationalités,* Paris, 1923; *Verhandlungen des zweiten deutschen Soziologentages vom 20. bis 22. Oktober, 1912, in Berlin,* Tübingen, 1913; Otto Bauer, *Die Nationalitätenfrage und die Sozialdemokratie,* Vienna, 1924; Karl Renner, *Der Kampf der österreichischen Nationen um den Staat,* 2 vols., Vienna, 1902; Karl Renner, *Der nationale Streit um die Aemter und die Sozialdemokratie,* Vienna, 1908; Koppel S. Pinson, *Bibliographical Introduction to Nationalism* (announced); and various books of Harry Elmer Barnes.

weak, and an older social formation needed military support from the masses to defend itself from invasion, the older élite exploited as much as possible of the place-, time-, and tradition-bound symbolism at hand. In Prussia the bourgeoisie never succeeded in capturing the language of nationalism from the monarchy and the feudality that rallied to repulse the French.

In the competition of merely local enterprises with one another, merely local differences are emphasized; hence effective nationalism could not appear until the expansion of the market made possible the concentrating of strong initiative in the hands of enterprisers who were situated at the principal metropoles.

The upper bourgeoisie at the chief marketing centers were receptive to the elaborated symbols of nationalism as they were developed by orators, journalists, poets, novelists, essayists, and systematists. The ideological incorporation of the lesser centers and the back country into the policy of the bourgeois state spread from the centers of dominance by means of the propagation of literacy and by the expansion of such secondary means of incessant stimulation as the press. The expansion of capitalist enterprise tended to promote the active widening of the marketing area for certain goods, like textiles, and, later, iron and steel products. The result was to facilitate the growth of a world-marketing area, which in turn set up many dialectical processes in the form of local opposition to foreign competition. These acute localistic reactions created groups which were favorably disposed toward new local nationalistic expressions. We notice the discovery of local identities throughout Europe, and beyond, as the nineteenth century wore on. The multiplication of state organization areas at the end of the World War is one of the residues of this process.

The emergence in an old organization area of a new élite which speaks in the name of the proletariat challenges the official symbolism of the ruling élites elsewhere. Unity of action would seem to be advantageous among these various élites in the face of the new threat, but intercapitalistic conflicts are still fostered by the importance of safeguarding foreign economic outlets and of uniting the community around nationalistic symbols; there is also a general tendency to doubt the immediate acuteness of the crisis.[17]

17. Many of the economic aspects of nationalism are well handled in Waldemar Mitscherlich, *Nationalismus: Die Geschichte einer Idee,* Leipzig, 1929; R. G. Hawtrey, *Economic Aspects of Sovereignty,* London, 1930; Walter Sulzbach, *Nationales Gemeinschaftsgefühl und wirtschaftliches Interesse,* Leipzig,

The calculation of pecuniary advantage is a highly "rational" process; yet the social patterns which permit this rational process to go on must be sustained by an irrational consensus. Hence the tension between the rational and the traditional is peculiarly high under capitalism, which requires consensus, yet fosters the rational analysis of every acquired symbol and practice. The rationalism of capitalism has rendered it peculiarly dependent for positive values, ethical imperatives, and unifying goal symbols upon its legacies from previous cultures. The vestiges of primitive folk culture (*Gemeinschaft*) have been drags upon the completely ruthless application of the principle of calculated pecuniary advantage in The Great Society.[18] The insecurities arising from the changes in the material environment have been augmented by the stresses arising from the decline in potency of the older religious symbols and practices. Nationalism and proletarianism are secularized alternatives to the surviving religious patterns, answering to the need of personalities to restabilize themselves in a mobile world.

The emergence of the last world-revolutionary pattern has intensified appeals to parochialism in the postwar world.[19] The older middle-class formations have revivified the national symbols at the expense of class or world symbols, and supplied blood, money, and applause to programs which have been designed to curb the "alien" and "radical" elements in the community. German Nationalism relies on the older middle classes. If proletarian strategists can devise ways and means of disintegrating the loyalties of the middle classes, proletarian struggles might in time of advancing economic distress eventuate successfully, short of the demoralization involved in prolonged or unsuccessful war. One of the tasks to be examined later in this book is that of controlling the psychological responses of the middle classes to rival symbols of identification.

1929; József Eötvös, *Der Einfluss der herrschenden Ideen des 19 Jahrhunderts auf den staat,* (from Hungarian), Leipzig, 1854; and in the writings of Bukharin, Lenin, and other historical materialists.

18. The relations between *Gemeinschaft* and *Gesellschaft,* first extensively developed by Ferdinand Tönnies, are carefully restated in Hans Freyer, *Soziologie als Wirklichkeitswissenschaft,* pp. 230–252, Leipzig and Berlin, 1930.

19. See Helen Martin, *Nationalism and Children's Books* (University of Chicago Ph.D. dissertation, 1934), which applies a rigorous technique to the study of the factors affecting the diffusion of children's books throughout the world.

Chapter III

THE BALANCING OF POWER; THE
EXPECTATION OF VIOLENCE

The purpose of this chapter is to analyze the significance of the expectation of violence in world politics. The assumption that men will settle their differences by fighting reacts powerfully upon the identifications, demands, and expectations of human beings, and leads to many overt changes in the material environment. Demands for colonies, ships, and treaty revisions are continually modified in the light of estimated changes in the relative fighting position of groups; estimates of fighting effectiveness are differentially modified by actual changes in the natural resources and technology; and identifications with this or that collective symbol are partially controlled by the supposed prospects of success of that symbol in the struggle for status. Any élite within an organized area is bound by a double set of relations to pay serious attention to the method by which conflicts are to be settled. Those who challenge the élite within the area may petition, declaim, demonstrate; or they may resort to overt forms of passive and active coercion. It often happens that a given élite is comparatively exempt from domestic attack; despite the frequency of uprisings, rebellions, and civil wars during recent years, the assumption that conflicts can be resolved short of violence is widespread. This assumption is less applicable to the relations among states; even where war is formally relinquished as an instrument of policy, the expectation in fact prevails that such declarations will not prevent the use of violence in the course of many conflicts.

Remnants of the World War alliances leave Great Britain, France, the United States, Japan, Italy, and Belgium pitted against Germany and certain succession states on various matters. The Austro-Hungarian succession states are divided, with suspicious eyes directed against the former wielders of authority, Hungary and Austria. The antagonism of France and Italy polarizes another set of hostile relations. Great Britain, looking suspiciously upon French hegemony on the continent, gives qualified support to a reviving Germany. The communist Union of Socialist Soviet Republics stands against the capitalist world, especially Great Britain, France, and the United States. The imperialist states (Great Britain, France, Japan, Netherlands, Italy) have much in common in retaining control over non-contiguous peoples of alien culture. Japan competes with Russia, China, and the United States in the Pacific. The United States inclines toward the leadership of an anti-Japanese bloc in the Pacific including Canada, Australia, and New Zealand, and complicates its relations with Great Britain. Spanish America and Spain regard North America with suspicion, and the debtors of the United States are sufficiently numerous and homogeneous to share common interests on many aspects of world economic policy. There are relatively passive, temporarily indulged states (satiated states), whose outlook is that of tenacious attachment to what they have, and there are active, deprived states whose objective is material and moral rehabilitation. The varied combinations which arise depend upon the nature of the values which are called in question in specific situations.[1] We have previously reviewed the world scene as a possible passage from capitalism to socialism, thus drawing attention to long-term processes which transcend events in particular organization areas.

The expectation of violence exercises a profound influence upon the distribution of other symbol formations and upon direct adaptations to the environment. The political processes which are favored by the expectation of violent conflict may be stated in these terms (an equilibrium analysis): The participants tend to array themselves in two conflicting camps (except a neutralized few who are protected by favorable positions with reference to the general balancing process, as is modern Holland). The dominating pivots of the two-

---

1. Details of the prewar and postwar alignments are to be found in Rudolf Kjellén, *Die Grossmachte vor und nach dem Weltkriege,* Edited by Karl Haushofer, Second Edition, Leipzig, 1930; Valentine de Balla, *The New Balance of Power in Europe,* Baltimore, 1932; William L. Langer, *European Alliances and Alignments,* New York, 1931; *Histoire diplomatique de l'Europe, 1871–1914,* Edited by Henri Hauser, Paris, 1929–; H. M. Vinacke, *A History of the Far East in Modern Times,* New York, 1928; P. J. Treat, *The Far East,* New York, 1928; George H. Blakeslee, *The Pacific Area,* Boston, World Peace Foundation, 1929; Francis Miller and Helen Hill, *The Giant of the Western World,* New York, 1930; W. Y. Elliott, *The New British Empire,* New York and London, 1932; Richard Hennig, *Geopolitik,* Leipzig, 1928; John Strachey, *The Coming Struggle for Power,* New York, 1933.

fold division are the strongest rivals. Putting the whole matter tersely, the process is:

    A seeks to associate C against B.
    B seeks to associate C against A.
    A or B, failing C, seek to associate D or E (and so on among the various participants).

It will be noticed that one consequence of this process is the tendency toward the universalization of the conflict until the position of all parties of similar status is defined with reference to it.

Another feature of the balancing process is that C may exact so much from A as a price of support against B, and from B as the price of support against A, that A and B may redefine their relations and pool against C, E, and F. This complex procedure comes about through the revision of demands in the light of the redefinition of the expectations of relative advantage to follow from the pursuit of demands in their original form. Hence the essential instability of the relations among participants in the balancing process; it is more accurate to speak of the *balancing* than the *balance* of power.

This essential instability is further shown when the implication is removed from the foregoing that participants in world politics act as units. Within each group there is a balancing process among all component elements. Within C at any given time the predominance may be exercised by a, b, and c. State A may be able to procure the cooperation of C at a cheaper price by assisting the combination b, d, and e to take control from a, b, and c. Indeed, the readaptation in the situation may come about more easily if the demands of A be redefined in senses more acceptable to such an alignment in C, and this may come about through a change in the predominating group in A from a, b, and c to some other lineup. In ultimate "microscopic" analysis the competitors in the balancing process can be presented as demand symbols in the name of persons as individualized entities, and demand symbols in the name of persons who invoke collective names. This means that the career line of the person can be said to include instances of demands made in the name of the primary reference symbol "John Jones," and in the name of the secondary reference symbols "John Jones, Catholic; Worker; Southerner; Democrat. . . ." Aspects of John Jones's personality are in rivalry with other aspects of the same personality, and each functioning aspect is significant for political analysis. The "individual" is not an

ultimate category of analysis in politics, although the events of ultimate reference are "individual."

When we view world politics as a whole, it is profitable to carry
the analytic process no further than rather coarse approximations.
Usually it is sufficient to characterize relations extensively rather
than intensively. Thus we may connect demands for protective duties
on agricultural products with the category "farmer" rather than
"manufacturer," and refrain from asking any more questions about
the categories appropriate to those who are "exceptions." If we
pushed our inquiry further, we should presently require data secured
by intensive personality study of representative cases.

The foregoing analysis adds what may be called the principle of
functional universalization to that of *geographical universalization* as
a characteristic of the play of the balancing process. All likenesses
and differences in interpersonal relations tend to be drawn into the
conflicting alignments.

Returning to the spatial aspects of the balancing process, we may
speak of the tendency toward geographical differentiation into two
major zones to stabilize into an encircling and an encircled distribution. Owing to the great variability of the balancing relations, this
encircling-encircled pattern is seldom approximated. The closest recent instance was in the later months of 1917 when the Central
Powers were almost entirely surrounded by hostile states, and when
most of the world was involved in the acute conflict then raging.

This approximate crystallization of the spatial zones into the encircling and the encircled marked a situation of maximum crisis,
which was resolved by shifts in two directions: the defeat of one
group of powers by a rival group; the defeat of those in control of
various organization areas by rival domestic élites, which were often
based on noncontiguous districts, and which were capable of appealing to noncontiguous districts within foreign areas. The latter process
of revolution was conducted by those who won support from the
residents of the poorer districts in cities, and sought to employ a
symbolism which would win approval among similar inhabitants
abroad.[2]

2. Besides the literature referred to on the balance of power in Chap. 1, attention is called to Ernest Nys, "La théorie de l'équilibre européen," *Revue de
droit internationale et de législation comparée*, 25 (1893): 34–57; Alexandre de
Stieglitz, *De l'équilibre politique du légitimisme et du principe des nationalités*, 3
vols., Paris, 1894, Part 1; Léonce Donnadieu, *La théorie de l'équilibre*, Paris,
1900; Wolfgang Windelband, *Die auswärtige Politik der Grossmächte in der
Neuzeit, 1494–1919*, Second Edition, Stuttgart, 1925; Olaf Hoijer, *La sécurité*

If certain conditions are fulfilled, the balancing of power process can maintain peace despite the expectation of violence. Many theories of the balance of power have been put forward as ways of keeping the peace where violent conflict is assumed to be constantly impending. The present point is that the process (including certain theories of the process) can conceivably preserve the peace. The conditions will be formulated as follows:

   a. If variations in power (fighting effectiveness) can be accurately measured;
   b. If variations in fighting effectiveness are convertible and distributable among participants in the balancing process;
   c. If variations in power are visible in the early stages of their development;
   d. If the estimating process can be sentimentalized.

These four conditions may be summed up as measurability, convertibility, visibility, and sentimentibility. The first requirement of measurability is peculiarly difficult of fulfillment; it needs no elaborate demonstration to show that the appraisal of all varieties of social change in terms of their implications for fighting effectiveness is treacherously complex. Historically very flagrant errors of judgment have been committed by those in responsible positions, especially when new technical developments were speedily occurring. The gross underestimation of the importance of modern industry led to such upsets as the Russo-Japanese conflict and the Franco-Prussian War. Great uncertainty characterizes our prevailing ideas about the relative effectiveness of the specialized tools of violence; witness the controversies over airplanes versus battleships, battleships versus cruisers, cruisers versus submarines, highly trained and mechanized mobile units versus large armies, and over the whole future of chemical warfare.[3] How difficult it is to evaluate the effect of trans-

internationale et ses modes de réalisation, 4 vols., Paris, 1930, vol. 1; Frederick L. Schuman, *War and Diplomacy in the French Republic,* New York and London, 1931, Chaps. 14–15. One of the most difficult problems is that of evaluating the influence of the various theories of the balance of power on the acts of public and private persons.

   3. Some of the current controversies are reflected in the following: *What Would Be the Character of a New War? Enquiry Organized by the Interparliamentary Union,* London, 1931; B. H. Liddell-Hart, *The Remaking of Modern Armies,* Boston, 1928; Neon, *The Great Delusion,* New York, 1927; Victor Lefebure, *Scientific Disarmament,* New York, 1931; Salvador de Madariaga, *Disarmament,* New York, 1929; K. L. von Oertzen, Editor, *Rüstung und Abrüstung,* Berlin, 1931, especially Part 3. The last is Vol. 45 of *von Löbells Jahresberichte über das Heer-und Kriegswesen.*

forming factories from peace to war is suggested by scanning the following list of substitutions.[4]

Peace Product	War Product
Files and saws	Army surgical appliances
Barbers' supplies	Army, dental, and surgical instruments
Brass goods	Artillery ammunition
Tractors	Tanks
Rubber goods	Gas masks
Watch springs	Time fuses
Carpets	Army duck and blankets
Furniture	Ammunition boxes
Ladies' waists	Signal flags
Fishing rods	Staffs for Signal Corps
Gears	Gun sights
Toys and novelties	Packing boxes
Jewelry	Military stamping
Black strap molasses and alcohol	Smokeless powders
Beer barrels	Marking buoys
Laundry machinery	Shell-loading machinery
Skates	Bombs
Cash registers	Pistols
Silverware	Surgical implements
Baby carriages	Balloon baskets
Cans	Steel helmets
Metal stampings	Hand grenades

The uncertainty which prevails in estimating material details is if possible augmented in considering the psychological or "imponderable" factors. Not even the fiasco of socialism on the eve of the World War has disposed of the lurking fear in Western Europe that next time the tale may be a new one; at least morale may be more quickly sapped as determined efforts are made to transform international into civil war.

The difficulty of foreseeing the nature of future political alignments adds to the uncertainty of all calculations. Should the French develop their naval policy on the assumption that they will cooperate with Great Britain in the next war? Regardless of ultimate aspirations, should Germany develop a re-armament program in connection with a pro-western or a pro-eastern orientation? Should the future plans of the United States include the protection of the Philippines?

4. Taken from Ralph H. Stimson, *The Control of the Manufacture of Armament,* p. 410, University of Illinois doctoral dissertation, 1931.

After having indicated some of the tasks connected with the accurate translation of social change into terms of fighting effectiveness, we are free to consider how to find a medium of exchange which can be used to readjust political demands in relation to these changes. Any participant who begins to suffer from a local disadvantage must be compensated promptly if the balancing process is to work harmoniously. Europe once sought to use the acre as the medium of exchange, since every acre was roughly equal to every other acre as a source of men and materials under agricultural conditions, allowing for crass exceptions, like deserts, waste lands, mines, and ports. Unsatisfactory as this standard was, the difficulties connected with it increased with the spread of modern industrialism, and the world is left today without a serviceable medium of exchange for the administration of those readjustments which follow from shifts in relative fighting effectiveness.

Any medium of exchange must be emotionally neutralized; each unit must be equivalent to every other unit. Since a stable object like an acre is readily sentimentalized, the reapportionment of the acre may be opposed; thus the growth of nationalism interfered with the previous methods of administering the balancing process. An impersonal unity, like a gold dollar, offers some advantages from the standpoint of emotional neutrality, but the task of estimating changes in society, first in fighting terms, and then in pecuniary terms, is inordinately complex; and if the sums in question are large, the "transfer problem" arises in ways made familiar to our generation by the efforts to handle reparations.

If changes in fighting effectiveness are measured and converted, difficulties will still arise in the balancing process unless the changes are visible. A change in the material environment does not necessarily precipitate immediate awareness of its implications, and a local change in the ideological situation does not necessarily modify the ideological situation elsewhere. The relations between material and material, material and ideological, and ideological and ideological are manifold and complex. Changes in technique may pass unobserved or unappraised owing to prevalent notions of what is important. And some changes, such as those involving patriotic sentiment, class consciousness, or optimism about the future are peculiarly "invisible." "Visibility" is thus a function of the overt change and of the reactivity of the estimators.

Unless the balancing process proceeds with no time lag between the change and its generalization in such a way as to preserve the status quo in fighting effectiveness, particular participants will enjoy advantages, narrow as they may be, at given times. This will increase their objective chances of using war successfully to modify their position, and if war itself is treated as a major value, war may be resorted to. War is already heavily sentimentalized in our culture, and treated as a value in itself; any alternative mode of resolving conflicts must therefore become a symbol which is sentimentalized. Positive affects must cluster about the process of "counting," to use H. N. Brailsford's happy phrase.[5]

The conditions of measurability, convertibility, visibility, and sentimentibility are only approximately realized in world politics. The most conclusive index of the discrepancies between the "possible" and the "actual" is the resort to violence itself. A supplementary indication of lag in the balancing process is immobility in the alignment of participants. Combinations against Charles V, Philip II, Louis XIV, and Napoleon I were themselves evidence of accumulated maladaptations between social change and the generalization of its fighting implications in such a way as to preserve the relative position of all participants in the world-balancing process.

It follows from what has been said in this analysis that research might profitably be directed toward examining the overt distribution of armed forces in the world at given times. Any immobilities may be viewed with suspicion as possible signs of failure in the balancing process; perhaps the act of presenting material organized from this point of view will interact in the world political process, and reduce certain instances of lagging adaptation. As usual, there is nothing completely new about this proposal for investigation. Every student of world affairs pays attention to the movements of armed forces during selected time periods in search of cues to the state of the balancing process. Army maneuvers in postwar Germany have very roughly indicated the state of the east-west orientation; France has reacted to Germany and Italy by concentrating army maneuvers in various regions, by constructing an elaborate line of fortifications along the eastern frontiers, and by maintaining garrisons at significant places; the naval concentrations and maneuvers of Great Britain and the United States when charted through time are obviously pertinent to the disclosure of the existing balance. Such indices need not be studied in isolation; combined with other indices of material and ideological details of the total configuration, they

5. See his *War of Steel and Gold*, Third Edition, New York, 1915.

may disclose the nature of the relationships among these various aspects of the totality.[6]

Suppose we examine with some care the nature of the insecurities which arise in the balancing process and which interact with other aspects of the whole to interfere with the smooth functioning of world politics. This necessitates the formal analysis of the ideological aspects of collective life. The meaning of any symbol to any personality at a given time depends upon its relative position in reference to the total structure of the personality; hence the meaning of any symbol to all the personalities in a given community at a given time is the relation of the symbol to all the personality structures involved.

One convenient principle of structural analysis examines the tripartite division of the personality at any specified cross section of career line.[7] Psychoanalysis uses for classificatory convenience the threefold division according to the biological needs, the socially acquired inhibitions and compulsions, and the testing of reality. Very few of the primitive biological impulses of the infant can be directly gratified, owing principally to the restrictions which are imposed by representatives of the particular social order into which the infant is born. When these restrictions are no longer dealt with as obstacles in the outer world, but are observed on the basis of an acquired modification of behavior, the individual has achieved the personality structure which is technically called the *superego*. The perceiving of external relations, the modification of impulse in the light of such current symbolizations of reality, are the special functions of the third division of personality which is named the *ego*. The impulses and their modifications which are unacceptable to the superego are called the *id*. The terms id, superego, and ego are very roughly equivalent to impulse, conscience, and reason, although much distortion is involved in this usage. The three main personality structures are not to be thought of as rigidly separated from one another; the superego and the ego are not categorically cut off from the impulses of the id, but are properly to be conceived as complications in original impulse which have arisen in the whole process of elaborating these drives in relation to one another and to surroundings. The id and superego aspects of reaction go on without conscious awareness

6. A definite piece of research will be discussed in the following chapter.

7. See my discussion of "The Triple-appeal. Principle: A Contribution of Psychoanalysis to Political and Social Science," *American Journal of Sociology*, 37 (1932): 523–538.

on the part of the person; full waking awareness of the nature of the primitive components of the personality can only be attained by means of special ways of using the total reactive structure.[8] Those memories and imaginings which appear at the focus of attention without correlative excitement are included within the ego structure of the personality; acute insecurities are produced when impulses are able to elaborate themselves so far as to modify directly the events at the phase of waking attention.

Symbols are often organized within the personality so that they are principally related to the ego, superego, or id, although it is clear from what has been said before that these connections cannot be exclusive. The symbol "Lenin" in one personality may relate chiefly to the ego, where it is connected with nonsentimentalized characterizations of historical facts associated with Lenin. In another personality the symbol "Lenin" may be reenforced from the superego compulsions to perform acts worthy of the great revolutionist. In still another personality the hatreds directed against "Lenin" may indicate the strength of the appeal which is made to the anti-authoritarian tendencies of the id, which clash with the superego, forcing the latter to mobilize all of its resources to maintain its control in conformity with other symbols.

When we desire to characterize the role of a given symbol in the personalities of those who live in a certain community, special terms are advisable in order to reduce confusion. Those culture patterns which appeal predominantly to the superego of most of the personalities in the group are the *mores;* the culture patterns which relate chiefly to the ego are the *expediencies.* This usage is desirable in order to keep the point clear that the mores are not universally embedded within the superego formation of every one in a designated community.

The mores of a community may include the objects and symbols called priests, generals, kings, policemen, churches, uniforms, ceremonial observances, and verbal admonitions to the "ideal"; the counter-mores may embrace revolutionists, prostitutes, prisoners, obscene and subversive talk; the expediencies may be musical or technological skills and debatable questions. It is possible and profitable to study the symbols and practices of a community in order to discover their meaning to representative personalities. An inventory of the relevant relations would consist of the following: person to

8. Free association techniques are devised by psychoanalysis to facilitate this process.

person, person to institution, person to occasion, person to policy, to practice, to doctrine, to myth, and to legend.

If the sampling of representative career lines can be satisfactorily executed, the symbols and practices prevailing at any selected time can be grouped in the following way:

Expediencies versus Expediencies
    (for example, disagreements about the relative effectiveness of land and naval armaments)
Expediencies versus Mores
    (for example, biological theory of evolution versus biblical literalism)
Expediencies versus Counter-mores
    (for example, efforts to reduce alcoholism in the interests of efficiency in production)
Mores versus Counter-mores
    (for example, authoritarian versus anti-authoritarian movements)

During periods of slow social change, an equilibrium is maintained among these forms of expressions through which human impulses pass. During periods of rapid social change, the direction and intensity of the readjustment may be predicted according to the following principle: Prolonged ego and superego indulgences (expediencies, mores) precipitate redefinitions in directions gratifying to the id (counter-mores); prolonged ego and id indulgences initiate redefinitions gratifying to the superego. In general the meaning of this formula is that periods of disregard of the prevalent body of authoritarian patterns generate insecurities which are favorable to the reimposition of new controls, or to the revalidation of the older controls; periods of intensified discipline generate insecurities which favor the spread of deviational symbols and practices.

Changes in the surroundings of selected people may be examined from this point of view in the search for dependable routines in reality. What is the bearing of this scheme upon the understanding of the readjustments which are connected with the balancing of power? How do changes in the environment impinge upon the career lines of those who assume that international and interclass differences may be settled by resort to violence? Restricting ourselves to interstate relations, our general expectation is that the balancing process produces insecurities connected with maintaining inhibition, and that the resulting tensions favor sudden redefinitions in directions more gratifying to the inhibited impulses.

The threat of loss to any portion of the personality tends to revive all the anxieties connected with previous threats to the personality system. Hence the assumption that violence may be involved in settling differences among the human beings symbolized by nations and classes exposes the persons who are identified with such symbols to repeated threats of loss. All personalities who have been studied by psychoanalytic methods reveal residues of the early anxieties which were connected with the establishment of inhibitions upon the free use of the body. Other sources of anxiety may be mentioned, but the anxieties connected with the threats of losing parts of the body, the "castration" anxieties, are particularly acute, and situations which reinstate them complicate adjustments to reality. It is quite reasonable to recognize that dangers are connected with affairs which involve groups in the name of which differences may be settled by violence. Many personalities are able to appraise these situations with objectivity, and to gauge the probabilities of conflict. But behavior is always more or less susceptible to modification from the earlier and less well-oriented components of the personality. Situations which involve objective loss are particularly prone to arouse the underlying and incompletely liquidated conflicts. While it may be assumed that professional soldiers will be much freer of irrelevant anxiety reactions in adjusting to immediate changes in fighting effectiveness, the study of specific cases show how even these highly disciplined personalities may be affected by the unwanted participation of primitive legacies from their infantile and childhood past. All that applies to them is applicable with greater force to persons who focus upon the play of the balance of power, but who have unchastened amateur standing in the interpretation of reality.

It is no doubt appropriate to show what is meant here by referring to some of the material presented by an American officer who was being analyzed during a period of stress in our official relations with Japan. The portentous meaning of the symbol "Japan" was reflected in a long series of reported dreams and nightmares. In one of them he was wrapped in an American flag which impeded his movements in trying to run away from a vile-looking Japanese officer who was chasing him with a huge knife in his hand. He woke up in a sweat and discovered himself under the bed, with the sheets wrapped round his legs. Free associations to the nightmare and to the other dreams produced a long array of reminiscences of imaginings in which the Japanese figured. But ultimately it appeared that the scowling Japanese, with their cartoon knives, had become connected with early situations in his childhood when threats were made to cut off his sexual organs if he continued to meddle with them.

This extract from a case history is not intended to convey the impression that all American officers were reacting to the prospect of a war with Japan with precisely this much castration anxiety. The precise significance of any symbol to any adult can be determined only by prolonged study by special methods, and generalizations about the distribution of specific constellations in a given situation depend upon applying these methods to personalities representative of the situation in question. All that can be accomplished by this fragment is to render a little more explicit the nature of the connections within personality which complicate the behavior of the adult by residues of past insecurity.

Owing to the assumption of violence in international and interclass relations, collective symbols are presented at the focus of attention under circumstances which are particularly prone to precipitate all manner of anxiety reactions. The meaning of these symbols is a function of the total personalities in which they occur, and they necessarily derive much of their significance from deeper and earlier sources than those connected with the immediate political situation.

Insecurities which are induced by threats of loss may be abated by direct acts of counterassertion. But in a world of limited opportunities the impulses toward boundless counteraggression which are elicited under such circumstances must submit to incessant chastening. Impulsive counterassertions are rarely consummated, and the most direct means by which the underlying anxieties may be removed are therefore unavailable. The continuing necessity of suppressing hostility, or of giving it indirect expression, means that a substantial measure of anxiety remains related to the secondary symbols. There are many ways of disposing of accumulated insecurities in relation to political symbols without directly implicating political symbols. Hence anxieties which arise from the rumors of foreign conspiracies may be effectively abolished by displacing hostilities upon wives, secretaries, or chauffeurs; or by orgiastic and diffuse release in orgasm, alcoholism, or pugilism. The routes to release are very numerous; they may be classified into acts which involve object orientations, reflective thinking, autism (moods and irrelevant fantasies), and somatic reactions (headaches and other bodily changes in which functional factors are important). Despite the rich variety of insecurity-abolishing alternatives, several circumstances conspire to connect world political symbols with anxiety reactions. The expectation of violence sustains an organization of communication which pays attention to what the various key participants in the balancing process are doing. Their names are continually before the population as targets for affective displacements of all kinds, and they are reported in connection with many events which directly expose the local symbol to the possibility of losing its independence, its material claims, or its prestige. Vested interests arise in connection with the special function of transmitting symbols in the press and elsewhere; and many of these vested interests extract direct advantages from emphasizing the threatening aspects of the world situation.

Although insecurities arising within the personality in its political aspects may be removed by nonpolitical acts, many of the reactions to insecurity are immediately relevant to politics. We have seen how the suppression of vigorous counterassertion in a world of many limitations sustains insecurities arising from the balancing process. Some of the aggressions which are mobilized and denied direct expression against the foreign environment are directed against the self. This is one of the most important dynamisms of our intrapsychic life, displaying itself in extreme form as suicide.

One of the chief immediate results of subjecting an ego symbol to external danger and of inhibiting counteraggression is thus the preoccupation of the ego with its own relations to the world. This represents a partial withdrawal of libido (affective interest) from the symbols of the surrounding environment. This growing absorption in the more central self-symbols reactivates the earlier, more primitive, less disciplined attitudes of the personality. The result is the elaboration of narcissistically gratifying fantasies of the self. A personality so reacting may create symbols to which he exposes others, boasting of the high moral worth and ultimate omnipotence of the collective symbol; or in the absence of autonomous elaboration, he may respond positively to such symbols when they are supplied by others in conversation or in print. A particular value is attached to acts of ceremonial deference to the collective emblem, since to personalities in such a condition each small detail seems to involve the fate of the whole collective symbol, and of national or class or race "honor."

One of the consequences of heightened ego preoccupation is that excessive demands are unconsciously made upon others for deference to the symbols of the self; the failure of the world to acquiesce in these demands creates a discrepancy which in turn complicates the stresses within the personality. Now it is of the essence of the balancing process that partners shall be subject to change with little notice, and while on the ego-reflective level there is no basis whatever for remonstrating with a participant who acts according to his idea of self-interest and changes sides, the deeper psychological consequences are not so lightly disposed of. Owing to unconscious demands for deference, which tend to place a sentimental overvaluation upon mere partnership, a change in partners provokes deep resentment on the part of those who have developed this overestimate. Resentful of having been deprived of full response (deprivation through emotional withdrawal), resentful of having been led into error (narcissistic wound at loss of independence by wrongly appraising the other, and depending on him for response), the "deserted" partner characteristically seeks revenge.

These are the reenforcing psychological dynamisms which help to explain the long standing reputation of Great Britain on the continent for great "hypocrisy"; the ruling élites have occupied a position in reference to the general balancing process which enabled them to veer here and there as their sense of the situation indicated. As Lord Grey commented, the intense unpopularity of Great Britain on the continent (prior to 1870) "has been due largely to the opinion that we were always taking a hand and never taking a side.[9] The Italians, whose pivotal position has likewise placed them where they have been able to adapt themselves to shifting balances on the continent, have accumulated a reputation for untrustworthiness.

Some of the stresses arising from the suppression may be relieved by the primitive dynamism of "projection"; part of the hyperassertiveness of the personality itself is imputed to other groups. Like so many of the elementary methods of dealing with insecurity, projection is not wholly successful; the fantastically remoulded environment of threatening groups recreates in its turn new sources of insecurity within the personality. Even without hypocrisy the perceptual processes through which contact is made with the environment are subject to deformations arising from the unconscious mental structure; details which corroborate the imputed threat are given special weight.[10] All sorts of fancied blows are cherished

9. *Twenty-five Years*, 2: p. 37, New York, 1925.

10. Many of the observations of President A. L. Lowell on the role of attention are corroborated and deepened by the analysis of the unconscious aspects of the reactive structure. See his *Public Opinion in War and Peace*, Cambridge, Mass., 1923.

against the personality, and the past and present are reconstructed as parts of vast plots against the integrity of the collective symbol.

The ego symbol of any selected personality within a class or nation is a highly complicated structure which includes symbols of all degrees of differentiation. The ego sentiments which are organized with reference to brothers, sisters, friends, professional associates, and neighbors are much fuller of nuance than those which refer to such secondary objects as nations or classes. The personality-in-relation-to-partner is controlled by many reflective considerations, since there is much tested knowledge available about the capacities and proclivities of the partner.

That part of the ego symbol which is organized in relation to the ambiguous "we" called our nation, or class, or race, is in most instances but slightly modified by knowledge. In view of the undeveloped character of such a "we" symbol, it may properly be called a *rudimentary* sentiment or symbol. The ambiguity of reference of these secondary terms and the residues of early emotional attachments and aversions combine to minimize the "reality critique." The resulting instability of judgment is displayed in the ease with which uncorrected swings occur between extremes of hostility and of admiration in relation to secondary symbols. A study by E. S. Bogardus of the attitudes of Californians toward various national and racial groups showed that it was not the Japanese who were the most hated nation, but the Turks, whom the subjects had never seen.[11] The absence of information about Belgium made it easier to build up a vast idealization of the Belgian people than of the British or the Germans.

It should be explicitly stated that persons who are well integrated in their immediate personal relationships may be poorly developed toward remote objects and, reversely, that people who are poorly organized toward primary situations may have acquired the special knowledge which chastens reactions in dealing with remote objects. Indeed one of the principal functions of symbols of remote objects, like nations and classes, is to serve as targets for the relief of many of the tensions which might discharge disastrously in face-to-face relations. The hatred of the physical father may be displaced upon the symbol of the monarch, enabling the person to keep on good terms with the person toward whom the early animosities were mainly directed.

11. See the articles on "Social Distance" by E. S. Bogardus in the *Journal of Applied Sociology* since 1925.

From this analysis it follows that the rudimentary self-symbols which are related to world politics may function in loose association with other aspects of the personality and, like all partly dissociated systems, may predominate in shaping overt conduct in situations which call them up.

The elaboration of regressive and fantastic processes in connection with the rudimentary self-symbols of world politics is favored by the weak superego formations which arise in consequence of the comparative absence of world mores. The assumption that the resort to violence is the ultimate appeal in world politics indicates the weakness of moral imperatives in this sphere of human relations. Impulses are permitted to discharge in elementary form owing to the fragmentary nature of world culture.

Strictly speaking, it is not legitimate to refer to rudimentary self-symbols as pathological expressions of the individual. Nor is it correct to oppose a sick society to a basically healthy person. Pathology is neither social in contrast with individual, nor individual in contrast with social; pathology is configurational. If the word is used at all, it may be defined as referring to events destructive of certain patterns defined as "normal" or "supernormal."

We have seen that one of the principal consequences of the expectation of violence in world politics is to build up insecurities which arise from the curbing of counteraggressive tendencies which are initially elicited by the dangers connected with the we-symbol in the balancing process. This prolonged indulgence of the reality-testing, cautious, self-controlling features of culture and personality favors the drastic redefinition of the situation in directions gratifying to the underindulged, unreflecting, incautious, and spontaneous patterns of culture and personality.

Chapter IV

THE WAR CRISIS: THE DEMAND
FOR SECURITY

The expectation that violence will ultimately settle the clashing demands of nations and classes means that every detail of social change tends to be assessed in terms of its effect upon fighting effectiveness, divides participants in two conflicting camps, segregates attitudes of friendliness and of hostility geographically, and creates profound emotional insecurities in the process of rearranging the current political alignment. The accumulating tensions between the repressed and the repressing structures of personality and culture create a situation favorable to orgiastic release through the violence patterns which are all along recognized as potential, and which appear to furnish release in maximal assertion against the unfriendly features of the environment. The flight into danger becomes an insecurity to end insecurity. The demand for security takes the foreground.[1]

As long as the expectation of violence prevails, war, whether civil or interstate, whether called "war" or rechristened with expedient circumlocutions, will remain a trait of our civilization. "Peace" is a latent period between major crises during which vital resources are in process of readjustment with reference to the most probable ensuing crisis. It is a distorted notion of world society to suppose that a slumbering giant of carnage springs fully panoplied among a lamblike population, or that a world "order" is precipitately threatened. The rank and file is always shocked by the outbreak of hostilities, but the rank and file, like the élite, can only be shocked by what is expected yet suppressed. One of the hard sayings of

---

1. Miss C. E. Playne writes that "the spirit which accepted the war in 1914 was in truth suicidal . . . There was a feeling abroad that life without great excitement was no longer tenable; that explosive forces to the right and to the left had become too threatening, too dangerous to tolerate, too intractable to coordinate, impossible to subdue." *Society at War*, p. 21, Boston and New York, 1931.

psychopathology is that people are shocked by what they want to have happen, but which they struggle to deny admitting that they want to have happen. Ordinary common sense discounts the sincerity of many widows who seem to overmourn their husband's death, and this insight, like so many others of everyday experience, is of more general applicability than commonly supposed. The basis of excessive shock in death or war is furnished by powerful unadmitted attractions toward the event. This applies with special force to the class war, whose contingency is ignored or denied by the ruling classes as long as possible; the "revolution" is invariably "Ten Days That Shook the World" and despite years of premonitory rumbling is greeted as a sudden clap of thunder.

Our immediate task is to consider the setting in which the demand for security guides mobilized impulses toward war and to develop some of the relations between such a symbol of demand, and symbols of identification and expectation, and certain aspects of the material environment. In this chapter our attention will be directed mainly to the security demands which express themselves in wars of states and nations, rather than class wars, although certain of these implications will be mentioned.

The distinguishing mark of warfare is the performance of acts of violence directed against persons outside the community, justified in the name of, and accepted by, the community. The clearest meaning of the term community is a group of people inhabiting a compact territory; a group is distinguished from an aggregate in that it is composed of persons who are bound by ties of counteridentification. The word community is very often used to designate groups which are not only settled together, but which have well developed culture patterns; an effort is sometimes made to reserve the expression for culture configurations in which the reflective element is at a minimum, and in which enough unifying symbols and practices remain to exercise an unescapable and preponderating influence in the molding of personality.[2] However we choose to use the word, all acts of violence cannot usefully be included in the concept of warfare; and all acts of violence which are justified in the name of, and accepted by, a contiguous body of counteridentified people cannot profitably be included, without bogging down the concept in a myriad of minute marginal cases. There will remain the question of whether

2. For the use of the word community in certain of the more comprehensive senses alluded to here, see the work of Ferdinand Tönnies, R. M. MacIver, Mary P. Follett, and E. C. Lindeman.

feuds among families occupying adjacent localities should be in-included, such as the famous feud between the Hatfields and the McCoys who were separated by a small river branch between Kentucky and West Virginia.[3] Conflicts with nonpacified tribes within a small district are not "legal" wars, but "political" wars, falling within our definition. Conflicts with areas which are striving to secede from a given organization area are wars in our sense of the term, regardless of usage in international legal discussion.

The evidence seems to show that the war pattern as defined above may be viewed as universal among all cultures. Hobhouse, Wheeler, and Ginsburg made a careful survey of ethnological literature a few years ago, and reported nine cases of "no war."[4] These were found among some of the lower hunters and lower agricultural peoples. It now seems reasonable to interpret these instances as those in which rather exceptional circumstances led to the relinquishment of the war pattern; very weak tribes have been in the presence of over-whelmingly superior tribes which for one reason or another have neglected to obliterate them. Among the Negritos warfare seemed not to exist; they were a nomadic people living in loosely organized groups, utterly without any prospect of successful warfare against their well organized Malay neighbors. It was discovered later, however, that the Negritos on the Andaman Islands, where they were alone, engaged not uncommonly in war. The Eskimos of Greenland are not said to show any organized violence, but the Behring Straits Eskimos fight ferociously among themselves and with neighboring peoples.[5]

If we give to the concept of war the definition so far used, it is rather thin in meaning. There is the same lack of differentiation as among the doctors of another day who diagnosed so many complaints as "fevers." It is important to determine the relative role played by the pattern in the lives of the people employing it. Fruitful com-

3. See my discussion of "Feuds" in the *Encyclopaedia of the Social Sciences*.
4. *The Material Culture and Social Institutions of Simpler Peoples*, London, 1915.
5. Harry Hoijer has reviewed the evidence in a Master's thesis at the University of Chicago prepared under the direction of Professor Fay-Cooper Cole, as part of the Causes of War investigation. See also S. Rudolpf Steinmetz, *Sociologie des Krieges*, pp. 22–31, Leipzig, 1929; Pitirim Sorokin, *Contemporary Sociological Theories*, Chap. 6, New York and London, 1928; Maurice R. Davie, *The Evolution of War: A Study of Its Role in Early Societies*, New Haven, 1929. For a methodological criticism of the last, see the review by Ellsworth Faris in the *American Journal of Sociology*, 35 (1930): 1114–1116.

parisons ultimately depend upon the analysis of the genesis and development of wars in relation to personality and culture.

Certainly we desire to distinguish between "war" in a culture where all the young men are supposed to collect a head in inter-village forays, as a means of demonstrating maturity, and "war" in a culture where each man may spend a lifetime without being expected to kill an outsider, but is always subject to the possibility that he may be called upon to kill to the uttermost, without regard for supposed kinship ties.

It is relevant to contrast a raid which involves a few men and ends when one or two men are killed with an operation which continues until large numbers are destroyed, and resources of all kinds are drastically depleted. In our culture we know war as an enterprise which may include a high proportion of the population as active fighters, and which depends upon the extensive organization of civilians in the services of supply.

Another contrast is furnished by the war which is unanimously accepted by the community and the one which is accompanied by reluctance and regret, dissension and strife. Some operations are in the hands of a small number of highly trained specialists; others involve the *levée en masse*.[6]

In some cultures the war pattern is invoked over property disputes, or insulting gestures, or the abduction of the chief's daughter; elsewhere the inciting incidents have to do with efforts to proselyte.[7]

Scanning our own culture, and limiting the scope of our study of organized violence to the interstate field, we may classify war crises

6. See L. Schraudenbach, *Psyche und Organisation des "Volkskrieges,"* 1916.

7. The following account of a war over "honor" is in Dr. J. G. Zimmerman's *Essay on National Pride,* New York, 1799: "In the year 1458 the Confederates were invited by the city of Constance to a shooting party; but unfortunately, near the conclusion of the diversion, a Lucerner and a burgher of Constance, being about to shoot for a wager, the Lucerner staked a small piece of money coined in Bern, which is called a Plappert; this the other in derision called a Kuhplappert (that is, a piece of cow dung). This was taken so ill that the Canton of Lucern immediately urged the whole Confederacy to join them in resenting the injury. The forces of the state affronted, the honour-loving Lucern, aided by those of Underwald, opened the campaign by the invasion of Thurgaw. They seized on Weinfeld, because the proprietor of that place was a near relation of the aggressor, and laid a contribution on the inhabitants of two thousand florins. The other Confederates prepared likewise for war; the forces of Canton of Bern were already on foot, and arms were not laid down till the city of Constance restored their pitiful honour to the Swiss by a penitential gift of three thousand Rhenish florins." (Essay X)

into insecurity crises, exasperation crises, and indignation crises. Every crisis involves the concentraton of impulsive energy, and the probability of explosive release in violence, but there are important differences in the distribution of attitudes toward the situation. Some crises arise among participants or combinations of participants who believe themselves substantially equal in resources; this is the insecurity crisis which is inseparably connected with the balancing process where the expectation of violence prevails. Such was the World War. There are also incidental crises in world politics which, while they are by no means emancipated from the play of the balance, have other primary meanings. Sometimes a strong power resents interferences by a weak and isolated people with the claims of citizens of the strong power; the accumulating annoyances may culminate in an exasperation crisis terminating in war, as in the relations between Great Britain and the Boer Republic. Sometimes the strong power has been aroused against the supposed brutality of another power; and, although there is no direct suffering from these acts, enough hostility may be built up to create an indignation crisis when a direct incident occurs. Such was our Spanish-American war crisis.[8]

The analytic basis has already been laid for considering the insecurity crisis as a delayed reaction to the changes which modify the fighting effectiveness of various participants. The uncertainties connected with the balancing process generate the emotional insecurities which culminate in the overwhelming demand for security. More specific demands are always current in world politics; these are in continual redefinition among themselves and in relation to general demands for security.

In general terms, demands may be said to vary in relation to ego perceptions and calculations, and to superego and id valuations. Ego values change according to expectations in relation to circumscribed ends. Shifts in technology are perceived to devalue Chilean nitrate deposits, and this in turn modifies the significance assigned to overseas communication, to South American friendships, and to a network of affiliated details.[9] Technical innovations alter the importance

8. See for details, Walter Millis, *The Martial Spirit; A Study of Our War with Spain;* Boston, 1931; Marcus M. Wilkerson, *Public Opinion and the Spanish-American War, A Study in War Propaganda,* Baton Rouge, 1932.

9. The dialectical relations between the technical change and the symbolic revaluation will not here be considered; we are looking at the intersymbol dialectic for the time being.

of super-dreadnaughts, of colonial possessions in the tropics; current expectations that specific demands are worth pursuing are thus open to constant revision.

Now there are some demand symbols which are relatively uncomplicated by considerations of simple expediency; these symbols are sentimentalized in conformity with the mores. Holy places and capital cities come in this category. Palestine has been a storm center through the centuries because of the importance attached to it by the Greek Orthodox Church, the Roman Catholic Church, the Armenian Christians; there are also the Jewish Wailing Wall and the site of the Mosque of Omar, so highly reverenced by the Arabs. Possible allies are sometimes provisionally or finally rejected as infidels, even when the ruling élite in a state fears no inner disturbances.

Certain political demands draw heavily from the counter-mores or id values, even though a veil of mores symbolism may be drawn around them. Hostilities which are mainly elicited in connection with domestic affairs may be deflected from the symbols and practices of the ruling élite and turned toward symbols of foreign civilizations.

The insecurities of the balancing process are heightened by the circumstance that there are at least two plausible orientations which may be rationally urged in nearly all situations. Since the nature of the process is such that it may be expedient to pass over instantly into the camp of the "enemy," it is relevant to preserve contacts in all directions. The history of foreign policy shows continuous bickering over alternatives of policy among cliques of ambassadors, ministers, permanent foreign office officials, army and navy staffs, influential journalists, and public figures. The ever recurring problem of East or West in Germany is provisionally settled at a given time on the basis of a complicated relation among the various specialized persons referred to. Wherever the ego is able to put up a good case on either side of a question, the superego and the id come into their own; this is the source of emotional deformations of all kinds in the judgment of persons of wide experience, and leaves the outcome of specific situations singularly dependent upon the more primitive and massive components of the personality structure.

A war crisis grows with the concentration of affective impulses upon world political symbols, and moves toward the explosive release of tension in concerted action. The insecurity crisis, as previously shown, arises in the suppression of counterassertions which are precipitated in the play of the balance. The prolonged indulgence of the rational and superego structures of the personality (and corresponding patterns of the culture) prepares the way for a sudden redefinition of the situation in directions gratifying to the suppressed impulses and patterns; this is the flight into action on behalf of security. The dash into the revalidation of the war pattern offers supposed opportunities for the orgiastic release of the blocked aggressions.[10]

The war crisis proceeds by redefining the world in terms of acute impending dangers. Symbols like "German," "French," or "War" are enormously inclusive; during the developing phases of the critical situation the war symbol is reworked in a myriad of forms: "Will there be war?" "Is there a way out?" "Are the Germans mobilizing?" "Can war be stopped?" "Is war inevitable?" "War may be localized." "Shall it be again?" "Sentiment conciliatory in

10. The war crisis in general is a particular class of *crowd* formation. Gustave Le Bon in the *Psychologie des foules,* Paris, 1895, called all kinds of collective behavior "crowds." Most of the literature since Le Bon has objected to this catholicity of expression. We may use the word to indicate a situation in which persons are excitedly oriented toward a common focus of attention. Some crowds are expressive (some theater audiences) and others are political presented with demands for action, or indulging in action). The *public* is a situation in which persons with a common focus of attention are making debatable demands for action; the political crowd is characterized by undebatable demands for action. See my "The Measurement of Public Opinion," *American Political Science Review,* 25 (1931): 311–326. In examining any instance of crowd behavior, the relation to the total context must be considered. Some are mainly in defense of a conventional order (crowds moving as mobs to avenge a sexual assault) ; others are mainly hostile to an established order (revolutionary mobs). Viewing the configuration as a whole, crowds of various relations to the dominant patterns may be discovered, and their frequency, direction, and magnitude may be employed in diagnosing the cultural situation. Our previous analysis has suggested that the dynamic relations are functions of the relative indulgence of different personality and culture patterns; the insecurity crisis is a particular example of what follows from the suppression of aggressive impulses. The emphasis which is here laid upon the significance of crowds in relation to the larger context is parallel with the work of Theodor Geiger in *Die Masse und ihre Aktion,* Stuttgart, 1926; but Geiger's specific results differ from our own. On the field of crowd psychology, the work of the following persons may be referred to: Scipio Sighele, Pasquale Rossi, Émile Durkheim, Franz Eulenburg, Willy Hellpach, B. Krăkovič, S. Freud, William McDougall, W. Trotter, E. D. Martin, F. Schneersohn, W. Vleugels, G. Flügge, S. Sieber, F. Kraus, Robert E. Park, Georg Stieler, N. K. Michailovsky (in Russian; cited by Hecker, *Russian Sociology,* New York, 1916); for critical summaries, see Fausto Squillace, *Die soziologischen Theorien,* Leipzig, 1911; for bibliography, L. H. Ad. Geck, *Sozialpsychologie im Ausland,* Berlin and Bonn, 1928, and texts by Kimball Young, L. L. Bernard, and others.

Vienna." "The crisis may be averted." All the symbols of states, nations, and classes are called into the focus of publicity; incidents are excitedly elaborated, and stern calls for firm protest on behalf of collective honor, interests, and security abound.

As the situation intensifies, the war symbol becomes more richly laden with its implications for killing, and very primitive anxieties are reactivated within the personalities of those concerned. Even in the disguise of collective terms like "Germany" versus "France," the bearing of the imminent future upon the fate of the individual becomes more evident; "war" tends to invoke the terrible anxieties which are connected with the possibility of that final emasculation which is death itself. The opportunity for release in aggression is also an opportunity for extinction.

The insecurities connected with the war symbol are partially disposed of by vigorously asserting the "we" symbol at the expense of the "they" symbol. Dangers to the safety, the material claims, and the deference demands of the "we" group can be tolerated no longer; these interminable provocations must cease; the incessant alarms of recent years must come to an end; our security must be preserved; our benevolence has been imposed upon by designing conspirators. Chauvinism is the most extreme form of truculent assertion; it is an excited demand for the limitless, violent expansion of the nation.[11]

Chauvinistic boasts, threats, exhortations, and adulations are part of the process by which aroused impulses become concentrated around symbols of the community, including the courses of action deemed essential. By means of such manifestations the heightened reactivity level is given more coherent organization around the words, persons, and practices necessary to concerted action.

The assumption of violence keeps some attention focused upon the implications of events for the future of nation or class. When an incident is suddenly presented at the focus of attention as a challenge to some aspect of the we symbol in the name of they symbols of the same status, the competitive position of such symbols in relation to the whole body of insecurities current within the community is greatly increased. The reactivity level (or "tension level") may be high or low because of recent changes in the cost of living and employment (plus a hundred other significant details); the commanding advantages of the symbols of world politics in

11. See my discussion of "Chauvinism" in the *Encyclopaedia of the Social Sciences.*

attracting attention vastly increase the probability that private in-securities will be displaced upon such symbols of public objects.

When the focus of attention is occupied by interpretations of incidents as provocations, an opportunity is created for the abolition of the insecurities arising directly from this attack upon aspects of personality by means of symbolic "we" assertions. Those verbalists, journalists, and cartoonists who provide symbols of counteraggres-sion supply the representations which tend to abolish some of the anxieties aroused by the partial damage to the collective symbol.[12] But if acts of provocation are reported as continuing, vehement representations are not enough; demonstrations and other acts begin to appear; these are construed as provocative abroad, in turn pro-ducing "provocative" words and acts. The consulate is mobbed; visitors are manhandled in the streets; foreign plays are booed off the stage; students refuse to study the foreign language; informal boycotts are inaugurated against foreign goods; neutral persons are beaten upon suspicion of being members of the detested foreign group. The range of events which are interpreted as provocative expands: a bridge is blown up under mysterious circumstances and it is rumored that the foreigners did it; a foreign waiter resigns from his job, and it is reported that the reservists are being mustered to the colors; a foreign lecturer comments upon the importance of violence in politics, and it is reported that his country is planning war; relatives from abroad cancel their trip, and it is suspected that they know war is imminent; a rape is committed by a foreigner, and is sensationalized as an instance of the degeneracy of his nation.[13]

The monopoly of attention upon political symbols itself facilitates the distortion of reality judgments. We symbols in the secondary world of contact are as a rule rudimentarily organized within per-sonalities. Relevant knowledge is less, and codes of proper conduct are less completely defined; all of these circumstances favor the reactivation of more primitive modes of dealing with the world, and foster the elaboration of narcissistic, persecutory, and other uncritical symbols.

We have indicated some of the complexity of the interplay of sym-bol with symbol, overt act with overt act, in the crisis. It is interesting to speculate whether the comparative analysis of crises would enable

12. See Randolph S. Bourne, "The War and the Intellectuals," pp. 22–46 of *Untimely Papers,* New York, 1919.

13. See Georges Démartial, *Le mythe des guerres de légitime défense,* Paris, 1931.

us to disclose some features of the developing situation which would enable us to predict its probable termination in war. Some disease processes can be recognized rather early as "benign" and others as "malignant," and this analogy may at least stimulate us to scrutinize with renewed care the details of crisis situations in world politics.

A preliminary exploration of this kind was conducted by Schuyler Foster, who compared the space distribution of war news in selected United States newspapers between 1914 and our declaration of war on Germany.[14] This was a case study of how a large neutral state came into a war which was in full swing among large powers. Participation in the war came as the climax of series of popular crises in the relations of the neutral to the belligerents; these minor crises were numerous, and they showed certain varying characteristics which may be pertinent to our quest for signs of "malignancy." As these crises succeeded one another, there were indications of increasing self-preoccupation in relation to the war. The very early accounts of the European War dealt with it as the spectator views disasters to his neighbor. Later on, the focus of attention, as reflected in the press, was taken up with self-reactions toward the crisis. The news had much to report about our diplomacy, our preparedness, our opinions about the war, our national interests.

There also occurred a focusing of attention upon the state which ultimately became the opponent. Originally the belligerents were dealt with *en bloc*, and the emphasis was often upon the "European family quarrel." As familiarity with the general fact of war was attained, the details began to assume sharper definition and Germany became incessantly the object of reference.

The terms used in referring to mutual demands changed from the language of "legality" to the language of the "ideal." The vocabulary of morality, of general security, in short, of universalized demand, became more frequently employed. As acts of the other became construed as attacks upon the self symbol, and counterdemands became buttressed by universal symbols, demands for the conciliatory settlement of differences diminished, and demands for bellicose action rose from zero to enlarging proportions.[15]

Another study of crises has been made by Ralph H. Stimson.[16]

14. University of Chicago doctoral dissertation, 1932. One of the studies in the Causes of War investigation.

15. See the careful legal analysis of crisis in Werner Braun, *Démarche, Ultimatum, Sommation*, Berlin, 1930.

16. *The Control of the Manufacture of Armament*, University of Illinois doctoral dissertation, 1931.

Rapid increase in the number of references to war in characterizing relations between the United States and another country was taken as the index of "war scare." The index was compiled from the *New York Times Index,* choosing such headings as "U.S.—Japan, relations with," and counting the entries where the word "war" was used. Certain other terms, like "hostility," "break," or "clash" were by definition included. This index of the war scare was compared with an index of naval publicity which included references to this form of armament in the same source. The study of the period between 1913 and 1922 disclosed a tendency for war scare peaks to precede naval publicity peaks; this was also true in 1926–1927, but not in 1923–1925 and 1927–1929, when the two peaks coincide, or show a reverse relation.

An effort was made to relate such subjective manifestations with overt changes in the environment by seeking to correlate war and armament publicity with ratios of naval tonnage. The data taken from *Brassey's Naval and Shipping Annual* were used to indicate total tonnage in each navy and total tonnage building for each navy. There seemed to be no correlation with the ratio of tons in the Japanese Navy and tons in the United States Navy, in connection with war or armament peaks; but a correlation was discovered by taking the ratio between the displacement tonnage of war vessels *building* for the Japanese and the United States governments. The anti-Japanese war scares in the United States were thus found to coincide with rises in the ratio of naval building for the Japanese Navy to naval building for the United States, with the single exception of 1916–1917. This method of analysis disclosed, for stated periods, the nature of those changes in the overt environment which were most certain to precipitate changes in certain symbols of expectation, identification, and demand; the war crisis was dynamically connected with very circumscribed shifts in the overt situation. The basis was laid for further study of these varying interconnections, especially in relation to the dash into overt reactions after the ideological reorientation had reached a certain phase. A close association was found by Stimson between drops in the price of balanced armament firm stocks (like that of Bethlehem Steel) and the rise of naval publicity. Detailed study of the naval leagues in Great Britain and United States disclosed interlocking personnel connections with armament firms, supplying some indication of one of the specialized vehicles through which these material and ideological reactions were consummated. The nineteen founders of the Navy League of the United States were mostly connected with the manufacture of war material. The Bethlehem Steel Corporation, the Carnegie steel group, the Midvale steel group, the Harvey steel group, and Colonel Robert Thompson's International Nickel Company were represented.[17]

Another piece of research may be selected to illustrate available methods of attacking the problem of crises. The Far East Crisis from November, 1931, through April, 1932, was studied in order to disclose connections between changes in the focus of attention, in attitude expression, and in the movements of armed forces during the period.[18] The general starting point was that the preliminary phases of the crisis would show an increasing amount of attention; that the increase in ego references (to the United States) indicated a shift from spectator to participant; and that this shift would be accompanied by overt moves on the part of government officials to offset a change in the world position of the United States.

Attention indices were devised by compiling the number of items per week which were listed in the *New York Times Index* under the heading *China, Japan, Relations with*.[19] The graph showed a gradual increase in attention during November and December, a slight slump in January, and a peak in the first week of February.

The monthly "Ship Schedules" of the *Army and Naval Journal* were used to depict the movements of the war fleet. From seventy to ninety per cent of the whole United States fleet was usually accounted for at any one time. For the last four months of 1931, when tensions were piling up, as indicated by the rising curve of attention, there were no significant fleet movements recorded. January saw the first indication of a shift toward the Pacific, and February, when the peak of attention came in the attention graph, had the largest number of fleet movements toward the Asiatic coast in both number and type of vessel. The sharp drop in March corresponded to the sharp drop in the attention curve. In this case overt movements of

17. See *Hearings before a Sub-committee of the Committee on Naval Affairs, United States Senate, 71st Congress, 1st Session, pursuant to Senate Resolution 114, Resolution to investigate alleged activities of Mr. William B. Shearer on behalf of certain shipbuilding companies at the Geneva Naval Conference and a meeting of the Preparatory Commission, September 20, 21, 23, 24, 25, 26, 30, October 1, 1929, January 11, 1930.* Printed for use of Committee on Naval Affairs, Washington, 1930.

18. Seminar paper of Paul E. Treusch, University of Chicago, 1932.

19. As a check on the relation between item counts and space counts, the actual space was measured to the nearest centimeter; the correlation was so high that the space measurement could have been omitted without damaging the results.

the armed forces followed the accumulation of tensions, and appeared to play some part in relieving them.

On the assumption that the increase in ego references indicates a definite shift in attitude from spectator to participant, it was considered worth while to group the *Times* items into "neutral" references, which impartially observed and recorded facts, and "non-neutral" references, which ranged from expressions of slight concern for the interests of the United States to hints at possible war between the United States and other powers. The non-neutral items advanced sharply in January and in February. Thus there appeared a lag between the increased focusing of attention and the development of non-neutral comment, as there was a lag between the growth of non-neutral comment and overt ship movements.

By confining our attention too narrowly to the more acute phases of crisis, we may overlook details of the developing intercrisis situation which may have high prognostic value. One scheme of thinking is to treat the acute crisis as a belated reaction to consummated changes in fighting effectiveness brought on by various social changes. From this viewpoint, the war crisis is an effort to reinstate an "equilibrium" relation which has become "disequilibrated" because of deformations in the balancing process itself. Perhaps we may be successful in finding some details in the intercrisis configuration which regularly multiply before the crisis begins to show itself. Perhaps there will be changes in the overt activities of men in relation to one another which can be used to presage the probable appearance of ideological readjustments closely related to political symbols. Of course, it is possible that such equilibrium analyses are inapplicable to our problem, since new constellations, new emergents, are constantly arising. We may find ourselves at sea in a multitude of indices with respect to which we have introduced so many assumptions that our ultimate findings will possess but a spurious specificity. But the precise ordering of the details of historically elapsed events may possibly indicate future regularities; although regularity in the past may only increase the probability of some sudden disappearance of the pattern, furnishing future historians with an instance of "leaping development."

The best effort to gather results in relation to the equilibrium style of thought was published just after the war by Slavko Šećerov.[20]

20. *Economic Phenomena before and after War: A Statistical Theory of Modern Wars*, London, 1919.

He takes as his starting point the general proposition that as long as the increased consuming capacity of the community is balanced by its producing capacity, there can be no disturbances of economic equilibrium, except through natural population growth, which because of "biological peculiarities of race" may not keep pace with production. As the production of primary goods is replaced by the production of secondary (manufactured) goods, the production of secondary goods soon overtakes the demand in a limited area; it is therefore necessary to supplement the available area of the community by new areas which produce primary goods, or else the economic equilibrium must be restored by entirely domestic changes.

To reestablish the economic equilibrium it is necessary to lower the consumption, that is, the standard of living, or to increase proportionately the production of primary economic goods, or to lower the increase of population, or to look for supplementary territories providing the necessary primary economic goods and offering a market for secondary goods. Now of these four possibilities, two are effective before war, that is the consumption is lowered and the rate of natural increase is depressed. But the equilibrium is effectively reestablished by war. War effects an actual diminution of population (killing, diseases), it lowers still more the consumption and the standard of living; it raises proportionately the production of primary economic goods in communities, particularly in industrial ones; it gives an opportunity to acquire new supplementary territories by a successful war, and it destroys or binds the capital wanting employment.[21]

Figures are extensively mobilized to show the following phenomena before wars: a decline of the rate of natural increase of population; a rise of consumption per capita, indicating a slight pressure of consumption in the years immediately preceding war; disproportionate production of primary in relation to secondary goods, and the consequent rise of prices for primary goods. Postwar tendencies are said to be: a decline of consumption and a lowering of the standard of life; a rise of the rate of natural increase of the population; a proportionate rise in the production of primary economic goods in relation to secondary goods. It is also endeavored to show that the "aggressor" in war shows the preceding evidences of disequilibrium more conspicuously than the aggressed.

This particular monograph is open to criticism but it states the equilibrium method clearly, and by its laborious application to quantities of data establishes strong presumptions. Its net effect

21. *Ibid.*, p. 39.

is to treat the demands for this or that detail of policy, together with excited demands for security, as transitional phenomena in a process of reestablishing certain relations among material contexts. The treatment is not developmental because it neglects to emphasize the dependence of the discerned regularities upon certain patterns which, if reversed, would modify the possibility of continuing the regularities specified. The terms employed cover changes which have complex relations among themselves; it is very difficult to hold constant the terms "primary" and "secondary," "consumption" and "production." Strong presumptions are, however, raised that the analysis of the various war crises must begin before the acute phases in order to explore the total configuration in which they are embedded.

Chapter V

INDEPENDENCE MOVEMENTS: THE DEMAND FOR EQUALITY

The demand to be emancipated from an inferior status is one component of those national, racial, and labor movements which have figured so prominently in recent history. The rejection of an inferior status may be joined with demands for equality with other collective symbols, as in independence nationalism. Or the rejection of an inferior status may be associated with outright demands for supremacy through the total destruction of rivals, as in proletarian socialism. Movements in the name of collective entities not infrequently change their character at different phases of growth, sometimes starting as protests against discrimination and developing into discrimination movements against others. Nationalistic agitations have sometimes begun as demands for equality, and expanded into imperialistic demands for supremacy over those of alien culture. Labor movements which have started to improve working conditions within the framework of the capitalistic order have become crusades against the social system as a whole; and, reversely, proletarian revolutionism has made peace with the forms of parliamentary democracy.

Fully developed independence nationalism is a mass demand to become, or to remain, a state which occupies equal status with other states. The symbol structure of independence nationalism represents a synthesis of identifications, demands, and expectations which displays important differences from one historical situation to the next. The varied manifestations for which the common name is used should be distinguished, even though the operation strips away the flesh of historical detail and leaves exposed the bare schematic skeleton.

What may be called *democratic* nationalism took root in organized states as an incident in the struggle of various social groups to supersede feudal and dynastic control. The alignment of gentry versus landlord, of bourgeoisie versus aristocracy, were conflicts to broaden the basis of access to governmental authority. Since the symbols which embodied the protest of these classes against the constituted order were made in "democratic" language, they were able to get the aid of all dissatisfied elements in their campaign against the accredited symbols and practices. This was, in effect, an overgeneralizing of the protest, since the rising social class was certain to be contented with less sweeping changes than were favored by the affiliated allies. At certain phases of the growth of the protest movement, control passed out of the hands of the moderate elements, alienating their support, and driving them into vigorous counteraction to liquidate the "excesses" perpetrated by their confederates. The bourgeoisie of France drew back from the "extremism" of the French masses, and they ultimately succeeded in bringing affairs to a moderate culmination. In the course of its growth in Great Britain, Holland, and France, democratic nationalism was elaborated until it came to include various demands for strong legislatures, wide suffrage, political parties, freedom of agitation, civil rights, economic individualism, small independent agrarian proprietorship, and church disestablishment. The bold French pattern of antimonarchism, anticlericalism, and antifeudalism was no doubt the least equivocal form of modern nationalism.

During the days of counterassertion against Napoleon, Prussia became the seat of *liberation* nationalism as the symbols of the older social order partially incorporated various features of democratic nationalism, and retained their control over the government. The dynasty, the bureaucracy, the army, legitimized themselves as defenders of the whole community against the invader, and nationalism became a mass movement of defense against a territorially segregated external enemy. The social structure of the community was such that the clash between feudal and bourgeois elements was not yet present on the grand scale which was exemplified in Great Britain and in France, so that fewer concessions were made to democratic forms than in the west.

As the nationalistic pattern spread during the last century, it began to appear where disunited groups which possessed traditions of cultural and political unity came to believe that they were discriminated against in politics, business, language, worship, and education. The work of organizing the random insecurities of the community around these particular demands for equal status was greatly facilitated by the intellectuals.[1] Such was the phenomenon of *oppression* nationalism.

Where traditions of cultural and political unity had practically faded away, the work of the intellectual in quickening the quiescent sense of cultural unity through cultural creation and political agitation was even more conspicuous and successful. In some instances the group concerned was not discriminated against until quite late in the growth of collective demands, and scarcely fits into the category of oppression, but rather of *resurrection* nationalism. Some of the history-less nations of Europe acquired a cultural personality, a language, a literature, a history, and a mission in the course of the last century. Frequently the diffusion of nationalist symbols came about in connection with the rise of the bourgeoisie and substantially recapitulated the social setting in which democratic nationalism first arose.

Another form taken by nationalism had almost as little to do with protest against gruelling oppression as resurrection nationalism. When people who share the culture of the ruling élite of a state live on the periphery of the state in noncontiguous areas, many processes of differentiation set in. The developing community has a different focus of attention for news than has the home country, and this favors distinctive forms of activity, organization, and sentiment. The growth of psychological separatism may be expressed ultimately in various conflicts over policy with the central authorities of the state, which may be generalized into nationalist movements. This line of development is *prestige* nationalism, and is exemplified in the history of Canada, Australia, New Zealand, and the thirteen colonies which later organized the United States. Genuinely nationalist movements are not to be confused with separatist demands which may be made in nationalistic vocabularies but with which the masses are not identified. A ruling élite may buttress its own demands by adopting a nationalistic phraseology, although the community remains aloof, which was true of some of the secessions from the Spanish and Turkish empires.

When revolutions at the center of the state provoke reactions on behalf of the older institutions at the margin of the state, we may be dealing with an instance of *separatist* nationalism. The conflict between the governments at the center and at the periphery results in centralizing both of them, and in uniting the populace around

1. See Sigismund Gargas, *Die Minderheit,* The Hague, 1926; H. A. Miller, *Races, Nations, and Classes,* Philadelphia, 1924.

their distinguishing symbols. Some recent, though incomplete, exhibitions of separatism occurred in the Rhineland and in Bavaria when Berlin was captured by "revolutionary" régimes in 1918.

The nationalistic movements in China and India are *anti-imperialistic in emphasis.* They arose among peoples possessing traditions of cultural and political unity, though incomplete in many respects; and they regard themselves as potentially powerful, despite the recent encroachments by cultures with superior physical and organizing technique.

In connection with the struggles which have arisen to restrict the spread of the last world-revolutionary pattern, and especially to limit the authority of the élite in control of the Soviet Union, *socialistic nationalisms* have been generated in countries with important middle-class formations. All these movements have emphasized parochialism (that is, nationalism) by emphasizing the *Russian* character of the world revolution and the local affinities of their own programs. They have, none the less, borrowed some of the vocabulary and the techniques of the revolutionary dictatorship. In turn, the assimilation of the élite in Russia to localism makes progress. The urges toward world revolution are principally linguistic; the policy is that of upbuilding Russia, which is presented to the community as the best way of reaching the goal of world revolution. The Third International has been inconvenient to the Russian élite in many respects, and has been cast in the shadow in the interest of survival within Russia. A study of the symbolism of the régime shows the deemphasizing of world for the benefit of local symbols.

If we use the term emancipation in the fullest psychological sense, as revealed through the intensive examination of specific persons, we limit it to the achievement of release from an internalized symbol of authority. The man who seeks to flee the clutches of a bandit is not emancipating himself in this deeper psychological sense because he is not bound by his own superego to accept the highwayman's authority. Submissiveness to an authority is achieved when many impulses in the personality are repressed, and when these repressions are maintained by the inner inhibiting structure which takes the place of the external agency which precipitated the original repression. Emancipation entails unconscious conflict between the repressed and the resisting structures of the personality, between the id and the superego, and is completed when certain of the older superego patterns are thrust aside, and the personality has been restabilized on a new basis.

Independence nationalist movements are seldom emancipation movements in the complex psychological meaning of the word. The Prussians who rose against Napoleon were performing less complicated acts than the Frenchmen who rose against the Bourbons, since the Frenchmen were breaking through the barriers of their own juvenile consciences which had been formed to revere the symbolisms of the dynastic, ecclesiastical, and feudal order. The Prussians were not bound by their consciences to obey the French. Oppression nationalism among the Polish nobles or intellectuals was much less complicated psychologically than among the Polish peasants, many of whom were often unconsciously bound to the authoritarian order around them. To stimulate nationalism among them was to encourage an act which in the fullest sense of the word was one of emancipation. Resurrection nationalism among peoples who had been absorbed in an organization area dominated by another culture also meant rejecting the principal symbols previously incorporated into the personality. Anti-imperialistic nationalism arises among peoples who are not emotionally bound to the outsider, but the growth of the movement depends upon rejecting many of the symbols and practices of the old culture, and the incorporation of the new. The profound disturbances which are involved in adapting Indian or Chinese cultures to the technology, democracy, and proletarianism of the West are due to the depth of the changes required in personality organization.

Even where emancipation adjustments are importantly involved in independence movements, they display varied forms from one individual to the next. When for short-cut purposes one speaks of an independence or an emancipation movement, the implication is not that all participants are passing through the same psychological process, even though the distinguishing psychological events are found often enough to justify the characterization. There are persons who act *on* the masses, but who are not psychologically acting *with* them. They go along with the collective movement for expedient considerations, often seizing the deference opportunities offered in the situation to rise to leading positions. I have the case history of one orator who could never understand why the masses always "fell" for him. He described to his physician how one part of his personality, his "real" self, seemed to sit sardonically commenting upon the rest of his self while it performed the curious laryngeal and gesticulatory operations that thrilled the masses.

Personalities often become emancipated from specific authority symbols associated with large groups like "nations," "races," or "classes." They are not "cosmopolitan" if this word implies emotional attachment to some symbol of world-wide order. They may be "individualists" who are emotionally released from large group names, although for expedient reasons they may play the public role of "American," "proletarian," or "Christian."

But these individual emancipations are too infrequent to be distinguishing marks of mass movements. Mass emancipations are passages from old to new symbols. They involve a new symbol rival to the old, which is legitimized by a sustaining myth, and executed by an élite which rises to the main posts of income and deference in the name of the new symbol and its mythological elaboration. During acute phases of mass movements, wholesale releases from superego and mores control occur, resulting in promiscuous killing, in orgiastic sexuality, and in wanton property destruction; but the completed movement reimposes restraints upon this behavior in the name of the new collective symbol.[2]

A detailed comparison of independence and of emancipation movements can be made with reference to the various possibilities of reaction which are disclosed by the intensive study of specific personalities. The dynamic possibilities in the readjustment of id and superego relations, which are revealed in personality research, may be used to guide our attention back to concrete historical patterns in order to see which of the segments of the gamut of possibility were realized in each specific pattern. The interplay of the intensive and the extensive perspectives may strengthen the total process of analysis.

Submissiveness is the total absence of conscious assertion in the name of the central ego symbol against the authority symbol which has been incorporated into the personality structure. In extreme cases this involves self-sacrifice to the point of self-destruction. When a relationship of slavery is psychologically complete, the slave is ready to lay down his life for his master. During times of crisis an authoritative secondary symbol may be invested with so much meaning within the personality that the central ego symbol asserts no separate claims. The self-forgetfulness in war and class crises when individuals rush into danger shows what is meant here; love of the primary ego symbol is insignificant; all is sacrificed for the secondary

2. The disordering and the reordering relations are formally stated in Pitirim A. Sorokin, *The Sociology of Revolution,* Philadelphia and London, 1925.

symbol. States of total infatuation in intimate life show the same characteristics; all is surrendered for the other.

Even in very extreme cases of submissiveness the central ego symbol may express itself indirectly, often in nonverbal forms. Many of the deeply intimidated (castrated) people oversmile, and discharge their tensions in music, dancing, games of chance and repetition, and in drug intoxication. Much laziness in work arises from the repression of hostility. Numerous techniques of passive aggression are worked out against authority. Lying is especially characteristic since this is one of the means of protecting the personality against complete domination, and occurs as an unconscious protection against the disclosure of underlying hostility. Adaptation devices are generated to "work" authority; the person appears pitiful, pleads, persuades, and thus elicits aid by exaggerating his dependent role. The fantasy world of the deeply intimidated person usually shows much preoccupation with the danger theme. Hostilities express themselves in dreams, day fantasies, and nightmares; the superego seeks to maintain order within the personality, and guilt reactions against hostilities are expressed in light feelings of insecurity, or in acute fear attacks. Sometimes the anxieties are referred to a single object in the environment; thus the person develops a fear of being in a closed room. Ceremonials, rituals, and charms are evolved to allay insecurities; the individual must clear his throat before speaking, put on his left shoe first, and carry a particular watch, or his embarrassment mounts to unbearable heights. The 'individual may become obsessively preoccupied with how much he should tip waiters, and spend hours in fruitless elaboration of considerations pro and con. He may doubt the utility of effort, and develop scruples about the completion of simple acts. All of these substitute reactions cloak hostilities of varying magnitudes, and handicap the person in different degrees in overtly adjusting to the requirements of the environment.[3]

The intimidated person displays his ambivalence toward other intimidated people of the same category, combining extremes of demonstrative affection and of hostility. The hostilities are particularly significant when the other person undertakes to play an authority role. This acting out of the inhibited impulses to overturn authority reawakens these impulses in the intimidated person; this precipitates defensive acts on the part of the resisting superego; and the person

3. On the role of the repression of the ego impulses, see Freud, *Civilization and Its Discontents*, New York, 1930. The development of the psychology of the ego has been greatly stimulated by Alfred Adler.

often seeks escape from these tensions by attacking the features of the environment which precipitated the crisis and which are vulnerable targets. Hence the aspiring one is ridiculed for "putting on airs" and "aping his betters." The rigid self-discipline of the superego extends in this manner to the disciplining of others who are closely identified with the self. The individual tends to continue to identify himself with the established order, and to ignore or to deplore challenging leaders who arise within his own group.

The characteristics of submissive conduct briefly enumerated here enable one to turn with new interest to the study of specific situations in which inequalities of status are involved. Do we find that those who submit to the dominant symbols display some of the characteristics which have been summarized from the intensive study of the strict id and superego relation? Those who have occupied an inferior status would be expected to show more of certain patterns of behavior than those who occupy or have occupied a superior status: more fawning smiles, more distrust of leadership arising in the group itself, more development of the danger theme in myth and legend, more satiric stories and tales ridiculing members of the same inferior group . . . (to enumerate a few representative hypotheses).

The process of becoming emancipated is that of expressing repressed impulses by casting aside older superego structures, and achieving a new integration. Emancipation means enduring the terrific insecurities which are generated within the personality structure as the older inhibiting devices seek to enforce themselves upon the previously repressed impulses. Anxieties are precipitated which must be endured before they can be abolished.

What is involved in the emancipation process may be indicated by reviewing some details from the intimate history of F, who was for many years the submissive admirer of a distinguished executive for whom he was private secretary. F was the companion of his chief at golf, billiards, dinner, and work. All the associates of the chief addressed F familiarly as "Ted" and treated him socially as though he were son rather than secretary.

The first sign of the emancipation process was slight embarrassment in the company of the chief. F began to avoid social engagements with him, and woke up in the morning depressed and lethargic. Bitter criticisms of this or that detail of the chief's dress, voice, or manner appeared in his reveries while he shaved and dressed. F began to tell himself that he wanted to be captain of his own ship and quit being cabin boy on somebody else's. He thought of John,

Tom, and Bill who were on their own in law, medicine, and advertising; in fact, the first twinges of discontent with himself came when he received the announcement that John was opening an office of his own, and overheard appreciative comments on John's ability from his chief.

F's bearing toward his superior became formal and slightly surly. One day his chief addressed him affectionately as "Ted" and jocularly told him that he was looking sour and needed a mistress to snap him out of it. F reddened and retorted that he was tired of being "Ted" this and "Ted" that, like a ten year old. The chief was puzzled and hurt, but passed the matter over with a tactful gesture. F flagrantly defied all the ordinary rules of sound judgment, threw himself with great vigor into his work for a time, did long hours of extra drudgery, and felt chronically tired and tense. He became more scrupulous about deciding matters of detail, and insisted upon more consultation with the chief and more formality in decision making. In some family troubles with the chief's divorced wife and son, F went out of his way to defend the claims of the son for more liberty than the father was willing to concede, although previously he had criticised the boy for undisciplined conduct. His moody fits increased in frequency and intensity; he pondered on the colossal futility of life and contemplated suicide. At times he felt powerful surges of anger at his chief, and was tormented by nightmares in which he awoke in the nick of time to escape from terrifying calamities. He began to dream of the death of his superior; one of his dreams showed an opera which was being conducted jointly by Paul Whiteman and Toscanini, who reached great pitches of enthusiasm as an old man—his own chief—was elaborately slain. There were also moments when he felt that he would never find anyone so strong, so understanding, so gracious as the chief; he became overdemonstrative and very apologetic for his erratic behavior.

Before his independence reactions arose, F had worked off his hostilities by nonverbal devices like tennis, golf, dancing, and music. He had also developed a ritual around a ring which was painfully small for him, but which he drew on and off a certain number of times in the process of dressing and undressing. F had been famous for his charming smile, and his thoughtfulness of others; he was continually being showered with gifts and favors from both men and women.

F finally bolted from his superior's organization, after provoking a violent altercation, and went over to the firm of an attorney who was cleaning up the city; F's former employer was partially compromised in the disclosures which followed this zealous crusade.

If we examine mass emancipation movements, we discover that the growing intensity of the struggle draws out reactions of the kind briefly described in the case of F. Withdrawal behavior displays itself in leaving the representatives of authority by themselves, and in developing more formal manners of dealing with them. Angry outbursts occur at "presumptuous" familiarity of superiors, concessions are demanded, and overscrupulousness indicates the growing strength of the unconscious impulses to damage authority. Hostile grumblings abound, and rumors are broadcast about the heartlessness of authority. Reports of cruelty and strength go along with rumors of weakness through dissension and immoral conduct. The unleashing of the impulse-life of the personality displays itself in the wider oscillation between contradictory moods and contradictory acts. Over-propitiatory gestures appear when the superego reasserts itself on behalf of the older symbolism; thus the peasants on certain Russian estates spontaneously gave extra gifts to their landlords just before the outburst of the revolution.

Instances of provocative behavior abound. Individuals dash into public denunciations of authority, seeking through hyperactivity to still their inner terror at the utterance of "dangerous thoughts." Ordinarily blasphemous or improper or subversive words and gestures evoke horror; this is explicitly akin to the revulsion of the inhibited child against impulses, images, words, and feelings connected with sexuality. The threats (of positive damage and of withdrawal of affection) administered by the early environment in establishing "proper" habits of language and gesture show their influence in the insecurities inflicted by the superego when violations, or strong impulses to violate, are activated. The child has the feeling of being befouled, irreverent, dirty, and damned; and this childlike attitude is organized about symbols of secondary objects like "constitution," "God," "commissars," and "emperor." Indulgence of the prohibited involves self-punishment reactions in the form of anxiety; often the self-punishment is achieved indirectly by provoking the environment into damaging the person, thus releasing inner stresses through the propitiation of martyrdom. Diabolism appears, which consists in reversing the previous taboos; the Bronx cheer supersedes the salute to the flag.

Some of the inner anxiety is disposed of by transformation into ecstasy, and murderous impulses become idealized in the service of a mystically held cause. The personality is sensitized toward the elaboration of the self symbol, which is reiterated and embellished; other symbols are charged with hostile affect. The recurring themes of we-symbol elaboration are: "We are of great worth," "We are unjustly situated," "We must revolt," "Victory is sure," "You neutrals should help," "You powerful should renounce your unjust power." When these symbols are connected with demands for merely equal status, the emancipation movement is an independence movement; when such symbols are connected with demands for the total subjugation of the other group, the emancipation movement is imperialistic.

The mythology of great or superior worth is stereotyped in pattern, although endlessly diversified in detail. Many collective symbols emphasize the location of the group "between" other people, and define the historic mission of the culture as that of mediating between two peoples, cultures, religions, or civilizations. In Paris you hear that the outpost of Eastern barbarism is the Rhine; in Berlin it is Poland; in Warsaw it is the boundary of the Soviet Union. In Southern Europe the term "Vlach" means dirty, backward, superstitious, Asiatic. The mission of many groups is the preserve culture against the "Vlach." The Dalmatians on the islands call the Dalmatians on the mainland "Vlach"; the mainlanders call the Bosnians "Vlach"; the Bosnians call the Serbians "Vlach"; the Serbians call the Roumanians "Valch"; and the Croats call all orthodox peoples "Vlach."

Some of the proletarian themes of emancipation are indicated in the following:

We are of great worth. ("We *work*.")
　　　　"We are the men who matter,
　　　　　　We are the working class."[4]
We are unjustly situated. ("We are betrayed by worthless promises.")
　　　　　"Work and pray, live on hay,
　　　　　　　You'll get pie in the sky when you die."[5]
We must revolt.
　　　　　"Enough submission and slavish love—
　　　　　　We'll drown the sufferings of the people in blood!"[6]

4. R. M. Fox, *An Anthology of Revolutionary Poetry,* Compiled and Edited by Marcus Graham, Introduction by Ralph Cheyney and Lucia Trent, p. 187, The Active Press, New York, 1929.

5. Words by Joe Hill, Tune, "Sweet Bye and Bye," *ibid.*, p. 84.

6. "The Anarchist March," Translated by Marcus Graham, *ibid.*, p. 349.

"Arise, ye pris'ners of starvation!
Arise, ye wretched of the earth."[7]
Victory is sure.
"The tyrant's chains are only strong
While slaves submit to wear them."[8]
You neutrals should help.
"If there breathe on earth a slave,
Are ye truly free and brave?"[9]
You powerful should renounce your unjust power.
"How long,
O cruel nation,
Will you stand, to move the world,
on a child's heart?"[10]

An emancipation movement that succeeds in capturing power has not completed the act of emancipation, since personalities continue to be partially controlled by their older unconscious formations. The external evidences of the older order tend to stimulate submissive reactions, and thus to maintain insecurities within many personalities. This is the dynamic basis for the wars of extermination which are conducted against symbols and practices associated with the old régime. The nationalities which achieved independence after the World War were notoriously loath to speak the language of their former rulers. In Prague it was good tactics for the visitor to address a policeman in Czech, French, or English, and very gradually to relapse into German; in Warsaw it was incautious to begin with Russian or German, although after nurturing the assumption that everybody understood French, the way was paved to the good fellowship which made German permissible. Metamorphoses were wrought in the names of streets, towns, schools, shops; signs changed on stores, street cars, billboards, railway trains; monuments and edifices intimately associated with the former superior were demolished. Forms of address, habits of dress, and scores of intimate details of living were modified in the various crusades to dissociate the new from the old. The sweeping transformations in Russia are symbolized in the passage from "St. Petersburg" to "Petrograd" to "Leningrad."

7. "The Internationale," *ibid.,* p. 309.
8. Charles Cole, *ibid.,* p. 58.
9. James Russell Lowell, *ibid.,* p. 94. Mr. Lowell was not a proletarian, but this is repeated by proletarians.
10. Elizabeth Barrett Browning, *ibid.,* p. 54.

The demolition of the older symbolism is usually accompanied by acts which alienate possible allies. Personalities who have risen to the level of their former chiefs often show powerful self-punishment reactions; taking the place of the earlier authority symbol is prohibited by the superego, and insecurities lead to inefficient or disgraceful conduct. The officiousness of the newly arrived, the insolence of the parvenu, are reaction-formations against the reinstatement of submissiveness. This conduct may damage the immediate ego objectives of the person by alienating possible financial and diplomatic assistance. There is persistent overestimation of the strength of the deposed authority, and unnecessarily harsh policies. The cultural supremacy of the Old South to the North left an inferiority reaction in the North which partially motivated the policies of reconstruction days. It will be recalled that F expressed himself overtly in the crusade against his former chief; he "paid out" presently by developing such serious impairments to efficiency that psychoanalytical therapy was necessary.

The spread of emancipation movements in society is intimately connected with changes in the division of labor. The rise of modern national, racial, and labor movements was dynamically connected with those innovations in the technique of production which expanded so rapidly in our culture. One of the principal consequences of the expansion of technology has been the diversification of the working conditions in society. Each new subdivision of activity furnishes a new environment, and each new environment creates a more or less distinctive focus of attention. The focus of attention in turn leads to the modification of the identifications, demands, and expectations of the personalities concerned. Many of the persons who saw new opportunities to extend their claims upon society for income and deference were blocked by traditional methods of poor relief or apprentice training. Some of these arrangements could be changed by controlling the dominant center of the organization area (the capital or the metropole). Innumerable instances of local frustration built up hostilities toward the symbols and practices of the central régime, creating receptivity for master symbols to universalize, legitimize, and coordinate these diverse impulses.

The work of elaborating the appropriate symbolism, and of inaugurating a division of labor specialized to its promotion, was characteristically that of "intellectuals." Hand in hand with the complication of the "technological" environment has gone the complication of the "symbolic" environment, and among the chief beneficiaries have been the intellectuals, who extract safety, income, and deference by using language in arguing, reciting contemporary and historical anecdotes, and poetizing future potentialities. The intellectuals are distinguished from other specialists on symbols by their concentration upon symbols of conflicting values. In more detail, the activities performed by this cultural-skill group are the following: proposing policies to the major élite or counter-élite; arguing over policies; redefining collective symbols; reporting and commenting on the policy implications of current affairs, transmitting the mythology of the group. It is obvious that the expansion of modern society has multiplied the opportunities for persons who have the skill and motivation appropriate to collecting news, writing history, teaching dogma, circulating editorial comment, elaborating revolutionary and counter-revolutionary symbols, and arguing over expediencies. The task of coordinating relationships in the new and variable world of modern technology has thus favored the expansion of the old legal profession. The problem of redefining ancient formulas to fit an unparalleled number of novel purposes has made the lawyer's skill quite as valuable in private consultation, negotiation, and agreement, as in court.

The "capital" of the intellectual is his learning, and he may be considered to be in competition with landowners, business enterprisers, and manual workers for safety, income, and deference in society. The absence of a common symbol of identification, and the struggles of intellectuals against one another, have somewhat obscured this common role. Intellectuals have elaborated symbols on behalf of nations, races, classes, religions, and all other collective entities; little wonder that Lenin dismissed them contemptuously as prostitutes. But their struggles with one another, conducted with words, allusions, theories, and all kinds of dialectical artifices, multiply the opportunities in society for this kind of activity. Analysts of culture have become more and more aware of the function of intellectuals in emancipation and counter-emancipation movements. All nationalist movements have exhibited the role of the skilled verbalist; but perhaps the most significant evidence of the rise of the intellectuals as a dynamic and reconstitutive class in society is furnished by the various labor movements. Indeed, the socialist ideal, which diffused so rapidly during the last century, depicted an administrative organization where intellectuals would have most of the desirable posts.

This interpretation of the role of the intellectual worker was generalized for labor movements by Waclaw Machajski (whose pen name was A. Wolski) early in the present century. Machajski spent ten years in Siberia for his activities as a revolutionary Marxist in Poland. He reflected upon his experiences and formed a theory which placed the orthodox ideologists on the defensive. He declared that the socialist theories of the nineteenth century expressed the class interest of the intellectual workers and not of the manual workers. The mental workers are a rising privileged class struggling for a place in the sun against the older landlord and enterpriser classes. Learning was their capital, and political democracy or revolutionary dictatorship, according to circumstances, were the steps in their advance toward power. They won over the manual workers by helping them in their early struggles for better wages, and by dangling before them the social ideal of equality.[11]

The development of ideological modifications in relation to new environments is a long drawn out interplay because of the vast number of reactions by means of which human beings are able to remove the insecurities arising from new situational requirements. Stresses arising anywhere in the personality system, it may be recalled, can be disposed of by bodily movements, autistic fantasies, critical reflections, or object orientations; and any new expedient of tension removal can be stereotyped and repeated. Hence political symbols must compete with all other symbols, together with all the channels of autistic and somatic release, for the control of personal energies. When particular symbols are incorporated within any personality, they immediately offer resistance to novel alternatives and elaborations, thus creating a maximum number of possible contradictions within the personality system, and with other personalities.

Changes in the material environment initiate such partial readaptations of the symbolic equipment of the persons seemingly affected, that "lag" becomes one of the conspicuous social phenomena.[12] Some material changes do not uniformly affect the focus

11. See Max Nomad, *Rebels and Renegades,* New York, 1932; Julien Benda, *The Treason of the Intellectuals,* New York, 1928; Hendrik de Man, *Die Intellektuellen und der Sozialismus,* Jena, 1926; Edouard Berth, *Les méfaits des intellectuels,* Paris, 1914; A. Cartault, *L'intellectuel,* Paris, 1914; T. G. Masaryk, *The Spirit of Russia,* 2 vols., London, 1919; K. Nötzel, *Die Soziale Bewegung in Russland,* Stuttgart, 1923; Hans Kurella, *Die Intellektuellen und die Gesellschaft,* Wiesbaden, 1913; Karl Jaspers, *Psychologie der Weltanschauungen,* Third Edition, Berlin, 1925; L. K. Tao, "Unemployment among Intellectual Workers in China," *Chinese Social and Political Science Review,* 13 (1929): 251–261; Max Handman, "The Sentiment of Nationalism," *Political Science Quarterly,* 36 (1921): 104–121.

12. Compare William F. Ogburn, *Social Change,* New York, 1922.

of attention of individuals exposed to them. Machines may be speeded in one factory practically without comment; the same material change in another factory may be publicly announced, immediately observed, and simultaneously evaluated. Persons who specialize in propagating new symbols of identification, of demand, or of expectation find it essential to repeat these symbols incessantly in order to increase the probability of their becoming incorporated within the personalities of the individuals affected. Since the specialist in reiteration may be able to extract income and deference from the environment in the shape of dues from an organization and approval in the press, the repetition of the symbol becomes a significant constituent of the division of labor existing in the situation. Since so many symbols are possible competitors, the contradictions of response are intensified by the growth of competing symbol specialists.

Indeed, the change of any provisional equilibrium induces substitutive reactions which may proceed through initial phases of insecurity, symbolization, crisis, and relatively stable readaptation. Propaganda, as the name for the self-conscious spread of symbols to mobilize collective action, thus tends to maximize insecurities, and hence crises. If the underlying environmental changes are comparatively slight, the catharsis function of propaganda may dissipate the available insecurities which are available for discharge; but if the insecurity level is more profoundly affected, propaganda hastens the discovery of contradictions, and may indeed precipitate a resort to the use of more coercive forms of adjustment than debate and enactment. The emergence of a pattern of world revolution appeals to the insecure elements in every other organization area. Propaganda support may indeed be forthcoming from the center of origin of the new élite-symbol relation, and the resulting challenge to foreign élites stimulates them to the maximum of defensive action, which implies the use of available means of propaganda, boycott, and destruction. The balancing process is such that locally inaugurated changes have always been restricted by the rapid mobilization of symbolic and coercive strength.

Readjustments of the material and the symbolic are partial, therefore, at best. One of the principal processes in the long series of partial adjustments is the creation of vested interest on the part of intellectuals in the repetition and elaboration of specific symbols which win an initial response. This is the general process which has been noted so often in the specific case of labor agitators and organizers, who have shown how vested interests can introduce contradictions in adjustive sequences. A little verbal radicalism, and the individual establishes a claim, modest though it may be, for income and deference, and thereafter behaves more circumspectly.[13] Movements toward emancipation, therefore, which emerge in connection with the insecurities generated from changes in the life situation of many people, tend to fall short of procuring large scale adjustments in the general situation on account of the vested interests which arise in the initial stages of adaptive processes. Insecurity reactions indicate that the accustomed channels of discharge are no longer available in the changed situation, and that "free energy" has been liberated from previous ties, and is ready to be "bound" around new symbols and practices. The reiteration of a new symbol may rebind labile energy, and secure relinquishments of income and grimaces of appreciation for the symbol specialist. This assuages the insecurities of the "intellectual" or "semi-intellectual," as well as the insecurities of those identifying themselves with the symbol and giving up income and deference to the agitators and organizers.

13. On bureaucratizing tendencies, see Roberto Michels, *Zur Soziologie des Parteiwesens in der modernen Demokratie,* Second Edition, Leipzig, 1925; O. H. von der Gablentz, "Industriebureaukratie," *Schmollers Jahrbuch,* 50 (1926): 539–572; Sylvia Kopald, *Rebellion in Labor Unions,* New York, 1924; Selig Perlman, *A Theory of the Labor Movement,* New York, 1928; Max Weber, "Politik als Beruf," pp. 396–451, in *Gesammelte Politische Schriften,* Munich, 1921.

Chapter VI

IMPERIALISTIC MOVEMENTS: THE DEMAND FOR SUPREMACY

Modern national imperialism is a mass demand for permanent control over peoples of alien culture, to be attained by force if necessary, and justified by allegations of mutual advantage. The expansion of a people into unoccupied territory or the pushing back of native inhabitants at the colonizing frontier are not imperialistic movements in the modern sense. When nothing but extinction is offered the natives, the mass movement is still comparatively uncomplicated.

National imperialism has little in common with the extension of overlordship by an élite which wins no popular support in its ventures. Conquests[1] by tribal chiefs and mercenaries are not imperialism unless the community adopts the venture as its own, and alleges some specific advantages to the other tribe. The urge to limitless expansion, which Joseph Schumpeter calls the essential imperialism,[2] must include assertions that values are sharable before it is modern imperialism.

What is involved here has been brought out in a felicitous comment by George Unwin on the reasons why Sir John Seeley's *Expansion of England* became a textbook of British imperialism. G. P. Gooch had previously said:

Its spirit was by no means that of unrestrained enthusiasm for empire or for the methods by which it was built up. . . . He draws a sharp distinction between the white colonies and India, the possession of which, he declared, increased our responsibilities, but not our power. He rejects the notion that the vastness of the Empire proves some invincible heroism or some supernatural genius for government in our nation.

1. See William Christie MacLeod, *The Origin and History of Politics,* New York, 1931, and article on "Conquest" in the *Encyclopedia of the Social Sciences.*

2. "Zur Soziologie der Imperialismen," *Archiv für Sozialwissenschaft und Sozialpolitik,* 46 (1918): 1–39, 275–310.

George Unwin remarks:

"His phrase about conquering half the world in a fit of absence of mind was a stroke of genius. British Imperialism bears the same relation to the imperialism of Treitschke or Bernhardi as the ambition of Macbeth bore to that of Lady Macbeth. Empire is congenial enough to the Englishman's temperament but it is repugnant to his political conscience. In order that he may be reconciled to it, it must seem to be imposed upon him by necessity, as a duty. Fate and metaphysical aid must seem to have crowned him. What he would highly, that would he holily—would not play false and yet would wrongly win.[3]

Such "soliloquizing on behalf of the national conscience" consecrated the *fait accompli*. The specific historic phenomenon which was the expansion and the defense of the British state was only partially imperialistic; much of its verbal justification has been retroactive, and has grown up in the struggle to defend rather than to extend. The British organization area grew in the battle with Spain and Holland and France; dynastic, commercial, and diplomatic expediencies were mingled with colonizing, proselyting, and kindred demands. Not the least delicate task of the historian of the expansion of England is the analysis of this subtle interplay with a view to assessing the role which the specifically imperialistic pattern played in the process.

The expansion of England embraced at no time a significant demand for world dominion. Extension, yes; universal empire, no. This comparative modesty of announced aim was no act of renunciation; the dream of universal empire was not taken up by the ruling élite of England. Accustomed to consider themselves on the periphery of Roman power, the ruling élite was relatively happy to maintain security, and to add some piecemeal possessions across the channel and beyond the seas. The ruling classes of England have been meek in their pretensions and they have inherited a sizable share of the earth. Never expecting to cut a wide swath in universal history, tacitly accepting the provincial role, their imaginations were never tantalized by the imperial phantom; little substance was wasted after the profligate manner of continental kings and kinglets in the illusory pursuit of the purple majesty that once was Rome. These yokels from the back provinces grew in power and flourished; but they revered the primacy of the Mediterranean and kept their station. Slowly and gingerly Englishmen began to dally with the Roman

3. See George Unwin's Introduction to Conrad Gill, *National Power and Prosperity*, London, 1916.

metaphor; they learned to revel in comparisons with the historic colossus, but they never quite believed themselves called to twist the strands of universal destiny around their fingers. It took the British generations to rise to the imperial manner, and the restraints of British style reflect the surface forms of the socially inferior. For generations the cultural primacy of the continent was secure, and the splendor of civilization irradiated from Vienna and Paris to London.

Since British political expectations have been limited to playing a chastened role in universal history, their demands have been modest, and their justifications have risen to no master abstractions in the field of political thought. The British have legitimized their place in the sun on the basis of individualistic toleration; they are glad to get on in the world, and they are not too envious of others who rise with them; they borrow their corroborative phraseology from Catholic and Protestant ethics and theology.

It was in France that the expansion of the state was a true mass movement justified by universally sharable values. Here the masses were organized around the symbols of democratic nationalism and sought emancipation from dynasticism and feudalism. As the élite which was sustained by the masses suddenly rose to power, their imaginations embellished the role which they were playing before the curtain of history. They believed themselves at the dawn of a new era when human society would be remapped by the human mind, when the aspirations breathed into the sail of "freedom" would waft the bark to the promised harbor of liberty. In the exultation of success, suddenly released from accumulated anxieties, they redreamed reality into the image of their hopes, and answered the imagined shout of the "subject" millions for emancipation. Armies went charging across the continent of Europe in the name of the universal good. If the "oppressed" resisted, some of them would be shot, the innocent victims of spiritual slavery to their masters, but the survivors would see the fiery dawn of liberty.[4]

The next great outpouring of energy in the name of ultimate values to be shared by force if necessary occurred in Russia. Here the language was no longer of the "people" but of the "proletariat," and "freedom" meant specific economic innovations. The extermina-

4. Clark Wissler has suggested that the sudden solution of any major cultural problem facilitates external expansion. See *Man and Culture,* New York, 1923.

tion of the capitalist class was alleged to be the means of inaugurating the classless society.

The political future of our world hinges in no small measure on the fate of the struggle between those who are identified with the symbols of "communism" and of "capitalistic nationalism." Communism, the spear head of opposition to the reigning order of society, is in a position to profit from the discontents which arise from whatever cause throughout the noncommunist world. The cardinal endeavor of revolutionary communism is to symbolize in itself release from insecurities, and to create such hyper-concentration of protest and faith that the "dictatorship of the proletariat" will spread over the peoples not already affiliated with the Soviet Union.

This struggle between communism and capitalism is world-wide, and must be viewed as a whole if we are to understand the imminent transformations in the balance of power and in the specific nature of political demands. The major symbols of conflict control lesser conflicts, and if we are to deal properly with the intricate interplay of personal, party, class, race, religious, industrial, agrarian, and national conflicts we are bound to view them in relation to the disjunction between those who are identified with the communistic and the capitalistic symbolism.

Now the future of any imperialistic movement no matter how inclusive the identifying symbol ("the people" or "the proletariat"), or how universal the language of justification, is compromised by the fact that at a given starting point it is *local* in extent, and impositional in method. When the secular religion of democratic nationalism arose, its symbolism was universal, but its material embodiment was French. No sooner did it achieve local success and seek extension by fire and sword in the name of brotherhood than countervailing influences consolidated in bringing about a halt. Dialectical processes were set in motion which presently frustrated all claims and all efforts on behalf of universality.

The specific process by which the universal was parochialized was that of partial adaptation and of countersymbolization. The French armies invaded territories where organized élites were accustomed to rule, and where propinquity had fostered cultural similarity. Enough identification reactions by the rank and file were connected with the authorities of the threatened areas to obstruct and ultimately to destroy the external threat. The ruling élite adapted themselves to the situation by borrowing symbols from the enemy. The new vocabulary resembled the language of revolution, but emasculated the substantive program of revolution. Many of those who were strongly identified with Prussian nationalism welcomed the strength which was made available in the struggle against the French by the older structures of government and society.

Thus one religion, as it sought to proselyte by imposition, provoked another religion into existence, a religion which deviated from it in several significant particulars, owing to the re-investment of old social forms and symbols with fresh meaning. Democratic nationalism fell short of creating a world state, or a world community of states, bound by a common mythology and relinquishing the monopoly of violence to a harmoniously circulating élite. This failure is to be attributed to the dialectical processes arising to block the expansion of authority from any local area, regardless of the inclusiveness of the symbols used by the authority.

If proletarianism follows the course of previous religions, it will fall short of universality. There is a sense of the word in which it will be successful. Insofar as enemies remodel themselves on the pattern of their strongest opponents, many varieties of socialism (national socialism) may be expected to rise and spread. Democratic nationalism was defeated as a road to world unity by its partial successes. It created many nationalisms and much local democracy, but it heightened parochialism and fell short of world brotherhood. Proletarianism may be expected to fail because of the same processes of restriction through partial incorporation. Hence there will be more ultimate equality in material income with no more brotherhood.

Although previous expansionistic movements have been halted by countervailing tendencies, we may consider whether new conditions guarantee new results. Students of primitive culture have generalized the connection between political and activity areas in the following terms: when the area of diffusion of material elements in the culture of a group outruns the boundaries of its political authority, there is sooner or later a pronounced tendency on the part of that group to extend its political authority along the lines of the zone of material diffusion.[5]

May it not be that the universalization of the world activity area will offer the preconditions of political unity? May not the material technique of western civilization expand until political authority will be developed to embrace the world area? Certainly it is possible to

5. See Clark Wissler, *Man and Culture*, New York, 1923. Suggestions about economic and political areas appear in Brooks Adams, *The Law of Civilization and Decay*, London, 1895; *The New Empire*, New York, 1903.

say that the history of the contacts between Europe and the rest of the world offers some corroboration of the tendency of control areas to follow material areas. Peripheral cultures which began to tolerate the penetration of European material technique presently awakened to the resulting dangers to their own cultural integrity. They therefore sought to impose obstacles upon further encroachments from Europe; the resulting crises have been settled by extending the political control of Europe. Disagreements over the meaning of contracts, resentment at having markets closed which once were open, desire for access to valuable resources, have contributed to the steady penetration of European control in the wake of trading activities.

This process has not proceeded uniformly, and the present indications are that European ascendancy has passed the zenith. Even during the day of Europe's greatest power, rival states were unable to unite permanently for the attainment of goals connected with trans-European affairs. The political disunity of the West persisted. Today the material technique of the West is being acquired by cultures peripheral to Europe, and the contradictions arising from diverse material and ideological conditions promise to defer the attainment of unity for an indefinite future.

The historical ascendancy of Europe in recent times has been commonly attributed to the culture formation called "capitalism."[6] Is capitalism irreparably tied up with "imperialism," and would the liquidation of the capitalistic culture pattern carry with it the extinction of imperialism?

The pattern of historic capitalism is a confluence of several details which may readily become dissociated. It is possible to distinguish the *application of impersonal energy to production* from the pattern of *industrial production*. The application of mechanical, chemical, and electrical resources to supplement manpower in production is not inherently connected with industrial production; the latter depends upon the use of fixed and highly specialized capital in great, concentrated aggregates (factories and power stations). Another turn in the technological arts may disintegrate the connection between impersonal power and industrial production, decentralizing the units of production and superseding both the factory and the central generating station. At the moment the alternatives dwell in the realm of simple fantasy; but it requires no great wrench of the imagination

6. In general, see F. L. Nussbaum, *A History of the Economic Institutions of Modern Europe: An Introduction to "Der Moderne Kapitalismus" of Werner Sombart,* New York, 1933.

to conceive of small appliances (fountain pens, let us say) which are capable of rendering enough energy available to satisfy the most varied requirements. Our present clumsy building materials may be abandoned when we learn how to rearrange the molecules of any available stuff by means of our highly portable utensil. Many innovations, far short of this omnipotence dream, could modify the amount of fixed capital required in production, and modify the importance of ownership of the instrumentalities of production. If by this time the aggregationalism of recent modes of production has stimulated great receptivity toward collectivistic symbols and practices, the manipulators of nature may have altered the technical basis of our social forms once more.

The capitalistic configuration includes the organization of *production for profit* rather than for *pluralistic values*. The pecuniary calculus is very difficult to apply where there is no smoothly functioning competitive market, and if the control of production is concentrated in the hands of those who have direct management of the coercing and propagandizing agencies of the community, pluralistic values are directly considered. Since there is no necessary relation between mechanical methods of production and free private enterprise, production can be run by hierarchies who are influenced by the need for specified commodities in order to strengthen military defenses, or to realize other cultural values. It is possible that *official* as distinguished from *private* control may be exercised to procure profit; in which case the capitalistic system survives despite the shift in management from free private enterprise.

The formation of that general pattern which we call capitalism was a fusion of many elements, which subsequently tended to diffuse together. The new technology, the factory, and the profits standard have been comparatively stable in recent history, although the new Russian régime looks forward to eliminating the connection of modern technology and the modern factory with the profits standard.

Imperialism is intimately connected with the assumption of violence in a cultural setting where fighting technique confers importance on the masses. The balancing of power is a process which antedates capitalism, and which has often resulted in generalizing demands into efforts to impose control on alien peoples. Since the growth of modern technology has democratized fighting, the loyalty of the masses has been sought by rival élites. This loyalty can be most readily secured in a society whose feudal bonds are breaking up by means of new naming and justifying symbols. Each élite must protect itself in the vocabulary of the general good. The promotion of loyalty through the circulation of symbols (propaganda) is cheaper than buying mercenaries or trying to coerce the populace. Imperialism as a mass demand for control over alien cultures, justified in terms of some inclusive value, can persist as long as the assumption of violence survives, and so long as the masses are necessary in war.

Rapid changes in the division of labor place certain persons in a position to take the initiative in making definite demands from which they can extract what they interpret to be advantages. A new way of making an article may cheapen the cost of production, and certain persons may see these possibilities and seek to take advantage of them for personal profit. It is worth emphasizing that it is by no means sure that new inventions will lead to these results: the inventor may be willing to extract no personal benefit from the new process, relinquishing it for nonprofit-making purposes to a guild or professional group. The income and deference of this group may rise owing to the handling of these processes, but such advantages may be much less than those possible had profits been the primary object. The development of western Europe has been such that the pursuit of individual profit has become an institutionalized pattern of conduct in relation to technical changes; but this pattern has not been exclusively followed in every instance owing to the survival of many values from the precapitalistic era.

When changes in the division of labor were taken advantage of for private profit, the bourgeois class developed in our Western World. Insofar as free private enterprise was more strongly motivated than official enterprise would have been, the expansion of the world activity area went on more rapidly than it otherwise would; and insofar as an enterprise of any kind was dominated by the profits aim rather than pluralistic aims, the profits pattern gave a distinctive direction to economic growth. These considerations must be kept in mind when comments are made upon the connection between capitalism and imperialism, since it is possible to demonstrate a close relation between the two for recent history, and to reach the incorrect conclusion that the elimination of capitalism means the extinction of imperialism. If socialism can be built in particular regions over the earth under conditions which preserve the assumption of violence in the regulation of interregional difficulties, the imperialistic pattern may persist.

Thus the various socialist theories which connect imperialism with capitalism may be historically sound and prophetically false.[7] It may be that imperialism is monopolist capitalism, as Lenin held, but that imperialism is not exclusively monopolist capitalism, and that imperialistic clashes may develop among socialist states. Assuming for the moment that the achievement of world unity depends upon ideological and material equality around the world, the analytical problem is how the existing differences in ideology and in material situation can be transmuted into ideological and material uniformity. What are the dialectical processes through which uniformities may be developed from dissimilarities?

Local movements toward uniformity are occurring in the Soviet Union with the elimination of the landed aristocracy and the rise of a ruling élite holding power in the name of the proletariat. The achievement of a socialist ideology depends upon modifying the present material situation of the peasants. Will the present élite retain sufficient motivation to bring about the material preconditions to the universalization of its ideology? Or will there develop a variety of vested material interests in the present period of "transition" which will transform the unrealized ideology into a phraseology? In view of the dialectical relations between material and ideological conditions, is it conceivable that the ideology of a small party group can prevail despite adverse material conditions? If the achievement of socialism in one locality is blocked by countervailing ideological and material influences, each socialist revolution may be but partially consummated, and the resulting differences may generate prolonged conflicts among semisocialized states. If this proves to be the correct

7. On socialist theories of imperialism, see N. Lenin, *Imperialism: the Latest Stage in the Development of Capitalism*, Detroit, 1924; N. I. Bukharin, *Imperialism and World Economy*, New York, 1929; the older writings of R. Hilferding, Rosalie Lübeck (Rosa Luxemburg), and Karl Kautsky. On the problem of inherently expansionist tendencies in capitalism, see Henryk Grossmann, *Das Akkumulations und Zusammenbruchgesetz des kapitalistischen System*, Leipzig, 1929, and the controversies in *Unter dem Banner des Marxismus*. A call for minute analyses is to be found in Albert Lauterbach, "Zur Problemstellung des Imperialismus," *Archiv für Sozialwissenschaft und Sozialpolitik*, 65 (1931): 580–599. See also B. J. Hovde, "Socialistic Theories of Imperialism Prior to the Great War," *Journal of Political Economy*, 36 (1928): 569–591; E. M. Winslow, "Marxian, Liberal, and Sociological Theories of Imperialism," *Journal of Political Economy*, 39 (1931): 713–758; Arthur Salz, *Das Wesen des Imperialismus*, Leipzig, 1931; E. Varga, *The Decline of Capitalism*, London, 1928. In general, See Parker T. Moon, *Imperialism and World Politics*, New York, 1926.

interpretation, the achievement of socialism lies much further in the future than is usually stated or implied.[8]

It is relevant to examine the Marxist symbolism itself in relation to other symbolism, since it is the most rapidly growing body of unifying mythology. For seventy-five years Marxism has been spreading over the earth, successfully outstripping utopian socialism, pure and simple trade unionism, and various forms of anarchism. Even though it has suffered by partial incorporation into the vital symbols of democratic nationalism, Marxism is today the strongest protest symbolism with revolutionary demands and universal claims. It is an emancipation demand which rejects equality of status in favor of imperialistic supremacy in the world of the future.

In common with all emancipation symbolism, Marxism inflicts deprivations (attacks, "castrations") upon the symbols and practices of constituted authority in precapitalist or capitalistic countries. All the persons who are in any degree identified with the ruling symbols are thus attacked; their ambivalences toward authority are stimulated, and the resulting insecurities press for relief. By offering new indulgence symbols as alternative targets for identification, the chances are increased that the insecurities will be utilized for new adjustments rather than for the vehement reaffirmation of the old.

The task of emancipation is that of dividing the superego against itself, thus permitting the redefinition of former authority objects as targets for hostile expression. In weakening the control of the superego, the old and the new are simultaneously redefined. The old is presented according to the superego categories of immorality, and the new is presented according to the superego categories of morality. This confusion increases the possibility that previously inhibited impulses will find release in directions favorable to the new symbols. In terms of our language of reference to the collective situation, Marxism facilitates the counter-mores patterns at the expense of the mores patterns, but seeks to break up the coherence of the mores patterns by presenting the old as incompatible with certain mores patterns, and showing the new as compatible with some mores patterns.

The preceding comments do not differentiate Marxism from other emancipation symbols, and it is necessary to proceed to distinguish-

---

8. The dialectical analysis of the "dictatorship of the proletariat" has been neglected by revolutionary theorists. Some relevant comments are in the book by Varga previously cited. The material aspects of the problem will be developed further in the next chapter.

ing details. Marxism differs from some protest ideologies by the sharp-
ness of the stress which is put upon the transitory nature of the
present social order. Some utopian symbols criticise the surrounding
world and predict its ultimate dissolution; Marx and Engels brought
together an imposing systematic body of material to justify the
treatment of the existing order as threatened with imminent doom.
This redefines expectancies about the future, for the dominant patterns of today are represented as weak, castrated, declining, decay-
ing. This picture of the reigning social order facilitates the projection
by each individual of the weak, devalued aspects of the self upon
the environment. Schematically this projecting process may be stated
so: "I am weak but I want to be strong; the environment is really
weak since it is ephemeral; it will be reformed to realize my wishes."
This lingual sequence does not unroll itself as a consecutive conscious
process; but the psychoanalytic procedure is capable of revealing this
structure by permitting the full elaboration of partial impulses at the
full focus of waking attention. The act of projection is a complex
operation of many components, and the conscious phase is but a
relatively small aspect of the whole. The intensive study of individual persons shows that the projection process as described is aided
by exposure to symbols which represent the environment as weak
and vulnerable, and the Marxist symbols which did this were incorporated in forms which heightened their authoritativeness. The
Marxist literature built up an elaborate theory of history and social
change which added the odor of plausibility to its general assertions.
A sense of inevitability was created by the sheer massing of detail
in the architectonic of *Das Kapital* and in the supporting publications. Certain patterns of historical scholarship and of economic
theorizing had grown in prestige by the time of Marx and Engels,
and they accreted the prestige of these patterns to their own central
contentions. The *Contrat social* of the previous century was impressionistic and vibrant; the major works of Marx and Engels were
analytic-systematic. They applied deference-producing apparatus appropriate to the new styles in culture and thus excelled the product of
competing theoreticians of revolt.

In Marxism the social environment is represented as immoral and
hostile. At certain phases of its growth capitalism grinds the faces of
the poor, driving them to want, prostitution, misery, and disease.
These consequences are "immoral" to the superego formations of
most people appealed to, and the juxtaposition of "moral" symbols
of authority with "immoral" symbols tends to create division within

the superego. The symbolization of the environment as immoral facilitates the projection of individual guilt feelings from the self to the symbol of the environment. The individual origin of the guilt feelings is not necessarily related by any rational link to the particular aspect of the environment which is criticized. Any obscure stresses between incompatible unconscious structures may generate guilt feelings, from which the individual may relieve himself by changing his symbolic definition of the environment. The process in question may be indicated, subject to the limitations previously made on such forms of statement, thus: "I am guilty of immoral impulses: I therefore deserve punishment; but the environment is immoral: the environment should therefore be punished."

Marx and Engels showed no greater skill in delineating the misery of the working classes than several other publicists, but what they said gained in potency owing to the concentration of attention upon selected features of contemporary society which seemed to aid in locating responsibility in the environment. "Surplus value" or profits, not the time worn "wealth" or "selfishness" became the root of evil. Such seeming specificity gave a new slant to an old complaint, and favored the projection of persecutory ideas on the outside world.

The immorality of the environment is represented as arising from its inhumanity, its impersonality. The Marxist literature is full of emphasis upon the routinizing, dehumanizing, quantifying consequences of the capitalistic division of labor and scheme of control. The capitalistic environment is complained of because it denies affectionate care and attention to the individual. Now any object which withdraws or denies affection provokes hostility. Anybody or anything that rebuffs our claims for intimacy or respect reactivates in some measure the earlier crises in growth when affectionate impulses were denied. Although resentment against the outside object-symbol is not the only response which arises under these conditions, it is frequent enough to be characteristic. The process by which aggressions become released against the external world is thus: "I love the environment; the environment does not love me. I hate the environment; I am not supposed to hate, but if the environment hates me, I can hate the environment." The Marxist complaints against the dehumanizing consequences of capitalism were thus remarkably well calculated to legitimize resentments against it.

Still another unfavorable aspect of the present world was said to be the discrimination in favor of persons who, though they have no more claim to superiority than the rest of us, profit from the fortuitous positions which enable them to accumulate "surplus value." Showing society in this light appeals to some of the deepest impulses in the personality. It implies the violation by the social environment of the "implied social contract"[9] by which the child renounces the direct gratification of his impulses on the tacit promise of ultimate gratification. The child's symbol of reference to the future includes claims for equal gratification with all who are comprehended within his own category. If the environment favors others of the same category, the superego is no longer able to maintain the older repressive structure, since the introjected symbol of the environment has been deprived of its positive value (libidinal cathexis). The Marxist presentation stresses the fundamental likenesses of men in all respects except their fortunate position in receiving the benefits of "surplus value." The pecuniary calculus strips the person of his human qualities (the dehumanizing consequence of capitalism) and enables some fortunate people, whose human qualities are irrelevant, to come into the most favorable posts. This vigorous characterization of capitalistic society appeals to the deeper psychological dynamisms outlined; the environment discriminates unjustly among people, and may therefore be destroyed. The individual is no longer bound to obey existing authoritative symbols. The Marxist analysis of the nature of capitalistic pattern shows why it must lead to inequitable results, and is therefore a far sharper indictment than the sentimental remonstrances of the utopians against the unfraternal characteristics of society. Marx found a diagnostic formula which aided in localizing responsibility in the social order, greatly strengthening the appeal value of his system in competition with its competitors.

The superiority of Marxism to utopianism arises also from the treatment of the future. Marx left the terminal situation ambiguous, and spoke of the class-less society as an utterly novel social formation totally incomprehensible by means of analogies drawn from class-bound societies. This left the future open for the gratifying of the fantasies most agreeable to the individual. The old style utopians tried to impose their private versions of heaven on mankind, and spent much of their time polishing off the celestial trumpets and refurbishing the celestial parapets, but Marx offered every man self-determination in utopias. In a rapidly expanding material and ideological environment, where words lose their mystery when they refer to technical details which are quickly superseded, such ambiguity is

9. This is the phrase of Franz Alexander and Hugo Staub in *The Criminal, the Judge, and the Public,* New York, 1931.

an asset. In relatively static situations, symbols of protest are most effective when concrete, as shown by the spread of certain religions among relatively static peoples.[10]

The ambiguity of the future frees the omnipotence cravings of the individual to transform the world in ways most gratifying to his yearning for strength. The person projects fantasies of power into the future and identifies himself with this remodeled symbol of expectation. The Marxist future is one of universal expansion and of untrammeled supremacy; all competing classes are wiped off the slate of history.

The vagueness of the class-less society symbol permits it to take on color according to the deeper yearnings for the reinstatement of that happy time in infancy when one was the center of the world which bent every effort to indulge one's whims. The yearning for maternal care, and, deeper still, for the quietness of the womb, may be gratified by endowing the future with joy without effort, with creativeness unbound by routine. The future is also a fraternal ideal, a commonwealth of brothers where no father-imago intrudes. This equality reduces the provocations for resentment against the more fortunate position of favored brothers.

The complex intellectualistic language used to encase Marxism derives prestige from its "scientific" form. One who identifies with it is free to glory in the supremacy of his intellectual furniture. He seems able to penetrate into the ultimate historical secret, to scan the omens and portents of universal evolution, and to divine the embryonic outlines of the future. The deeper sources of curiosity within the individual, including primitive sexual curiosity, are gratified partially in this all-encompassing perspective.

One of the most potent reenforcing appeals of Marxism lies in its "objectivity." The words which allude to the past and future are not handled as tentative conjectures but as overwhelming compulsions of the world historical process. The primacy of the material environment in the control of ideas reduces the individual to an episode in the triumphant evolution of reality. Dialectical material-

10. On different aspects of historical utopianism see Ch. Renouvier, *Uchronie* (*l'utopie dans l'histoire*), Second Edition, Paris, 1901; Fritz Gerlich, *Der Kommunismus als Lehre vom tausendjährigen Reich,* Munich, 1920; Josef Leo Seifert, *Die Weltrevolutionäre, Von Bogomil über Hus zu Lenin,* Zürich, Leipzig, Vienna, 1930; Lewis Mumford, *The Story of Utopias,* New York, 1922; J. O. Hertzler, *The History of Utopian Thought,* New York, 1923. Concerning religion among primitive peoples, see the writings of Robert H. Lowie, Paul Radin, and Wilson Wallis.

ism is the reading of private preferences into universal history, the elevating of personal aspirations into cosmic necessities, the remolding of the universe in the pattern of desire, the completion of the crippled self by the incorporation of the symbol of the whole. No competing symbolism rose to such heights of compulsive formulation.

The accessory dogmatism of Marxism is a defense against the doubts which its intellectual virtuosity seems to foster. Only highly skeptical minds could have emancipated themselves from the bonds of authority sufficiently to devise the novelties of Marxist theory. The effort to confine subsequent intellectual creativeness to the elaboration of detail by means of chronic impatience with "small bourgeois" doubts of fundamental postulates show how difficult it is to use doubt to aid faith and then to banish the doubt on behalf of faith. The escape from the insecurities of analysis to the relative security of affirmation is facilitated by the device of treating the preferences to be criticised as external coercions imposed by historical evolution. Hence many personalities come to peace with themselves by locating their private struggles in the world outside, identifying themselves with the fantasied outcome, and refusing to reconsider the act of projection itself. There are personalities which achieve something other than dogmatic unification in this process; they arrive at serenity precluding doubt. The basis of such differences in reaction is an unsettled question among specialized students of personality.

The foregoing interpretations of certain of the appeal values of Marxist symbolism rest upon intensive studies of personalities who have been differentially exposed to Marxist and to competing symbols, and upon the general dynamic relations disclosed in psychoanalysis. The observations necessary to show the relative applicability of these particular relationships to a specific time-space configuration may be made by the psychoanalytic study of representative instances, or by the careful interpretation of the results adduced by less intensive methods in the light of the fully studied cases. This means that psychoanalysis must be systematically utilized in the diverse culture contexts now accessible, that the relation of its results to those secured from ordinary autobiographical and similar methods must be discovered, and that the comparative findings must be used in construing historical fragments.

Intensive techniques need to be supplemented by extensive procedures, since the dialectical connections between the two are developmentally productive.[11] The term "proletariat" is an identifying symbol whose future depends upon maintaining its integrity as a nonparochial term. The proletariat must include the world proletariat, or else fail to achieve the inclusiveness necessary for the realization of socialism. It is embedded in an imperialistic symbolism which possesses many of the general advantages just summarized; but its future depends upon the dialectical relations between the ideological and the material, with all the implied complexities.

11. The following books use extensive techniques mainly, but there is some effort at comparative "career" studies: Roberto Michels, "Psychologie der anti-kapitalistischen Massenbewegungen," *Grundriss der Sozialökonomik,* 9, Tübingen, 1925 Georges Sorel, *Matériaux d'une Théorie du Prolétariat,* Paris, 1919; C. Bouglé, *Les idées égalitaires,* Paris, 1908; J. Delevsky, *Antagonismes sociaux et antagonismes prolétariens,* Paris, 1924; R. Broda and J. Deutsch, *Le prolétariat international; étude de psychologie sociale,* Paris, 1912; Aurel Kolnai, "Die Machtideen der Klassen," *Archiv für Sozialwissenschaft und Sozialpolitik,* 62 (1929): 67–110; Goetz Briefs, "Proletariat," *Handwörterbuch für Soziologie,* 441–458; H. G. Wells, *The World of William Clissold,* 1: 152–189; Gertrud Hermes, *Die geistige Gestalt des marxistischen Arbeiters und die Arbeiterbildungsfrage,* Tübingen, 1926; Lewis L. Lorwin, *Labor and Internationalism,* New York, 1929; the works of Werner Sombart previously cited.

Part III

CONDITIONS

Chapter VII

GOODS AND SERVICES: THE EFFECT
OF ECONOMIC CONDITIONS

Using symbols of identification, expectation, and demand as starting points for the consideration of world politics, the previous chapters have repeatedly referred to the "material" aspects of the environment. This section of the book will vary the procedure by beginning with the conditions and passing to the symbols. The exchange of goods and services, of peoples, and of communications are the environmental features which have been selected for distinct analysis. Attention will also be given to the inter-connections between political symbols and practices, in the narrowest sense of the word, and the general patterns of personality and culture. Although the discussion of specialized instruments of violence falls within the scope of this section, such problems have been excluded, since they were discussed at some length in the chapter on the balancing of power.

For the sake of analytical clarity, it will prove expedient to distinguish between economic conditions, economic considerations, political conditions, and political considerations. Economic conditions are the relations of persons to goods and services; economic considerations are subjective adaptations to economic conditions. Under conditions of relatively free competition, profit is the principal economic consideration. When individuals evaluate their environment in terms of their fighting effectiveness in relation to it, political considerations are involved; the threat value of this environment (viewed by an observer who arrives at an appraisal) is the political condition.

It is evident that the correlative nature of the economic and the political forbid their too rigorous separation. Under certain circumstances the individual can neglect the political aspect of his economic relationship to others: when there is general acquiescence in the exchange practices which are current, when acts of coercion against individuals who break their contracts or who object to other fundamental principles of the social order are spontaneously approved, when the exercise of violence is specialized in the hands of duly constituted authorities (policemen, armies, courts), and when the occasions for the large scale exercise of coercion are few. If these mutually related conditions are absent, calculations of fighting effectiveness assume greater importance.

Our general problem is to trace connections between changing economic conditions, economic considerations, political conditions, and political considerations. In the interests of precision the term "political" has been assigned a more limited meaning here than elsewhere in this book. Politics as the analysis of the value patterns in general has as one of its branches politics as the analysis of the conditions and the calculations of fighting effectiveness.[1]

The varied interrelationships between political and economic conditions and considerations may be profitably studied during such major crises as the Russian Revolution. Political considerations are paramount in the minds of any new élite which has abruptly assumed control of the armed forces and the administrative agencies of the community. During acute phases of conflict every social detail is instantaneously translated into its supposed influence on fighting effectiveness. The new rulers are constrained to sustain themselves by violence, but this is costly business; ideological support is cheaper. If the community can be induced to emotionalize a common myth, the élite can readily elicit deference reactions and income relinquishments from the population.

The development of ideological support for the Russian élite demanded fundamental changes in the conditions of Russian life.[2] The peasant as a sociological type had to be abolished and his place taken by workers in collective enterprises. Every effort to create the economic basis for the approved ideological formations generated profound resistances. Peasants sought to protect themselves from the pressure for production under the new system by resorting to slack work. Since the ruling élite required some efficiency in production in order to protect itself from inner disturbances arising from food short-

1. Compare Arthur Salz, *Macht und Wirtschaftsgesetz. Ein Beitrag zur Erkenntnis des Wesens der Kapitalistischen Wirtschaftsverfassung,* Leipzig and Berlin, 1930; R. G. Hawtrey, *Economic Aspects of Sovereignty,* London, 1930.

2. In general on Russia, see the works cited in the bibliography of works in German published outside the Soviet Union since 1917, *Die Soviet Union 1917–1932,* Ost-Europa-Verlag, Königsberg Pr. and Berlin, 1933; Maurice Dobb, *Russian Economic Development since the Revolution,* London, 1928; Calvin B. Hoover, *The Economic Life of Soviet Russia,* New York, 1931.

age, in both peace and possible war, the élite was strongly tempted to concede to individual demands for differential reward.

The immediate survival necessities of the élite are thus in some degree contradictory to the long-run purposes of those who desire to reconstitute the bases of Russian society, and ultimately of world society. Immediate efficiency depends upon concessions to individual differences which are anathema to all who adhere to the rigid theory of the Russian revolutionary mission. The toleration of differences in material income favors the proliferation of materially contrasting environments, multiplying the diverging foci of attention in the community, and hence hastening the growth of separate symbols of identification, demand, and expectation. Concessions are especially dangerous from a revolutionary standpoint, because it would be easy to modify the present régime into a "peasant republic," where the contradictions between rich peasants and poor peasants would intensify, though enabling the richer peasants to give active support to the factions within a compliant élite.

Oscillations in policy have been inseparable from the tensions generated by the contrasting requirements of immediate efficiency and ultimate ideology. The élite has seized power in the name of a theory of history which stresses the primacy of material conditions over ideological formations; the material conditions in their position of éliteship include many features which tend to dissipate their ideology. Can the ideology which was a serviceable means to power survive the material conditions of power?

Certainly there have been steps toward socialization followed by steps toward capitalism, or precapitalism. Unconscious as well as conscious slacking-off plays the role in generating shifts in Russian economy which has been played by certain technical maladjustments in capitalistic societies. The "crises of abundance" of capitalism are succeeded by the "crises of scarcity" under communism.

Let us explore the possibility that the oscillating concessions and reaffirmations so far exhibited by Soviet policy will presently cease. Will the ideology of socialism (to be distinguished from the phraseology of the movement) be relinquished by the Communist élite? Will the material conditions connected with survival, including efficiency in production, so modify the effective ideology of the élite that the effort to create the broader material conditions which are prerequisite to the triumph of the ideology will be relinquished?

As it is, individualizing tendencies are constantly cropping out among party members. Some of them devise ways of securing exemption from the voluntary duties which they are obliged to perform in addition to their regular jobs. Some of them argue that they can be more useful "building socialism" if they have more free time to study, or if they are able to rest and muster their energies for the strenuous and vital posts they hold in administration. Skilled members can and do demand preferred housing facilities on the ground that they have sacrificed to acquire a technique which enables them to contribute more to the constructive tasks of the régime than those who are less self-sacrificing and studious. Once a member of a skill group, the individual presses for the rewards which his sacrifices "entitle" him to. Constant initiatives are taken to get better pay for the skilled workers, thus fostering the material differences in society which nurture ideological contradictions.

Party members who are closely connected with groups of non-party skilled workers are able to increase their prestige by using their influence to modify party policy in the direction acceptable to the skilled group. These tendencies have displayed themselves incessantly in the "deviations" of the trades union members of the party; they appear in connection with demands to raise wages in the cities high enough to compensate for the higher prices charged for farm produce at the markets where some measure of private trading is permitted, subject to intermittent interference. [By reducing the supply of commodities to the factory stores, and routing the commodities through special channels of distribution, the revenues of the state are increased by this multiple-price system.]

The ideological reactions of skilled workers to their special material conditions are paralleled by those party members who are associated with different collectives, or with special categories of collectives.

Constant pressure is exercised to include friends within the party, and personal considerations of expediency and congeniality often take priority over the original ideal of a professional class of self-selected élite who are selflessly devoted to the consummation of socialism. An expanding party roster reduces the ideological intensity of the party, strengthening the tendencies to concede to immediate expediencies in the whole field of public policy.

Such diluting processes do not pass unchallenged, and they are held in check by the countervailing influences which have hitherto been sufficiently strong to create significant counter-movements. There are invariably "fundamentalist" elements in revolutionary movements who distinguish themselves by rigorously and censoriously applying what they conceive to be unalterable principles to the conduct of their party comrades. These fundamentalists are also abetted from time to time by dissatisfactions emanating from those who begin to suspect that their material position is threatened by the concessions made to skill in the interest of efficiency. The central nucleus of party leaders is able to take advantage of the stresses within the party structure to expel inconvenient factions, and to displace responsibility from themselves for current difficulties by casting out the "devils." The specter of external threat, so capable of being revived for disciplinary use, elicits no small measure of acquiescence in the exercise of power by a few, and so long as this external threat can be plausibly relied upon, party purgations can be readily accomplished.

The difficulties which would arise with prosperity in the Soviet Union are forecast in the foregoing analysis of the stresses within the party. Multiplying goods and services would confer added strength upon the skilled groups in improving their position by developing separatist policies. The functional antitheses behind the unified façade of the state would be intensified with increasing security arising from well-being and the pursuit of individualized objectives. Acquiescence in central discipline would dissolve and the "cleansings" of the party would doubtless become less thorough and less frequent.

Whether war would strengthen the equalizing or the differentiating tendencies within the Soviet Union depends upon the relative importance of the need for efficiency and the urge to sacrifice. The need for efficiency would stimulate the differentiation of income unless the mass emotions of war would stimulate enough coordinated self-sacrifice to cover all production requirements. At the start of a popular war, the equalizing tendencies would be reenforced by the renewal of loyalty to the régime; but if the war should draw out, other tendencies would be expressed.

The "withering away of the state," which is the prerequisite of a socialist society, as distinguished from a socialist state, would be a situation in which very little coercion would be exercised by the central authority, and in which enough consensus would prevail among functional elements in society to enable them to reach amicable working arrangements by negotiation. As long as the community is part of the world-balancing process, living among states which assume the resort to violence, central control of violence will continue. The central élite, moreover, will be able in the interest of discipline against danger to check the growth of rival functional organizations, except insofar as functional differences find expression within the factional movements of a somewhat enlarged party.

The possible appearance of revolutionary dictatorships beyond the borders of the Soviet Union would not necessarily accelerate the appearance of socialist societies, since differences in standards of living and in forms of production would exercise their usual effect in fostering and in preserving ideological contradictions. The survival necessities which are associated with the introduction of local dictatorships place premiums on efficiency, and upon the emasculation of the movements toward a socialist society.

The conclusion is that the contradictions which are inherent in the transition from capitalism to socialism tend to stereotype development at an intermediate phase between the dictatorship of the proletariat and the socialist state, and to defer progress toward a socialist society. The tendencies toward democratization which would mark the socialist state proceed concurrently with tendencies toward the preservation and the multiplication of material conditions which obstruct the attainment of the socialist society. The balancing of power processes generated by the localized emergence of a revolutionary élite function to postpone to an indefinite future the achievements required by the revolutionary ideology.

Most of the writing about economic and political conditions and considerations has had to do with better understood relationships than those obtaining under revolutionary dictatorships. We are on much more certain ground in characterizing the focus of attention, and the symbols of demand, expectation, and identification which are associated with an élite of large landholders. It is usually said that the large landholders think in terms of expansion by annexation, rather than by penetration, since they lack the mobile capital which is essential for the latter policy. Expansionism in the United States during the pre-Civil War period was common among the Southern landholders, who brought pressure to bear against Mexico to relieve the situation which developed as soil was exhausted in the older cotton states. The élite of prewar Russia craved distinction in the form of added acres, which both pointed and restricted Russian policy. The situation is admirably reflected in the report to Isvolsky which was once made by a Russian chargé d'affaires at Peiping:

Should we be sufficiently powerful economically it would be simpler to direct all our efforts to the conclusion of an economic treaty. If, however, as I fear, we should by so doing only be of service to foreigners and ourselves be unable to secure any profits from what

had been achieved (thus we have for instance in reality been unable
to profit by the extraordinary advantages embodied in the Commercial Treaty of 1881), then there is in my opinion no reason to
depart from the basis of the policy we have followed hitherto, that
of territorial acquisition.[3]

The rise of the bourgeoisie has been characterized by the technique
of economic penetration abroad, and by a series of alliances with
other social formations which have had some measure of influence
on foreign affairs. The bourgeoisie has at times combined with the
monarch against the aristocracy; at other times with all disaffected
elements against the monarch and the aristocracy. More recently, as
the bourgeoisie has begun to suffer from insecurity feelings with the
growth of the proletariat, it has combined with the older institutions
and classes, often abandoning the forms of parliamentary democracy
which were useful at an early stage in its historical development. Occasionally the bourgeoisie has been aroused against foreign states
where very obvious remnants of older feudal and monarchical forms
survived. But the exigencies of the total situation have been such
that if parliamentary Great Britain stood beside parliamentary
France, it likewise marched with Czarist Russia.

Much of the detailed description of the relations between "economics" and "politics" in modern capitalistic societies has pivoted
around such questions as these: To what extent do governmental
officials allow their official acts to be influenced by calculations of
material advantage to themselves? To what extent do officials rely
upon the commands or the representations of people who are pursuing material advantages? To what extent do officials undertake to
influence the income-making activities of others as a means to the
attainment of official purposes? To what extent do changes in the
conditions of production and exchange modify the behavior of
officials?

It must be conceded that until recently the literature on these
topics was anecdotal and impressionistic. The published studies of
"corruption" are still in this phase of development, and the appropriate qualifications for times and places are rarely introduced. In
February, 1928, it was made public that the chief of the Eastern
section of the British Foreign Office, John Duncan Gregory, was a
speculator. Baron Holstein operated on the exchange during his long
career at the German Foreign Office. These, and many other episodes,

3. *Entente Diplomacy and the World World,* Edited by G. A. Schreiner,
documents of B. von Siebert, Document 22, London and New York, 1921.

can be culled from recent writing; but the subject has thus far eluded masterly and well-balanced treatment.

No doubt this will continue to characterize the handling of some of the more elusive connections between the "interests" and the officials. The official élite is usually bound by ties of upbringing and specific advantage to the prevailing property system, and the exercise of official discretion follows the general pattern appropriate to the time and place. Since the official, propertied, and cultural élites are partially coincident, ties of family association and friendship operate selectively upon the versions of reality which are circulated among them. People of "standing" who are "accepted" are listened to, with little attention paid to the possibility that their behavior may be governed by the conscious pursuit of material advantage, or by insidious unconscious adaptation to courses of action which advance material interests. This sort of interrelationship can be given flesh and blood by means of specific instances, but it is extraordinarily difficult to work out a valid method of sampling the relative intensity of such influences in numerous situations.

No doubt an episode like the dreadnaught scare of 1909 in Great Britain can be usefully cited in order to depict the uncritical acceptance of interested advice by men high in authority. It may be recalled that the 1909 amendment to the German naval law produced something like panic among politicians, career men, and publicists in Great Britain. It was at once said everywhere that the future of the Navy depended on the dreadnaught and that the Germans were leaping ahead with their huge construction program. By chance this great dreadnaught scare can be traced to men who, although connected with the armament companies, were relied upon for expert advice. It was Mr. Mulliner, managing director of the Coventry Ordnance Works (in which John Brown and Company and Cammell, Laird, and Company held the bulk of shares), who made the statements upon which Asquith, Grey, McKenna, and others based their solemn warnings to Parliament. The whole affair was later characterized by Alan Burgoyne, M. P., editor of the *Navy League Annual,* as "one of the most portentous pieces of parliamentary humbug ever practiced on the electorate."

I am not implying that Mr. Mulliner deliberately lied. It is entirely conceivable that he was himself stampeded by some overexcited technician upon whom he in turn relied. The point is that his lack of self-criticism was no doubt facilitated by a predilection to believe anything conducive to his profitable and prestigeful career.

It is equally evident that cabinet members were insufficiently sensitive to the possibility that their sources of information were deformed by such influences.[4]

Partly as a reaction against the anecdotal technique of dealing with economic and political interrelationships, and partly as a reaction against the gross exaggeration of "simple" economic interpretations of public policy, a new crop of scientific monographs has been prepared which carefully stresses the extent to which business men are directed by the diplomats, though without attempting to minimize the instances when business men direct the diplomats.[5]

Frederick L. Schuman's analysis of a series of carefully chosen episodes in the diplomatic history of the French Republic led to the conclusion that

> . . . diplomacy bends business to its purposes quite as often as business controls diplomacy for objectives of its own. In none of the episodes analyzed . . . could it be said that private business interests pushed the Quai d'Orsay into a course of action which bore no relationship to considerations of national power vis-à-vis other States, and which was adopted exclusively for the benefit of the business groups. In every case—even in that of the imperialism of Ferry—patriotism and profits went hand in hand and it is naïve to assume that the values of patriotism are mere rationalizations of the economic interests of private groups of individuals.[6]

Care must be exercised in interpreting the relevance of these results to theories of class and skill struggle. The fully self-conscious and carefully calculated subjective aims of the businessman or the diplomat are but details of the total problem of analyzing the relationship of technical social change to changes in the relative strength of classes. Frederick the Great may stimulate the spread of industry in Germany, and Joseph the Second may encourage industry in Austria because they want to increase their strength in relation to the members of the élite with whom they are on competitive and emulative terms. If the effect of their measures is to strengthen or

4. A valuable analysis of official policy is the monograph by Eckart Kehr, *Schlachtflottenbau und Parteipolitik, 1894–1901*, Berlin, 1930. The personal role of Von Tirpitz is brought into sharp relief. See also H. C. Engelbrecht and F. C. Hanighen, *Merchants of Death*, New York, 1934.

5. Jacob Viner has been especially active in this matter. See his "Political Aspects of International Finance," *Journal of Business*, 1 (1928): 141–173, 324–363, and elsewhere. See the forthcoming volume by Eugene Staley.

6. *War and Diplomacy in the French Republic*, p. 395. New York and London, 1931.

weaken the aristocracy or the bourgeoisie, this effect is the test of the pertinence of their behavior to the survival of class formations through history. Perhaps the significant criterion is conveyed in the expression "class consequences" instead of "class struggle," much as the proper orientation is suggested by speaking of "class attitude" instead of "class consciousness."[7]

The modalities of the behavior of business men and officials can be studied in the future with more precision than in the past. New definiteness can be given to statements about the connection between specified "economic" and "symbol" changes by the selection of representative instances, and the use of precision techniques. Manifestly an increase in foreign competition within the American domestic market may be expected to arouse hostility against foreigners among the American producers who feel endangered. It may be possible to discover the range of change within which the maximum symbolic adaptation occurs. If the foreign share of the domestic market rises from 10 to 20 per cent, the symbolic reactions may be much more intense than when the change runs from 40 to 50 per cent during a comparable time interval. At certain points along the curve of the "material," we may have much refocusing of attention and much self-assertiveness, much viewing of the future with alarm and many demands for drastic countermeasures.[8]

The profound importance of waves of prosperity and depression in conditioning the past and future of political development is sufficient to justify the extended consideration of how insecurity levels respond to changes which have become so intimately associated with the expansion of industrialism.

From the simple formula that prosperity is a time of indulgence for the prosperous and depression is a time of deprivation for the impoverished arise many profound social consequences.

When human impulses are dealt with indulgently, as in prosperity, the resulting sense of power and achievement strengthens self-confidence, fosters individuality, nurtures differentiation. Deprivation, on the contrary, blocks the outflowing energies of the personality,

7. On these questions, compare Georg Lukács, *Geschichte und Klassenbewusstsein*, Berlin, 1923.

8. Studies of this kind are under way for boots and shoes, and other selected industries. Expressions in trade papers, conventions, newspapers, and the *Congressional Record* are sampled periodically; these data are plotted in relation to the marketing shifts. Regional studies will also prove highly valuable. See Bertil Ohlin, *Interregional and International Trade*, Cambridge, Mass., 1933.

frustrates the primary ego, constrains the weakened individuals to seek strength in concerted action.

So potent is the urge for individualization in prosperity that orthodox symbols and practices are neglected for the sake of a steadily expanding myriad of individual demands. New operations collide with old restrictions. Lured by new hope of tangible advantage, enterprisers view delay with impatience, often facilitating by bribery, if necessary, the readjustment of ancient rules to emerging conveniences.

Personal assertiveness is not confined to professional activity; it is generalized against the traditional pattern of sexual, familial, and intimate morals, manners, and styles. In the growing, subdivided, and anonymous urban community, all of the potentialities of the human personality gradually unfold, receiving corroboration from a few other persons, at least, and gradually supplementing, superseding, and disintegrating the moral standards of the rural, small town, and primitive folk culture.

The threat to the established order follows a different course during adversity. Accustomed outlets of the assertive impulses are blocked, precipitating serious emotional tensions, since the first effect of frustration in the external world is to turn aggressive impulses back against the primary self, a process which, in the extreme case, results in that most acute and irrevocable of all self-aggressions, which is suicide.

Some of the alternatives to suicide bear no direct relation to social and political symbols. An unhappy person may react in extremely neurotic ways and develop bodily infirmities whose basis is "psychogenic," that is, attributable to emotional conflicts rather than organic lesions. Incapacitating headaches and gastro-intestinal disorders often fall in this category. Another neurotic alternative consists in the elaboration of fantastic reveries rather than disabling physical symptoms; the sufferer indulges in depressed, melancholic periods, or cultivates delusions of reference, of persecution, or of grandiosity. Among the other extremely neurotic solutions are resort to the excessive use of drugs, like alcohol and morphine, and flights into various pathological character formations.

These relatively private ways of resolving emotional stresses generated by deprivation stand in competition with collective solutions which involve the use of symbols and practices connected with the institutional order. Instead of bodily symptoms or private obsessions, however, the personality may socialize its symptoms by means of collective symbols in mass movements.

Being thrown out of a job may be construed by the victim as the expression of the private malevolence of a hostile foreman; but such an interpretation does not survive indefinitely in competition with other interpretations when the army of the unemployed is swollen during depression. The deprivation now appears as an incident of one's relation to the whole social order, and when this degree of generalization is once accepted, the probability is increased that the person will seek to resolve almost any of his emotional problems by means of institutional symbols.

Toward these symbols of the secondary environment the individual may exhibit that primitive method of coping with deprivation which is the retaliatory withdrawal of affection. If it goes to extremes, the withdrawals of love from symbols of the real world can be as incapacitating to the personality as the turning of aggressive impulses against the primary self. The person who withdraws his love from the symbols of country, race, class, and specific people in his immediate environment, concentrating all affection on himself, is in a profound pathological state, suffering a narcissistic neurosis or psychosis. The pathological ultimate, however, is seldom seen, except in the back wards of mental hospitals, since substitute targets of love are readily available in the real world. Thus if I can no longer love the king, I can love mankind; if I can no longer love God, I can love the nation; if I can no longer love the country, I can love the proletariat.

The emotional task of damaged people, therefore, is to discover new outlets for assertive and affectionate impulses, short of suicide and narcissism. During depression the solution of personal difficulties by the use of secondary symbols is favored by the ease with which attention may be drawn to others in the same plight, and to the contrast between those who suffer and those who benefit from the established order. During prosperity disasters as well as triumphs are more individualized. Bankruptcies are more dispersed and less synchronized; the bankrupt bears more responsibility for his failure; hence suicide and similar private solutions are favored. These private expedients are less common in the later stages of depression, relative to the total number of those who suffer deprivation.

The simultaneous heightening of emotional tension in depression not only increases the probability that institutional patterns will be utilized in discharging tensions, but also the probability that the ruling order itself may be the target of attack. In the name of some utopian symbol, possibly of the class-less society, revolutionary mass movements may divert collective aggressions against the patterns formerly held in esteem. Such revolutionary eventualities may be avoided if the exponents of the old are able to outcompete the proponents of the new in meeting the psychological exigencies of the population.

Depressions, as we have had reason to show, are far more serious than the loss of goods and services; they involve blows to the self-esteem of those affected, and the victims require psychological no less than material relief.

Any deprivation arouses unconscious fears of further loss, and induces various efforts to allay the resulting anxieties. In some degree, the loss may be compensated by eliciting solicitude from the environment. Even authorities who are associated with the disaster from which people suffer may be exempted from attack if they express enough solicitude for the grievances, complaints, and suggestions of the victims by words and gestures of condolence.

Why are these solicitous operations so potent in allaying anxiety and neutralizing loss? The urge to be listened to is deeply implanted in every personality, springing from the dependence of the small, weak, and inarticulate infant and child upon the environment. The frustrations which arise in the arduous process of learning an adequate set of communicating symbols emphasize the importance of speech, and the circumstance that those who listen to our verbal productions in the early years are typically those who shower care and affection upon us leads to the chronic overestimation of the emotional interest of those who listen to our verbal outpourings. The monarch or the president who appears accessible and understanding permits a reactivated attitude of dependence upon the parents to strengthen his ascendancy. Relief administrators are well advised to lend an ear as well as to distribute loaves and fishes. A great deal of mothering and of understanding paternalism on the part of the persons in authority is required by those who react to deprivation by a species of psychological invalidism.

The ideal of the successful self is in sharp contrast with reality in depressed times. The assertive impulses which were externalized according to the idealization of the self are frustrated and take it out on the primary self by fostering morbid reveries of failure. These acute internal tensions can be alleviated if it is possible to project responsibility for this apparent failure away from the primary self and on to some symbol of the outside world, thus gratifying the primitive yearning for irresponsibility, and for the recovery of the earlier juvenile status of limited responsibility in relation to adult standards of social attainment.

This scapegoat function can be performed by a prodigious array of competing symbols, some of which are very personal and specific, like "my wife is to blame"; others of which are remote and inclusive, like the "Jews," "bankers," "grain gamblers." Others rise in the scale of impersonality and abstractness: "perversity of human nature," "godlessness," "occidental materialism," "business cycle," "oversaving." For all but highly specialized people, these are psychological equivalents of "I got a raw deal" because "He done me wrong." Systematic anthologies of the word forms used by those in power and out of power during depression would be useful supplements to the data upon the comparative incidence of suicide, dyspepsia, obsessional neurosis, drug addiction, and other competing alternatives.

Passing over such important aspects of behavior in depression as the exorbitant demands for praise, for justification, for hope, for action, for destruction, we may single out for special comment the rather remarkable passivity which characterizes so much conduct at such times. In part this depends upon uncertainty about the depth and significance of business recession, but it is also fortified by unconscious components. Clinical psychology has shown that those personalities who are consciously emancipated from twinges of remorse about novelties of conduct may suffer from obscure self-punishment reactions which arise from the surviving remnants of the childhood conscience. Since prosperity means for so many the substitution of luxury for simplicity, of borrowing for thrift, of speculation for investment, of laxness for abstinence, unconscious guilt feelings intensify. In prosperous times the "pay-off" to the conscience is comparatively easy; money can be spent on charity, on ecclesiastical and educational architecture, and on the embellishment of symbols connected with the mores. But in crises many persons revert to the symbols and formulas of childhood. If these formulas are mainly ceremonial, the individual may dispose of his tensions without working overt changes in the environment; but the reactivation of these fundamentalist patterns is frequently associated with militant demands for action.

Fundamentalist movements during prosperity are principally laughing matters for the metropolitan sophisticates. An H. L.

Mencken may scoff at the "Corn and Bible Belt" and make sport of a monkey trial. But in depression this sort of thing has serious meaning for political developments. With the declining economic power of the cities, and the search for soul-satisfying security in hard times, a substantial part of the population, especially in the provinces, may become incited to action around symbols of "The Old Time Religion," and the ancient code of familial and personal morals, manners, and styles. All the accumulated hostility of those who have hated the immoral cities may discharge in the fanatical revitalizing of these forms. Political leaders may capture many fundamentalist symbols, as did the National Socialists in Germany, whose attack on "cultural bolshevism," coupled with an idealization of primitive German virtues, expressed itself as a provincial upsurge before inundating Berlin at the crest.

The mass movements of depression favor the emergence of leaders of the agitational type common to all social crises, men who convey to the masses the impression of courage and decisiveness. Frequently those who perform the agitational function are pathological personalities whose verbal fluency, hyperexcitability, and mimetic gifts furnish the masses with that pantomime of their own yearnings which affords partial catharsis and partial corroboration of their emotional demands.[9]

Turning from the main possibilities in the interconnection of the "material" and the "symbolic," we may briefly consider the effect of attitude changes arising from economic oscillation upon the spread and the restriction of the last world-revolutionary pattern.

It is tempting to dispose of the connection between economic oscillation and revolution by the formula that depression fosters the revolutions that prosperity postpones. In a world divided into states whose ultimate differences are to be settled by violence, prosperity expands markets, intensifies contact, sharpens conflict and war. It is the threat of war which counteracts the individualizing tendencies unleashed in prosperity. The exigencies of war, and especially of defeat in war, lead to the partial adoption of patterns borrowed from

9. For studies of the effects of unemployment, see H. Lazarsfeld and H. Zeisl, "Die Arbeitslosen von Marienthal," *Psychologische Monographien*, 1933; E. Wright Bakke, *The Unemployed Man*, London, 1933; Dorothy S. Thomas, *Social Aspects of the Business Cycle*, New York, 1927; Gabriel Almond and Harold D. Lasswell, "Aggressive Behavior by Clients toward Public Relief Administrators: A Configurative Analysis," *American Political Science Review*, 28 (1934): 643–655.

the most recent revolutionary prototype, or to the emergence of a new constellation.

During the last century, every curtailment of the flow of credit from capital-exporting countries (an incident of depression) lit the fuse of discontent in capital-importing countries; but in many, if not most, of these instances, the spread of social revolution was hindered by older social formations which were often able to reassert themselves against the rising industrial, mercantile, and commercial agrarian elements which had been weakened or partially discredited by the collapse of values.

The emergence of the Russian revolutionary model vastly stimulated the exertions of the discontented elements abroad. In some degree direct propaganda assistance was obtained from the new Russian élite. Unless the non-Russian élites were immediately overthrown and incorporated into the Soviet Union, differentiating processes went forward rather rapidly, and the total diffusion of the new pattern was restricted.

Failure to overturn the local élite in the name of the symbols associated with the Third International weakened the prospects of immediate success, and strengthened the chances of those who could identify themselves with some local symbol and with some insecure local groups. As hope of immediate revolution receded, contradictions were heightened between labor organizations which used the Russian symbols, and were affiliated with the Third International, and labor organizations which invoked non-Russian symbols, and stressed their local connections. This found expression in the clashes between social democratic parties, unions, cooperatives, on the one side, and communist parties, unions, and cooperatives on the other. Meanwhile the middle-class formations were drawn into active political participation around parochial symbols (nationalistic, patriotic); their leaders struggled against the new middle class of proletarian origin composed of socialist party politicians, journalists, and trade union secretaries. Important elements of the landed aristocracy and the plutocracy aided the new movements which appealed to the older middle-class elements by means of their nationalistic, antiforeign, and anticommunistic vocabulary. The antiplutocratic or antiaristocratic symbols which were commingled in these movements were not taken very seriously by the plutocracy or the aristocracy, whose principal immediate objectives were to restore their sense of security by eliminating "alien" and "radical" influences from the nation, and by destroying the power of trade unions to engage in effective collective bargaining on a national scale. In some instances, some of the animosity which might have been directed against the older "capitalistic" structures was deflected against racial and religious minorities. The insecurities, intensified by clashing propaganda, were partially resolved in crises from which arose dictatorships utilizing language partly borrowed from the Russian pattern, and partly refurbished from the store of traditional symbols in the culture. The methods of the dictatorships displayed many features in common with the methods of the original dictatorship in the name of the proletariat.

The function of depression in this process of partial restriction and partial diffusion of the last pattern of world revolution was to precipitate localizing and dictatorial adjustments. A characteristic of depressions not attended by revolution is a double process of disillusionment and reillusionment among the protest elements. Where Leftist aggressions against the established order were blocked, they fell back on the Leftist movement itself, discrediting recent slogans and tactics, and attaching utopian expectations to new expedients. It will be recalled that as capitalism expanded through the merchant-capitalist, industrial-capitalist, and banker-capitalist phases, labor slogans and tactics were buried, as well as born, in every depression. The impotence of revolutionary leadership during depression is often the result of an unpropitious relationship to the external balance of power. Sensing the probability of foreign boycott or military intervention, the Left leadership may fail to seize revolutionary opportunities. Sometimes the policies of class collaboration may be signalized in coalition cabinets, but occasionally the parliamentary tacticians will seek to avoid any assumption of responsibility. In either case, disillusionment is cumulative, although the leadership seeks as well as it may to divert attention to plausibly radical issues. In Sweden, and in certain other countries, labor parties, having attained about the optimum of voting strength by available electioneering methods, finding it advisable to eschew militant revolutionary action, have sponsored various antimilitaristic and pacifistic measures which are more tributes to their impotence than to their humanitarianism.

Depressions, therefore, have actualized the contradictions implicit in the various material and ideological configurations existing at various distances from the Soviet Union. Anti-élite movements which were connected with the Soviet Union were doomed to suffer reversals as the hope of world revolution was deferred. Under the stress of economic adversity, the welling tides of discontent have discredited in turn the movements whose primary appeal was to the workers. The expanding and oscillating material and symbolic environment prodded ever widening circles into active participation in politics: the upper bourgeoisie, the workers, the small bourgeoisie. The vigor displayed by the older middle-class formations may in turn vanish as dictatorships fail to coincide with prosperity, and these classes will return to the neutralized role in relation to the class struggle which was usually imputed to them by historical materialists.

Modern industrialism emerged in a precapitalistic world where it was taken for granted that differences between states would be settled by violence, and hence where social changes were construed by ruling élites with reference to their meaning for relative fighting effectiveness. Modern industrialism increased the number of those preoccupied with calculations of pecuniary profit; and as the expanding division of labor drew the world into more intense contact, accumulating contradictions once more entailed the vigorous reappraisal of change in terms of fighting effectiveness. The balancing process universalized participation in politics around the world and among various classes, presently drawing the world into two hostile camps; the World War witnessed efforts to split the world division of labor into two self-sufficient systems, and the postwar epoch has continued the fractionalization and parochialization of economic life. Diminished material income has provoked efforts to increase psychological income by restoring a new sense of significance to damaged personalities, justifying their existence in relation to the building of a "Socialist Society" or a "Third Reich"; new substitutes for bread are supplied by self-selected specialists on the manipulation of symbols, the modern masters of political propaganda. If the present trend is not reversed, the complex division of labor which is the heritage of generations of effort will be progressively disintegrated; but lessened external contact may itself be a precondition for revivifying of contradictory influences.

Chapter VIII

MIGRATION, TRAVEL, AND POLITICAL ATTITUDES: THE ROLE OF PRIMARY CONTACT

The political consequences of face to face contact among peoples of alien race and culture are as manifold as the processes which are initiated in direct personal intercourse. When two persons come together, all the free energies of the personality are available in the relationship. Certain characteristics of the opposite person may be incorporated within the reactive equipment of the other through conscious imitation or unconscious identification and introjection. The phenomenon of assimilation occurs when the borrowing process goes far enough to include many of the practices and the collective name exemplified in the personality of the model. When the collective name is excluded, something short of assimilation takes place, in the form of either friendly or hostile attitude. Hostile attitudes, which imply negative identification, may result in the brusque rejection of many traits of the other.

A wealth of human experience is available for the study of primary contact. Casual or permanent connections with the indigenous population have been made by successive generations of immigrants, fugitives, proselyters, traders, students, travelers, tourists, officials, and reporters. Despite the dearth of systematic material, enough impressionistic observation has been made to warrant extended consideration, and to reveal where intensive study would repay the effort expended.

There are certain general characteristics of primary contact situations which may be profitably discussed before analyzing more specific configurations.[1] "Fear of the stranger" is so widespread that

---

1. In general, see Georg Simmel, *Soziologie,* Third Revised Edition, pp. 509ff., Munich and Leipzig, 1923; Roberto Michels, Chap. 3, "Zur Soziologie des Fremden," *Der Patriotismus,* Munich, 1929; Hermann Levy, "Der Ausländer: Beitrag zur Soziologie des internationalen Menschenaustausches," *Weltwirtschaftliches Archiv,* 2 (1913): 273–298; and the writings of the American social psychologists Charles H. Cooley and George H. Mead.

it has often been treated as if it were an inborn reaction uniform throughout the human species. Experimental study of infants now shows that it is more truly considered to be an acquired trait; but, like most of the traits of the human animal which have been presumed by many competent observers to be imbedded in the germ plasm, the removal of the trait to the postnatal history of the child is of little practical importance if early developmental conditions almost universally lead to its implantation. Even children who are carefully handled show episodic or chronic revulsions against strangers, without apparent reason. The psychoanalytical study of the growing person has shown how the struggle of the child to modify the direct expression of his primitive impulses generates much inner anxiety. The child is compelled by the exactions of the social environment, either in the form of direct punishment or of the withdrawal of affection, to give up the direct gratification of impulse, and the external limitation is internalized as the inhibitory formation known as the superego. The forms of impulse organization which are put at the disposal of the superego in this process are mobilized against the less modified forms of impulse expression; this is the inner incompatibility which precipitates the anxiety reactions of the child. One means of relieving these insecurities is to project part of his own "evil" nature upon the environment. Strangers are very common and convenient targets for such projections since they are human, yet they are otherwise undefined in previous specific experience.

Since the primary environment of any individual is highly circumscribed in available national, racial, sociological, and personality types, the deficiencies are made up by vocabulary. All sorts of naming systems organize reactions of growing children toward persons who are far beyond the range of direct experience. Fairy tales and folk lore, funny stories and derisive epithets, all organize attitudes toward people who are black, dwarfed, foreign, strange, Chinese, German, Irish. These prearranged reaction patterns are organized categorically.

The adult environment characteristically uses value symbols of remote persons and groups in order to sanction the inhibiting system which it fosters in the child. Thus during a period when England was under the shadow of possible invasion by Napoleon, nursemaids frightened unruly children with these verses about "Old Bony":

Baby, baby, naughty baby,
   Hush, you squalling thing, I say;
Hush your squalling, or it may be
   Bonapart may pass this way.
. . . . .
Baby, baby, he's a giant,
   Tall and black as Rouen steeple;
And he dines and sups, rely on't,
   Every day on naughty people.
. . . . .
Baby, baby, he will hear you
   As he passes by the house,
And he limb from limb will tear you
   Just as pussy tears a mouse.[2]

In any face to face contact all the reactions by category are threatened by the free libidinal impulses which are activated in the situation. The other person simply does not stay put in the vivid whites or blacks of reaction by category; saints and devils thrive on distance. The other person is an object which may call out the whole range of personality reaction. Very primitive impulses may be involved here, such as curiosity about the structure and functioning of the sexual organs. Primary contacts thus corrode the preorganized categories, and the symbols of the other become redefined on the basis of the concentration of impulse in the developing situation. That this will always terminate in primarily friendly association is not to be assumed, although positive identifications are always possible components of any interpersonal reaction.

One of the reactions to strangers which has been the subject of much wondering comment is the confiding of intimate problems to them. Most of us have had total strangers approach us on shipboard or at hotels or at week-end house parties, insist upon unburdening their whole past life and present quandaries, then vanish in the mass once more. This behavior has been illuminatingly studied by psychoanalysts; it is a particular case of the general urge to confess in order to relieve the feelings of anxiety and guilt arising from inner conflict, and it occurs when some feature of the stranger facilitates the projection of the confessor role upon him. If the stranger is courteous, the chances are that the urge to relieve inner tensions may be so acute that this superficial social behavior will be elab-

---

2. H. F. B. Wheeler and A. M. Broadley, *Napoleon and the Invasion of England. The Story of a Great Terror*, 2: 39, London, 1908.

orated into the fantasy of a wise, helpful, kindly soul who has all the traits which were imputed by the child to the responsive persons in his early environment.

Turning to the more specific consideration of situations of contact, it is evident that the preorganized attitudes of the stranger toward his new environment are influential, but that the newcomer tends to respond to the attitude taken toward him by the native inhabitants. Hatred of the old environment may have led to an idealization of the new, to which the immigrant clings despite hostile acts by the local people. Sometimes the political refugee has no choice but to take any alternative available to him, and he may spend his time bending every effort toward the control of events in his native land, remaining as indifferent as possible to the new home.[3]

Complexities arise when the new environment shows both hostile and indulgent reactions. Some verbal ridicule may be encountered; but, if there are chances to buy land, to send children to free public schools, to get jobs if needed, and to worship freely, the substantial ties which are thus developed will ultimately obliterate the effect of the initial verbal assaults.

Negative identifications which arise in direct contact may have great potency in stimulating the elaboration of rival symbols.[4] Many Italians in America who encountered epithets like "wop" or "dago" were stung by this provocation to contribute to the Fascist movement, thus indirectly avenging themselves by developing bigger and better symbols with which to associate themselves. Many of the movements of national independence which were so prominent in the last century may be traced to the activity of students of philology and history who were educated abroad, and who reacted against more or less goodnatured ridicule or indifference when their cultural origin was mentioned. They took over the technical equipment of the older environment in order to present a claim to distinctive speech and distinguished history.

Thus Finnish students who went to study at Upsala University came in contact with the rising self-assertiveness of the Swedes. As one student wrote, who became an initiator of Finnish nationalism:

3. See Oskar Blum, "Zur Psychologie der Emigration," *Archiv für die Geschichte des Sozialismus und der Arbeiterbewegung,* 7 (1916) 412–430.
4. Interesting data are assembled in Robert E. Park, "The Immigrant Press and Assimilation," Chap. 3 of *The Immigrant Press and Its Control,* New York, 1922; and in various chapters of Robert E. Park and Herbert A. Miller, *Old World Traits Transplanted,* New York and London, 1921.

We would like to show the Swedes that we can exist without their language or their customs—yes, even without their Thor or Odin. . . . If we ever want to obtain the respect of foreigners, we must be ourselves, and not try to be everything, for that means trying to be nothing . . . (Much must be done in order that) our posterity will not be a meaningless compound of a Russian and a Swede, which means zero,—but a nation independent at least in the realm of the intellect and the spirit.[5]

Another student exclaimed:

Oh, to have a real fatherland, to be a citizen of a State, and not a squatter in a mangy province governed by stupid asses and sly foxes.[6]

The students took over the identifying symbols of a nationalism and the techniques which enabled them to elaborate their own symbol. As Van Gennep remarks:

The sciences created and developed by western and central Europeans have in turn provided the people of other regions with the reason for asserting themselves. The truly scientific history—of the Slavs, the Arabs, the Persians, the Armenians, the inhabitants of China, of Japan, and more recently of the Bantu Negro—is owed to the Europeans by these people; and it is against the Europeans that they are now turning this history and our principles of liberty and equality.[7]

The adjustment of the stranger to the new environment is strongly influenced by the relation of his cultural technique to that which he finds there. Immigrants whose native language is similar grammatically or phonetically to the new tongue assimilate readily even though they have but mediocre command of their native tongue, owing to inadequate schooling or to dialect. Thus the South Italians quickly assimilate in Spanish speaking countries. Where the stranger's language is so little used that it must be dropped in order to secure an economic foothold, assimilation is also expedited. Even conquerors who settle down to live among a people of complex, literate culture take over this culture; so it was with the Norse con-

5. John Henry Wuorinen, *Nationalism in Modern Finland*, p. 70, New York, 1931.

6. *Ibid.*, p. 47.

7. *Traité comparatif des nationalités*, 1: 43, Paris, 1922. See also G. P. Gooch, *History and Historians in the Nineteenth Century*, New York and London, 1913; Richard T. La Piere and Cheng Wang, "The Incidence and Sequence of Social Change, (In China)," *American Journal of Sociology*, 37 (1931): 399–409.

querors of what became Normandy, and the Mongol and the Manchu conquerors of China. The carriers of a complex, literate culture in a less complex culture usually maintain their identity.

The reception which is given by an environment to strangers must be considered in relation to the broader configurations against which the significance of the stranger is defined. In very sweeping terms, the reception accorded to the stranger is a function of the world balance of power, the internal balance of power, and the local standards of propriety and morality.

The cultural affiliates of a political enemy in the world balance are treated with hostility, as were the Germans who arrived in the United States after the World War, or who lived in the United States during the war. In Turkey, Armenians were viewed as outposts of western encroachment and suffered accordingly. Cultural affiliates of former rulers are in very exposed positions while the process of emancipation is completing itself; such was the unfortunate lot of the Germans in postwar Czechoslovakia and in some of the Baltic states. Those who are connected with powerful groups in other lands may be viewed with alarm far out of proportion to their actual numbers in the immediate environment. Arabs see the Jews in Palestine the forerunners of endless inundations; the Jews elsewhere are under constant attack on account of their international affiliations.[8] Anti-foreignism may be a general function of insecurity which does not lay too much stress upon the nefarious characteristics of specific groups of foreigners. The barring of immigration in America was stimulated by the general insecurities arising from our new role in world affairs and from internal transformations;[9] the anti-foreignism of Asiatic and other non-European peoples has been defensive against penetration by stronger techniques.

The play of the balance determines whether refugees are well received; all who are expelled by the enemy are ipso facto friends, and those who are associated with allies have a presumption in their favor. A favorable attitude may be generated toward foreigners in

8. See Fannie Fern Andrews, *The Holy Land under Mandate,* 2 vols., Boston, 1931.

9. See the literature on deportation policy: L. F. Post, *The Deportations Delirium of Nineteen-Twenty,* Chicago, 1923; William C. Van Vleck, *The Administrative Control of Aliens,* New York, 1932; Jane Perry Clark, *Deportation of Aliens from the United States to Europe,* New York, 1931; Reuben Oppenheimer, *Report on the Enforcement of the Deportation Laws,* President's Law Enforcement Commission.

general when a country is intent upon the rapid exploitation of its natural resources.[10]

The history of exclusion, expulsion, and colonization policies confirms the importance of the interstate, and also of the internal balance of power.[11] The ruling élite is necessarily sensitive to the implications for its own position of every minority. When John VI of Brazil decided to encourage colonists, he turned in 1818 to Switzerland, not only because the country was weak, but because he desired Catholic families in order to prevent the growth of a Protestant opposition.[12]

The hostilities which developed in the United States against Irish immigrants were partly due to the strategic significance of New York in national elections, and to the strategic position of the Irish voters in New York. Whenever political "radicalism" is generated among alien groups within the community, it inspires defensive measures on behalf of those identified with the ruling patterns. The Germans got into trouble in Texas because of their activities in favor of the abolition of slavery in pre-Civil War years.[13] It is worth observing that political "radicalism" flourishes among members of rationalistic cultures[14] who encounter obstacles in their new environment; many Swedes who were social democrats at home became communists in the United States, and some German democratic liberals became socialists in the United States. Many Jews who were members of the small bourgeoisie in Europe identified themselves with movements of political and economic protest in the United States. Their culture is highly rationalistic, and protests readily express themselves in abstract form.[15]

A ruling group may need a scapegoat for the diversion of accumu-

10. See Isaiah Bowman, *The Pioneer Fringe; Pioneer Settlement,* by Twenty-Six Authors, American Geographical Society, New York, 1931, 1932.

11. Concerning the postwar developments, see Stephen P. Ladas, *The Exchange of Minorities,* New York, 1932; Charles B. Eddy, *Greece and the Greek Refugees,* London, 1931; C. A. Macartney, *Refugees,* London, 1931; R. D. McKenzie, *Oriental Exclusion,* Chicago, 1928; Yamoto Ichihashi, *Japanese in the United States,* Stanford, 1932.

12. Imre Ferenczi, *International Migrations,* Vol. 1 (Statistics), p. 137, Edited by Walter F. Willcox, National Bureau of Economic Research, New York, 1929.

13. Edith Abbott, *Historical Aspects of the Immigration Problem. Selected Documents,* p. 500, Chicago, 1926.

14. Cultures which encourage the dialectical defense of their postulates. Jews and Calvinists may be contrasted with Catholics in this respect.

15. See George Soule and J. M. Budish, *The New Unionism,* New York, 1920; Werner Sombart, *The Jews and Modern Capitalism,* London, 1913.

lated discontents and use an alien element in the community for this purpose. The Jews were convenient targets for dynastic-feudal-catholic hostility in old Russia, and the German bourgeoisie have hated the "Jews" as an alternative to hating "capitalism."

The ruling élite may modify the process by which the élite is recruited in order to preserve its own position aganist alien encroach-ment. The appearance of the Negro in northern cities of the United States created no special problem when their numbers were small. They were welcome to Republican machine politicians who could depend upon them to vote for Mister Lincoln. But the postwar influx led to results which threatened democratic formalities. In Chicago it is now impossible to run Negro candidates for offices which were open to them a few years ago; the insecurity of the white rulers of America is one of the factors favorable to a Fascist development in the United States.[16]

When the balance of economic power is threatened by a foreign group, hostile acts are directed against it. Thus the free blacks of Baltimore protested against the competition of poor white immi-grants from Germany.[17]

A welcome is accorded to like class refugees by all whose class consciousness has become explicit. The foreign aristocracy did what it could for the homeless aristocrats of France and of Russia.[18] Bour-geois and labor groups were very sympathetically inclined toward refugees from the revolutionary actions of 1848; and all Americans were disposed to offer asylum to defeated democrats everywhere.

The significance of the stranger in terms of the balance of external and internal power varies with relative numbers and relative rate of introduction. If the members of a foreign culture are few at first, the chances for the growth of friendly ties are much greater than when mass inundations appear. Housewives like their maids of all work,

16. For the general place of the Negro in American politics, see C. E. Merriam and H. F. Gosnell, *The American Party System,* Second Edition, New York, 1929. H. F. Gosnell is engaged in research upon the Negro in politics. See Donald S. Young, *American Minority Peoples,* New York, 1932; Paul Lewinson, *Race, Class, and Party: A History of Negro Suffrage and White Politics in the South,* New York, 1932.

17. Edith Abbott, as cited, p. 463; see also J. Legouis, "Les problèmes d'émigration devant l'opinion mondiale," *Revue économique internationale,* 18$^{me·}$ année, 4, No. 1, (1926): 36–65.

18. See Fernand Baldensperger, *Le mouvement des idées dans l'émigration française (1789–1814).* 2 vols., Paris, 1924; Hans von Rimscha, *Der Russische Bürgerkrieg und die Russische Emigration, 1917–1921,* Jena, 1924.

even if they speak contemptuously of "Swedes," householders like their valets, even when they distrust "Japanese," gardeners dislike losing efficient assistants when antiforeign agitation comes, libertines resent interferences with their favorite prostitutes, people of good will dislike to surrender their benevolent labor among the strangers within the gates, colleges dislike the loss of lists of foreign students, impresarios oppose losing the prestige of foreign artists, hotel keepers and caterers view with regret interferences with trade, and social climbers dislike obstacles in the way of snaring lions.

It has been possible to conduct some preliminary studies into the relation of numbers to defensive acts in the case of the American Negro.[19] The tabulation of results showed that per ten thousand population the Negroes are safer from mob deaths in the old Black Belt, where more than half of the population is Negro, than any-where else in the South. They are relatively less safe in counties with from one-fourth to one-half Negro population, while per ten thou-sand Negro population they are in the greatest danger from mobs in counties where the proportion of Negroes is less than one-fourth. The plantation system of production prevails in the first group of counties, and the Negroes are needed as hands; in the last the Negro more often owns a small farm or competes more directly for employment with the whites. The old Black Belt, despite its high percentage, is an area of great stability where the interracial situation has reached a provisional equilibrium. Florida with its phenomenal population growth in recent decades shows a lynching rate of 4.5 per ten thou-sand Negroes during the 1900–1930 period, a rate which is nearly twice as high as that of Mississippi, Georgia, or Louisiana, more than three times the Alabama rate, and six times the South Carolina rate. But the greatest danger of mob deaths exists in the sparsely settled rural counties of the South. An inhabitant of the South's most sparsely populated two hundred and fifty counties is in sixty times as much danger of mob death as a person living in or near one of the South's half dozen largest cities.

It is manifest from this survey that positive findings can come from the study of the rate and magnitude of introduction of alien elements among an indigenous population. Such researches may hope to provide the basis for a technique of statesmanship for the

19. *Lynchings and What They Mean, General Findings of the Southern Commission on the Study of Lynching,* The Commission, Atlanta, Ga., 1931. Arthur Raper, *The Tragedy of Lynching,* Chapel Hill, N. C., 1933, describes cases.

management of population contacts. That the simple numerical factors represent but one dimension of the situation is evident from what has already been said about the significance of the external and domestic power relations.

Reactions on the part of the local population to aliens, based upon estimates of the world balance and the domestic balance of power, are modified according to the prevalent standards of morals and propriety. Visible violations of the mores arouse hostile acts of defense. The Irish immigrants to America were visibly anti-Protestant, since they held to the Catholic ritual; they were often visibly drunk, quarrelsome, and garrulous; and they often formed parades, danced merrily, and gesticulated wildly and sometimes obscenely. All this clashed with the less expressive American patterns, as it also clashed with the English standards.[20] The Irish brought the pattern of violent action along with them from their struggles against authority, turned the Molly Maguires against the bosses in the anthracite coal fields, and stuck together with that unanimous hatred of the informer which is characteristic of conflict groups.

That aliens often become prominent in countermores activities need cause no astonishment. On account of the amount of discrimination against such activities, they often pay well, and the foreigner needs an economic basis. The prominence of Negroes in gambling and vice, of the Chinese in drugs, gambling, and vice, of the Jews in the theater and in "rackets," is not only due to the psychological fact that the native population tends to notice their presence, but to the fact that individuals from alien culture environments are less under the control of the local mores than the native population. Also those who depart from the environment in which they have developed show varying degrees of personal disorganization in the new environment. In the original situation the family, the church, school, fraternity, and neighborhood were recurring stimuli for the preservation of the acquired inhibitions. In the new environment external supports to the superego are often missing; indeed, the older symbols of ecclesiastical, dynastic, and paternal authority may not only be missing, but they may be treated with obvious disrespect by the new milieu. Restraints on behalf of sexual abstinence, regularity in work, regularity in saving, respect for property, and the like, may prove ineffective in preventing counter-impulses from expressing themselves. In fact, the environment may offer advantages to those who

20. See the interpretations of this and similar points by Paul Cohen-Portheim, *England the Unknown Isle*, New York, 1931.

engage in activities which were countermores in the old community; work may be offered on religious holidays, and readjustments to new possibilities may extend to the demoralization of the whole reaction pattern.

The future course of interpersonal relations is deeply influenced by the initial contacts which set the pattern. A superiority reaction is organized in the resident population when the first jobs taken by the alien are menial tasks. The Polish harvest hands created the same impression in Germany as the Irish in America when they were employed in railroad construction camps; a whole nation is characterized as filthy, intemperate, and shiftless when the first arrivals are unskilled and occasionally intemperate. The aliens are accused of deficient initiative when they develop petty business enterprises or go into personal service, and it is not until increasing wealth breaks down the barrier to power and culture that old insinuations die away. Those Americans who know the Swedes as servant girls, the Italians as fruit vendors, the Germans as cooks, the Greeks as restaurant keepers, the Chinese as laundrymen, or the Polish Jews as junk dealers have no glimmer of the cultural richness of the civilization in which these immigrants originated.[21]

The primary contacts so far discussed have shown the effect of preorganized attitudes upon the newcomer and his reception, and emphasized the influence upon the resident population of initial responses, of the external balance of power, the internal balance of power, and the standards of morals and taste. When we consider transitory rather than permanent contacts, we find the same analysis applicable.[22] During economic stress the foreign tourist, student, business man, and traveller is treated as a menace by many local inhabitants. Foreigners are "parasites" that live off the fat of the land; they raise prices by paying outrageous sums for what they

21. On early contacts, see George H. Danton, *The Culture Contacts of the United States and China: the Earliest Sino-American Culture Contacts, 1784–1844,* New York, 1931.

22. The proselyter may be in permanent or casual contact with a foreign environment. See Maurice T. Price, *Christian Missions and Oriental Civilization,* Shanghai, 1924; Chao-Kwang Wu, *The International Aspect of the Missionary Movement in China,* Baltimore, 1930; K. S. Latourette, *A History of Christian Missions in China,* New York, 1928; and other standard volumes. For travelers, business men, explorers, students, tourists, see Arthur Percival Newton, Editor, *Travel and Travelers of the Middle Ages,* New York, 1926; Roberto Michels, *Der Patriotismus,* pp. 109ff., Munich and Leipzig, 1929; Adolf Reichwein, *China and Europe: Intellectual and Artistic Contacts in the Eighteenth Century,* New York, 1925.

fancy. Naturally this complaint does not come from the catering groups, but from the middle classes and the workers who see no direct gain to themselves from the foreigners, and who imagine from instances of conspicuous profligacy that they suffer loss. The cry against the foreign profiteer, blood sucker, and exchange speculator resounded over Europe after the World War as one nation after another dropped into the trough of acute economic difficulty. Sharp reversals of sentiment occur when the world balance of political power is suddenly and visibly rearranged, or when a change in the inner balance of power sends new exiles abroad and furnishes asylum to others. Native hostilities accumulate against visitors who violate their standards of morals and propriety. The Americans who complain of the lack of bathtubs and telephones in Europe or the Englishmen who inquire superciliously if there really is culture in America are both in their little way doing their mite to estrange nations.

The preorganized attitudes of the foreigner cover the gamut from reverence to contempt. Many American school teachers who approach France with enthusiasm show startling reversals of attitude when they struggle over supplementary charges on the hotel bills, find themselves short changed by taxi drivers, and see private necessities publicly relieved. Those who undervalue their own culture but who are disappointed abroad may come back into the arms of the mother country with relief. A new identification may occur which profoundly affects their subsequent conduct. If foreign travel sometimes modifies a simple-minded over-estimation of one's culture, it not infrequently leaves nothing but a conviction that all is better at home. As Roberto Michels remarks, the technical perfection of modern travel renders impressions of foreign countries yet more superficial as one speeds from one place to the next carrying much of his environment with him. One often notices the tendency to overpraise foreign countries as means of attacking the policies, parties, or institutions of one's own community; and this may lead to the excusing of all sorts of hardships and inconveniences during the period abroad. Thus American democrats once overpraised France, and foreign communists today overpraise the Soviet Union.

It is possible to continue this inventory of possibiilties, but no special purpose is served; what is needed is the development of research whch shows for selected periods the relative importance of various possibilities. What was the net effect, immediately and ultimately, upon American soldiers (of different social origins) of their experiences with Frenchmen during and after the war? What attitude changes follow first-hand contact with the Soviet Union on the part of Kansas school teachers, Chicago factory workers, New York engineers, Middletown high-school students, New York actors, Main Street business men and wives? What is the effect of contact with various details of American life upon foreign students from different nations and classes? What is the background of the expatriates?[23] What was the selective process lying behind immigration to America, and the development of various degrees of incorporation into American life?[24]

Of direct interest to students of government is the study of contact at official conferences and in continuing international agencies. The advantages which are expected to arise from the conference in general are those which C. K. Webster has summarized for the conferences of the early nineteenth century.

> The sovereigns and statesmen of the different countries had lived a common life for almost two years. They had shared trials and triumphs and even board and lodgings for long periods together. Those who had experienced the emotions produced by the final overthrow of Napoleon never completely lost a peculiar intimacy such as statesmen of Europe have possessed at no other time. With all their jealousies and intrigues they had been, as it were, comrades for a considerable period. Since 1813 Alexander, Metternich, Hardenberg, Humboldt, and numbers of lesser men had lived a common life for long months together at camp fire and council board and there undoubtedly existed between them something of that spirit of connection and obligation which bind together men who have rowed together in the same boat or lived at the same college.[25]

Mildred Moulton has undertaken with the encouragement of Pitman B. Potter to analyze in detail the conditions affecting the course of

23. See Percy H. Boynton, *The Rediscovery of the Frontier,* Chap. 5, "The Backtrailers," Chicago, 1931.

24. Despite the rich monographic studies now available, little effort has been made to indicate the relative frequency of the possibilities described. From a methodological standpoint the best study remains that of William I. Thomas and Florian Znaniecki, *The Polish Peasant in Europe and America,* 2 vols., Second Edition, New York, 1927. New methods are now available to apply to the study of contemporary contacts, ranging from new types of questionnaires to observational notes, qualitative and quantitative, by participant observers, and prolonged (psychoanalytic) interviews to supplement other personal documents.

25. *The Foreign Policy of Castlereagh 1815–1822,* p. 63, London, 1925.

international conferences. Her first publication succinctly deals with nine types of peace-time conferences and with the Versailles Peace Conference as representative of those at the end of war. Peace-time gatherings are concerned with (1) Legal Questions (London Naval Conference, December, 1908, and February, 1909; (2) Nonperiodic Political (Washington Conference on the Limitation of Armaments, November, 1921, to February, 1922); (3) Politico-Economic (Porto-rose, November, 1921); (4) Economic (Pan-American Financial Conference, May, 1925); (5) Administrative (Communications Conference, Barcelona, March to April, 1921); (6) Periodic Conference on Social Questions (Washington Labor Conference, October, 1919); (7) Nonperiodic Conference on Economic Questions (Geneva, May, 1927); (8) Nonperiodic Conference on Political Problems—To be Called at some Future Date after Extensive Preparation (Preparatory Commission, League of Nations Disarmament Conference); (9) Nonperiodic Conference on Political Problems Called Without Preparation (Geneva, June to August, 1927).[26] In the general psychological sense there is no reason for excluding the assemblies of the League of Nations from this list.

The methodological problem in studying the conference as a form of contact is to keep separate the indices which describe the reactive situation at the beginning of the conference from the indices which describe the reactive situation at the end, and which delineate the changes occurring at the conference itself. The initial problem is to assess the strength of the demands and the nature of the expectations entertained at the outset by the various participants. The redefinition of these demands and expectations is one of the chief consequences of contact. Sometimes the general sense of emergency is so acute and the line of concerted action so self-evident that the conference as a method of contact is incidental; but where the sense of common need is less, adroit handling of the details of conference layout and of symbols may produce overt results.

26. Mildred Moulton, *The Technique of International Conferences,* New Jersey College for Women, 1930. See also Eduard Rosenbaum, "Ueber diplomatische Konferenzen als Mittel zwischenstaatlicher Beschlüsse," *Kölner Vierteljahrshefte für Soziologie,* 5 (1925): 157-170; Edward Eyre Hunt, *Conferences, Committees, Conventions, and How to Run Them,* New York and London, 1925; R. Doré, *Essai d'une bibliographie des Congrès internationaux,* Paris, 1923; Sir Ernest Satow, *A Guide to Diplomatic Practice,* 2 vols., London, 1917; N. L. Hill, *The Public International Conference,* Stanford University, 1929; F. S. Dunn, *The Practice and Procedure of International Conferences,* Baltimore, 1929.

Official agencies offer opportunities for fruitful study. *Special fact-finding* committees, like the Lytton Commission, have their public relations problems, as do the *Regular fact-finding* agencies, like the permanent sections of the League of Nations. *Supervisory* agencies add evaluative judgments and proposals to the collecting of facts.[27] The *coordinating* agency has a thorny problem when the principals are states.[28] The *mediating, conciliating, and adjudicating* agencies do their work in international crises, and are often improvised to meet the situation.[29] *Control* agencies range from military occupations, emergency relief services, plebiscite supervisions, customs administrations, to "advisers" of all degrees of power, dealing with diplomatic, financial, military, or minor questions.[30]

More systematic efforts have been made to examine the role of the ambassador than of any other specialized agent of contact.[31] The study of special occasions of international contact, of fairs, exhibitions, sporting events, musical festivals, dramatic spectacles (Oberammergau), resorts, and unofficial congresses and committees has not progressed very far.[32] More has been said about shrines and holy places as congregating points for people of diverse culture, and the role of war in facilitating contact has been repeatedly stressed.

These special topics finally draw attention back to the massive literature which reports upon contacts among specific peoples at definite periods. Topics like the crusades, the mass migrations, the

27. For much detail see H. R. G. Greaves, *The League Committees and the World Order,* New York, 1931.

28. See Sir Arthur Salter, *Allied Shipping Control,* Oxford, 1921.

29. For guidance to the literature, see J. H. Ralston, *The Law and Procedure of International Tribunals,* Revised Edition, Stanford University, 1926; *International Arbitration from Athens to Locarno,* Stanford University, 1929.

30. See N. L. Hill, *International Administration,* New York, 1931.

31. In the old literature Monsieur de Callières retains his high place, *On the Manner of Negotiating with Princes,* (Translated from the French by A. F. Whyte), Boston and New York, 1919. See also Jules Cambon, *Le diplomate,* Paris, 1922; Mendelssohn-Bartholdi, *Diplomatie,* Berlin, 1927; A. A. Friedländer, *Diplomatie, nationale u. internationale Psychologie,* Halle, 1919; Severus Clemens, *Der Beruf der Diplomaten,* Berlin, 1926; R. Finger, *Diplomatisches Handeln,* Stuttgart, 1931; François Charles-Roux, *Trois ambassades françaises á la veille de la guerre,* Paris, 1928.

32. See O. Brandt, "Zur Geschichte und Würdigung der Weltausstellungen," *Zeitschrift für Sozialwissenschaft und Sozialpolitik,* 7 (1907): 81–99; Guy Stanton Ford on "International Expositions" in the *Encyclopaedia of the Social Sciences,* and Joseph Kulischer on "Fairs" in the same place. For sports, see G. A. E., Bogeng, Editor, *Geschichte des Sports aller Völker und Zeiten,* 2 vols., Leipzig, 1926.

culture contact of the Mediterranean world with the East and North, the interrelationships at the historic centers of culture (Nile Valley, Tigris-Euphrates Valley . . .), the spread of the European culture pattern, the function of historic routes of communication, all provide pertinent information in definite perspectives.[33]

The analysis of varieties of direct contact requires careful study of the preorganized attitudes of participants, the specific pattern set by initial contacts, and the significance of the stranger for the external and internal balancing of power and the standards of morality; each term used must be defined in relation to the material and symbolic details of the total context.[34]

33. See F. S. Marvin, Editor, *Western Races and the World,* London, 1922; George Young on "Europeanization" in the *Encyclopedia of the Social Sciences;* Richard Hartmann, *Die Krisis des Islam,* Leipzig, 1928; and the general literature on culture contact.

34. For an application of the configurative analysis to a specific problem of primary contact, see the forthcoming study of South Slavs in America by Dinko Tomašić.

Chapter IX

NEWS CHANNELS AND ATTENTION AREAS: THE ROLE OF SECONDARY CONTACT

Changes in the division of labor initiate other modifications in the world when attention areas are redefined. The attention area is one of the psychological areas whose interrelation with areas of activity and organization deserves systematic analysis. The *environment* may be technically defined as the world of objects as viewed by an observer who does not take into account the symbolic relation of others to those objects. The *milieu* is the world of objects which are referred to in the symbolic processes of selected persons. The town hall is the environment of all who reside within a defined geographical area, but it is part of the milieu of those who look at it or think of it. People develop reference symbols to objects which are beyond their own experience; Chicagoans speak of New York or of Bombay, without necessarily having been there; in some degree these objects are part of the milieu of Chicagoans. People may refer to objects so far removed in time, or so dubious in nature, that they cannot enter into any contemporary experience, like the Greeks of antiquity and the Holy Ghost.

When attention is directed toward similar objects, the symbols of these objects compete in the personalities involved for positive and negative affective impulses; hence the focus of attention guides the sentiments, and those who share a common focus of attention may pass over to the sharing of common sentiments. The growth of a sentiment area releases impulses toward the control of the outcome of events; the spectator self becomes a participant self. The reported inhumanities inflicted upon the Cubans by the Spanish fixed attention in the United States upon Cuba, fostered hostility toward Spain, and released demands for liberation of the Cubans. These demands could be debated at first on the ground that we had no business interfering with other people's affairs, but the emotional entanglement was such that the demand for liberation with American help grew intolerant of dissent; the changed focus of attention thus favored the organization of sentiments which fostered the growth of a public and the ultimate dissolution of the public into a crowd.

Speaking formally, the public is composed of those who make debatable demands for action; the crowd, of all who make undebatable demands for action. Since collective action is likely to be precipitated by means of the common focus of attention, the control of the milieu is a matter of great practical urgency. Allusion has already been made to an instance in which the focusing of attention upon a common set of reference symbols led ultimately to changes in the activity of troops and ships, and to the organization of a certain area (Cuba liberated from Spain). Now such changes occur concurrently and reciprocally; the focus of attention is usually guided in rough conformity with existing organization and activity areas. The national capital supplies legal news; the movements of the armed forces or of the wheat crop challenge attention. What we find is no invariable sequence, focus-sentiment-demand-activity-organization, but covariation, complex redefinitions through the same time interval. Since the control of the focus is so pivotal for immediate reaction, it invites extensive study.

How shall we measure the attention area in relation to other significant areas? Exposure through time to a symbol is one process which can be examined. Where a newspaper press exists, it is possible to study the circulation of the paper among various groups, to analyze the contents of the press, and to find out how much time is given by the reading public to each category of printed matter. It is possible to find figures which show how some newspapers are concentrated in high rent or in low rent areas in cities, or circulate extensively in the suburbs. It is comparatively easy to measure the amount of space given to news which refers to various social objects, and something can be found out about the time spent reading foreign news, national news, suburban news, city news, cartoons, and features. The relation between the time spent reading newspapers can be compared with the time spent talking about the world; by special study one might find how much the newspaper influences the conversation, or other expressive acts.

Several technical procedures have been devised which have been applied, or which can be applied, to the survey of the attention areas of the world. Such a survey would seek to discover the frequency with which persons were exposed to symbol representations of various objects. It might disclose that the middle-class citizen of Chicago spent ten minutes a day reading news about Europe, the upper-class citizen spent fifteen minutes a day, the middle-class Londoner spent five minutes reading about the Empire and five minutes reading about the rest of the world beyond Great Britain (for selected days for designated years). Such a survey would show the extent to which Geneva, London, Moscow, Shanghai, New York, Tokyo figure in the world news, and indicate the amount of time given by readers to various personalities, types of events, and places.

The direct study of the space content of the press is useful insofar as it furnishes clues to the distribution of attention, but it is obviously subject to several limitations. Reporting a certain amount of print about a given social object does not show how much time is spent by the reader on this amount of space, and it requires supplementary information to disclose whether different papers are read by the same people. Some papers are still read aloud in the Turkish cafés to those who listen, some are read by all members of the family, and some are discarded by the wage earner on the way home after work. Some are laboriously deciphered from beginning to end and others are cursorily inspected. Certain papers are thrown aside with little attention to their political news, owing to general knowledge of the censorship. Caution must be exercised in interpreting the significance of space results from newspaper measurement since the relative role of the paper to other channels of communication may be highly variable. In some localities word of mouth, letters, radio, magazines, all play important parts in drawing attention to social objects.

The orderly study of newspaper space has been conducted for the purpose of showing variations in the amount of space given to foreign news. Julian L. Woodward[1] found that the proportion of space devoted to news from abroad for forty newspapers each weighted by its own circulation was 5.15 per cent. Of the foreign news printed by the forty newspapers in the sample, 58.5 per cent was furnished by the Associated Press. The *New York Times* and the *Herald Tribune* published by far the most news (measured in centimeters). The papers of Pittsburgh and Cleveland published very little. Using relative percentages instead of absolute amounts, the *New York Times* retains rank one, but the *Chicago Tribune* climbs to third place. Woodward suggests that this tends to refute the supposed provincialism of the Middle West in reference to foreign affairs. The provincialism of New England is said to be corroborated by the small

1. *Foreign News in American Morning Newspapers,* New York, 1930.

relative amount of space given to foreign news by the two Boston papers of largest circulation, the *Post* and the *Globe*. If New York papers are eliminated from consideration, the differences between seaboard and inland papers become insignificant. The Hearst chain of papers showed no uniform policy.

The relation between psychological areas (as defined by the focus of attention) and organization areas can be studied for districts of varying size. The analysis of the space of the Pittsburgh and Cleveland press with reference to a twenty-five mile commuters' area adjacent to the city limits gave these results: 5 per cent of the Cleveland press was devoted to the suburban belt; 8 per cent of the Pittsburgh press. A sample of the Chicago press showed that 2.8 per cent of its space referred to the suburban belt.[2]

Space-counts divide newspapers rather clearly into those which follow world affairs with some system, and those which report episodically. The systematic papers include the small number published for the business and political groups closely concerned with the world of affairs. The variations in the handling of the news in the London press of the crisis which was initiated by the assassination of the Archduke in 1914 were great. The London *Times* ran something on the development of the situation every day of publication from June 29, 1914, to August 1, 1914, even though the total amount sank as low as a quarter column on July 18. The *Daily Mail* printed nothing (or less than an eighth of a column) from July 8 to July 24, except a quarter-column editorial July 14, and a quarter-column dispatch on July 22. The papers which, like the *Times*, followed the crisis consistently were the *Daily Telegraph, Morning Post, Daily News and Leader,* and the *Manchester Guardian*. The papers which gave practically no attention to the situation between the assassination and the ultimatum of the Dual Monarchy to Serbia were the *Westminster Gazette, Chronicle, Evening News, Standard, Star, Pall Mall Gazette, Daily Express,* and *Daily Graphic*.[3] It is little wonder

2. Cleveland and Pittsburgh sample for July 12–25, 1929, using Cleveland *Plain Dealer*, Cleveland *Press* (no Sunday edition), Cleveland *News*, Pittsburgh *Post Gazette* (*Telegraph* on Sunday), Pittsburgh *Press*. Chicago sample for July 6–12, 1930, using *Tribune, Herald-Examiner, Journal of Commerce, Daily News, Post, Evening American*.

3. For a list of English newspapers with circulation figures and qualitative data see Walter Zimmermann, *Die Englische Presse zum Ausbruch des Weltkrieges*, Verlag "Hochschule und Ausland," Charlottenburg, 1928. See also Jonathan Scott, *Five Weeks*, New York, 1927; Friederike Recktenwald, *Kriegsziele und öffentliche Meinung Englands 1914–16*, Stuttgart, 1929. The data just summarized are from one of my manuscripts.

that the masses of the population greeted the outbreak of the acute phases of the world crisis with such consternation, and took their cues from the simplest interpretations.[4]

Besides newspapers (and magazines) the printed reports of deliberative bodies may be used to indicate the focus of attention. Allowances must be made for variations in reporting practice from year to year within the country, and for differences in the relative significance of legislative debates from country to country. Commentators on the problem of legislative control of foreign policy have frequently lamented the lack of interest in foreign affairs on the part of elected representatives, and a few space measurement (time measurement) investigations have been conducted.[5] William Ballis analyzed the contents of the *Journal Officiel* from the convening of the 1927 Chamber on January 11 to May 10, and found that 7 per cent of the contents referred to foreign affairs, and 16 per cent to "quasi-domestic affairs," namely military, naval, and colonial matters. This was a relatively quiet period, and it is interesting to see how these results would vary through time, and how this particular index would compare with indices based upon newspaper content, magazine content, book publication, and the like.[6]

Some of the shortcomings of data collected from space analysis can be overcome by examining the circulation districts of the me-

4. Besides showing variations in the amount of attention paid to local, national, and world affairs, space studies may indicate interesting differences in the regional or class attention to continents, countries, regions and topics. The technique of reporting space counts is being perfected in order to show the comparative results produced by alternative modes of procedure. One has the choice of reporting space in number of words, linear inches, or centimeters (with multiplier for extra wide columns), number of mentions, quarter or eighth column estimates, per cent of page, per cent of total space, per cent of general news. The Pittsburgh, Cleveland, and Chicago data are expressed as proportions of general (non-departmentalized) news. The unit of mention may be the item or the identifying word. In seminar reports the possibilities of the measuring unit called the *ment* (mention) have been explored; this counts an item as a unit.

5. See Francis R. Flournoy, *Parliament and War,* London, 1927; J. S. Henderson and H. J. Laski, "A Note on Parliamentary Time and the Problem of Devolution," *Economica,* 5 (1925): 89–93; Eber M. Carroll, *French Public Opinion and Foreign Affairs 1870–1914,* New York, 1931.

6. Mr. Ballis in his seminar paper classified 17 per cent of the space, measured in column centimeters, as "procedural" and 60 per cent as "domestic." 27 per cent of the "foreign affairs" were classified into "topical" and 73 per cent into "geographical" categories. The geographical distribution was 31 per cent "noncontiguous European states," 5 per cent "American," and 46 per cent "Asiatic."

dium. The United States has been divided into metropolitan regions by Charles Newcomb, working under the direction of R. D. McKenzie, for the President's Commission on Social Trends.[7] The morning daily with the largest circulation was chosen for each metropolitan center, and gradients were calculated in all directions where the paper furnished fifty per cent or more of the metropolitan circulation of each city and town. The cities with the widest territorial spread were New York, Chicago, New Orleans, Los Angeles, and Seattle, and the boundaries remained very stable between 1920 and 1929. By classifying circulation according to social groups the definition of the attention area can be rendered much more precise.

The starting point for attention studies may be the social object itself. On May 18, 1932, Pope XI issued his encyclical called "Caritas Christi," warning the faithful of the dangers of communism and of militant nationalism and exhorting them to prayer to end the economic depression. Measuring the number of words given to the encyclical in papers of the largest circulation in the 42 metropolitan areas disclosed in the Newcomb-McKenzie survey, it appeared that the most attention was given by the newspapers in the Middle West. According to the Catholic Directory of 1932 Catholics are more numerous in the northeastern states. Cities like Boston and Baltimore do not appear in the maximum attention group, despite their large Catholic populations, and some southern districts played up the encyclical although there were few Catholics there. Such apparent discrepancies raise interesting questions for further research into the distribution of news.[8]

Now what is the nature of the relationship between changes in the focus of attention and changes in other details of the environment? Can we study the interrelations between attention areas and areas of sentiment, action, and organization? Suppose that we consider the connections between the movements of armed forces and the focus of attention. We have already seen from the study previously made that one sequence of relation showed the involvement of attention prior to the movement of armed forces; but our general knowledge leads us to desire other sequences to be investigated where the choice of maneuver areas initiated the events which guided the news. To what

7. "The Rise of Metropolitan Communities," Chap. 9, Vol. 1 of *Recent Social Trends,* New York, 1933. Studies of this kind have been stimulated by Robert E. Park.

8. Data from the seminar paper of Robert Zolla.

extent do rearrangements of the armed forces follow or precede changes in the focus of attention?

Another very general relation is that which may exist between areas of economic activity and areas of attention. Perhaps, over various time periods, the focus of attention is profoundly affected by changes in the relative volume of imports and exports passing between a given community and foreign communities. When a single country is studied, allowance must be made for the proportion of the total volume represented by the trade with this country. Perhaps it will be discovered that changes in exports are more influential than in imports, or that changes in the relation of manufactures to other commodities will evoke the most response. Research may show that items in the balance of payment such as security issues, tourist expenditures or remittances will be particularly sensitive. Changes in money value rather than physical volume may be influential in modifying attention.

Analyses of the gross amount of space alluding to selected social objects can be supplemented by analyses designed to show relations between *mode of representation* and response. How does the particular manner of reporting, commenting, cartooning, or photographing define the responses of those exposed to these stimuli? The focus of attention tends to influence expectations, demands, and identifications, and in turn to be influenced by the existing body of attitudes. Notoriously a newspaper which lampoons a political figure may arouse its readers to sympathy with the victim. Notoriously, also, newpapers are limited in their reporting practices by the standards of discrimination current in the community. American editors censored out many references to sexual perversion among the leaders of the Hitler movement, although such matters were rather freely handled in Germany.

What indices of the manner of presentation and of the effect shall we select? Difficulty arises because the category of "manner of representation" is usually somebody's guess about the effect to be expected. If some people are asked to arrange dispatches, editorial statements, pictures, or cartoons according to their surmise about its "tendency" to influence attitudes, the question arises whether people in the year 1935 can be expected to guess correctly about the influence which items in the New York *Times* had upon readers in 1930, 1925 . . . 1900? Can people who judge these items again in 1940 be expected to guess parallel to those who guessed in 1935? How shall we issue specifications for the choice of people who will be precisely comparable in exercising the judging function in 1940 and in 1935?

Despite such limitations, this method is being applied to the analysis of newspaper contents. The method has particularly interesting possibilities when the materials so appraised are actually applied to samples of the group reached by the medium. It is possible to elicit response data from readers of a paper by uniform procedures: subscribers to papers of sharply contrasting bias (measured by the consensus procedure) may be asked to fill out questionnaires designed to expose their tendencies to act favorably or unfavorably toward different symbols; they may be asked to vote a "straw ballot," to express themselves categorically when directly questioned, to give their free-word associations to the symbol (the associations to be classified by a consensus procedure as plus, neutral, or negative); or they may be given an opportunity for the indirect expression of preference in the course of an interview. Observers may record the spontaneous comments which occur through selected time intervals when crowds are viewing news bulletins, or when a subject is broached at dinner. The further question arises of the relations between specific indicators of response and the total response-in-situation. Does the person who expresses himself volubly against Germany in response to a given topic of conversation prove to be a person of whom it may be said:

> He is among the group from whom contributors to anti-German associations can be secured; he will advocate the election of candidates hostile to Germany; he will drill in order to be ready for war; he will welcome danger for himself and son in crises with Germany; . . . .

The significance of each detail of reaction is continually being assessed by the observer with respect to its significance as an indicator of other aspects of the total pattern, with special reference to critical situations which are more or less clearly envisaged. Since the orderly study of stimuli and reaction is comparatively new in society, about all that can be said at present is that it is a matter of growing interest to scientists and practitioners.

Among the pioneer efforts to deal exhaustively with the language in circulation through time in connection with world politics is a book by George Carlslake Thompson which was published in 1886.[9] Thompson carefully distinguishes the opinion which is *predominant*

9. *Public Opinion and Lord Beaconsfield, 1875–1880,* 2 vols., London, 1886.

from that which is *public*. The course which the state actually follows shows the first; the latter has the characteristics of wide diffusion, persistence, intensity, and reasonableness, which he defines by saying that one element of reasonableness is *"elaboration,* which term may be used to denote either on the one hand *definiteness with regard to practical action,* or on the other the degree to which the opinion in question results from a thought-out political theory; let us say its *theoretical completeness."* Classifying opinions according to their definiteness with regard to practical action, he distinguishes a general preference (*biases*), a wish for a particular end or course of action (*notions*), and a belief as to the best practical means for achieving those particular ends which are desired (*policies*). For the most part policies are mutually exclusive, but some notions can exist simultaneously in the same mind, since they are so nearly allied. These are called *views.* Certain other terms are used for the purpose of classifying the standard of conduct, the conception of England's role, and the nature of the motive involved in the expression.

The "notions" which were grouped together in the anti-Turkish view are: crusading spirit; historic instinct; humanity; England's special responsibility for Turkey's behavior (Turkey our watch dog, Turkey supported by our money, policy of Crimean war makes us responsible); nationality is the best foundation for states; the open sore must be healed; the concert of Europe must be preserved; a barrier can be erected against Russia. The implied standard of conduct in some cases was international law; in others morality or historic taste. Certain notions showed that England was conceived as a European power. Sometimes the notions were sustained by motives which were sentimental; at other times diplomatic. This remarkable book classifies the entire public output of the time according to this nuanced and sophisticated arrangement; the work was far ahead of its age in the detailed study of modes on representation.[10]

Secondary contact raises in most acute form the problem of completing acts of communication. In face-to-face experience over a protracted period personalities with parallel biopsychic structures and cultural technique may communicate extensively. An act of

10. For modern efforts to measure attitudes, see the literature cited by D. D. Droba, "Methods for Measuring Attitudes," *Psychological Bulletin,* 29 (1932): 309–323. See especially L. L. Thurstone, Floyd Allport, Stuart A. Rice, E. S. Bogardus, Gardner Murphy, Goodwin Watson. Also Hornell Hart, "Changing Social Attitudes and Interests," *Recent Social Trends,* Vol. 1, Chap. 8, New York, 1933.

communicating is bilaterally complete when two autobiographies knowingly concur in the frame of reference of symbols. When the experience of an observer in Berlin is translated into expressive symbols which must travel through various intermediaries until brief dispatches appear in a Chicago newspaper, the chances are slight that the act of communication between the reporter and the reader will be complete. The act of communicating in the anonymous-one-to-the-anonymous-many relationship is brief, and peculiarly handicapped by the thinness of the transmitted stimuli. Written dispatches lack the correction which comes from listening to intonations and watching the play of gesture; they suffer especially from the difficulty that the same words phonetically or orthographically are not the same words culturally or psychologically.

Thus the dispatch which speaks of the assassination of the President of the French Republic is at once equated by the American reader with the assassination of a President of the United States. Yet in important particulars this is a misconstruction of the seriousness of the situation, for the French president is a ceremonial executive, and the implications for policy of his death are slight. When a news report speaks of the triumph of the "Radical Socialists," the American reader assumes that the aggressive revolutionary elements are gaining. That the "Radical Socialists" are neither socialist nor radical in policy, being shopkeepers and independent farmers, does not appear from the use of the party label. A dispatch about the German Center Party has to do with a phenomenon for which there is no political equivalent in American experience. Our formal governing is still done through the Republican and Democratic parties, and the floor of the House and Senate has not been redefined from "Left" through "Center" to "Right." Of course a parallel can sometimes be found for a foreign attitude. The Prussian view toward the Polish corridor can be faintly indicated to the American by letting him imagine that the Japanese occupied Canada, and that they were given at the end of a war a wedge of territory which cut off New England from the rest of the United States.[11]

11. The troubles which arise from inadequate knowledge of those elementary approximations to common meaning which are the common words of a foreign language do not need to be elaborated. A less tragic instance than some is recited by Shane Leslie in a letter to the London *Times*, published June 3, 1927: "Thousands of Englishmen have learnt French in the last few years and thousands of Frenchmen have learnt English and even talked it, so that one is not prepared to read the amazing English translations afforded for the titles in the apparently official guide to the French Salon this year. For instance, it

There are many reportorial devices which can be used to convey the proper impression. The lobby activities at Washington are so vitally connected with our practice of government that they deserve to be more regularly handled by our Washington correspondents. The felicitous tag, "The Third House of Congress," has already been invented to name the new phenomenon.[12] Many techniques are available for heightening the word-consciousness of the newspaper reader. News from Asia and Latin America can frequently indicate the significance of "bandits" by putting the quotation marks around the word, and perhaps alluding to an official spokesman. The French press and foreign papers which were influenced by the French spoke of the "Ruhr operation" in 1923, while the hostile elements in the British press referred automatically to the "Ruhr invasion" or the "Ruhr adventure." American correspondents often repeated these tags without indicating just who was talking. The French spoke of "taking pledges" which put the "Ruhr operation" in the same class as a foreclosure proceeding against a bad debtor.

Often the phrase "national interest" is used when what is meant is that a certain bank wants the state department to do something. Since foreign correspondents can increase their space by emphasizing the national angle, an episode is generalized by lifting Mrs. Brown's trouble with a cab driver to "American Woman Insulted by Frenchman."

The act of communicating within the terse limits set by the one-to-many relation prevailing in the reporter-to-readers context is efficient when rough equivalences are found. Language is replete

---

requires the picture itself to help us to translate such as:—'Storm coming at the day breacky,' 'dress of a pole lady.' But a few versions are so screamingly funny that we commend them to our linguists with the original attached:— 'Ship's goat with subsists' (*Le canot aux vivres*). Rather disappointing it is to find that 'fantasy in night gown' (*en robe de soir*) is only an evening dress, and the Italian Ambassador will be humbled to be called 'messenger of Italy in Paris.' Doubtless 'the lafe chas Smith' will be recognized by his widow, but a certain Mr. de R— has every reason to be angry to find *Madame de R— et ses enfants labeled* 'Mistress de R— of her children'! Only Scriptural knowledge enables us to interpret such affecting scenes as 'under the tig tree' or 'return of the profuse child' (*l'enfant prodigue*) . . . Finally, we offer a prize for any reader who can guess the subject, or even hazard a vague resemblance to a picture, which has been solemnly labelled and set forth to the admiring Anglo-Saxon world as: 'The Pediometry at the drop of milk of Belleville.' "

12. For details, see E. Pendleton Herring, *Group Representation before Congress,* Baltimore, 1929, and Peter H. Odegard, *The American Public Mind,* New York, 1930.

with positive and negative terms which facilitate this process, and the reporter is guided by sound conceptions of his task when he uses them freely in creating the desired effect. Accurate reporting to the lay public necessitates colorful language; the reporter is an observer-translator who must experience in himself the equivalence of one cultural detail in terms of another cultural setting, and externalize the result.

The task of reporting for the specialized and semispecialized public has shown few innovations in method. The anecdotal technique still prevails in handling political news, although in certain fields the anecdotal method is supplemented by totalistic symbols. There are probably few business men of reputation in the United States who rely entirely for their ideas of economic fluctuations upon the casual incidents which happen to float into the current of gossip around the office or the club, or which make the headlines. They have gradually grown accustomed to the idea of correcting personal knowledge of specific details by continual reference to symbols which show the total movement of economic changes. Business graphs are part of the standard equipment of business executives in the modern world, and whatever may be their limitations, they are permanent instruments of adaptation in our civilization. The existence of totalistic symbols does not imply that the executive ignores his own direct observations. He need not forget the details of how the X company failed, nor ignore the complaint of his local shopkeeper about hard times. Such particulars gain new significance by finding a place in relation to the trends of economic life as a whole.

The modern man has passed from the anecdotal to the totalistic method in governing his relations to the weather. If the day after tomorrow is golf day, the news of old man Jones's rheumatism is disquieting if it is a famous sign of rain. But one is no longer bound to rely upon the sensitiveness of the old man's bones, for it is possible to scan the weather chart and estimate the proximity of the approaching "low." The simple lines of the weather chart offer an epitome of the atmospheric conditions over half a hemisphere and the ensemble aids in reaffirming or in rearranging the plans for day after tomorrow. Weather details of direct and limited observation are still pertinent, but they are always evaluated in relation to the totalistic symbol.

Such new devices have not been extensively applied to the reporting of political news. A dispatch relates that a great Communist demonstration has been held in Paris in memory of Lenin, or that

L'Humanité has published a fervid eulogy of revolution. Perhaps the report includes a statement that the incident is of no importance. The episodic and categorical character of this report is not easily put in perspective by the semi-instructed reader, since totalistic symbols have not been invented and standardized to indicate the comparative significance of diverse political trends in world politics. What proportion of the population respond favorably to the Communist symbol and where are they located?

The present almost exclusive reliance upon the anecdotal method of handling political news is fed by the proprietor's desire to be exciting in order to sell copies in order to raise advertising revenue. But it is also due to simple failure to extend techniques from one field to another. The result is that uncorrected caricatures so readily flourish in the political public. France passes for reactionary or revolutionary, Germany is vengeful or conciliatory, the Soviet Union is one thing or another; the habit of balancing political characterizations on opposite ends of an ideological teeter-totter is fatal to the steady perception of totality.

Technical ideas about the nature of totalistic symbols are forthcoming from experience in charting many details of the universe in their distributive aspect. Epidemiology, meteorology, human geography, business forecasting have been particularly rich in experience.[13] In developing "weather maps of public opinion"[14] new devices would be needed, but so great is this body of existing graphical aids to presenting data that such problems are sure of ready solution.

The real task is to organize an agency capable of executing a continuous survey of world attention. The press is only one channel of communication, but the task of classifying and rendering the output instantly available is obviously huge. It would be necessary to select papers for all regions of the world, to allow for factors affecting the relative significance of the press, and to standardize methods of correlating data in compact symbols. At present there

13. See W. G. Kendrew, *Climates of the Continents,* Oxford, 1928; H. H. Clayton, *World Weather,* New York, 1923; Karl Karsten, *Charts and Graphs,* New York, 1923; and standard volumes on statistical procedures.

14. Apparently this possibility was first foreseen by A. A. Tenney. See the *Independent,* 73 (1912): 895. He wrote: "What is needed is a continuous analysis of a large number of journals. Data would then exist for discovering the exact relation which may obtain between press attention and public action. The records in themselves would constitute a series of observations of the 'social weather,' comparable in accuracy to the statistics of the United States Weather Bureau."

are private clipping services which go through much of the press of the world, and all the leading foreign offices have comprehensive summaries of the world press. Such private agencies as the French steel trust and newspaper research institutes have extensive collections.

It seems probable that the launching of a continuing survey of world attention depends upon subsidies. On account of political complications, it is undesirable for an official agency to sponsor the work. The World Attention Survey should be under impartial, research auspices. It is quite possible that such a world service could presently sustain itself, partly from "weather map" service, and partly from special reports privately sold. Entirely apart from its value as a method of handling current intelligence, the proposed agency would arrange material of great historical and social scientific utility.[15]

The execution of an act of secondary contact involves an elaborate subdivision of function. It represents a multiplication of agency relations with distortions of meaning possible at each relay. All those who perform specialized roles in connection with secondary contact deserve careful study in relation to the apparatus which they use, and to the factors influencing their recruitment and motivation. We require the analysis of the foreign correspondent, the foreign editor, the managing editor, the proprietor, the advertising manager, the circulation manager, the reader. We must ferret out the effect of changes in telephone, telegraph, radio, cable, postal services, printing and publishing. Spies, foreign services, and specialized official and unofficial propagandists need to be investigated. Despite many sporadic, qualitative, and descriptive articles and books, most of the systematic research remains to be done.[16]

15. On the basis of estimates received from various experienced people in 1924, the cost is put at $250,000 a year. Thirty-five offices could be set up at an average cost of $6000.00, allowing for one chief, one assistant, one reader and stenographer, one cutter and sorter, office rent, office facilities, and communication expenses. $40,000 could be allowed for central office expense and for organization expense.

16. For leads in various directions just designated, see Charles Hodges, *The Background of International Relations*, Chaps. 22 and 23, New York, 1931; Paul F. Douglass and Karl Bömer, "The Press as A Factor in International Relations," *Annals of the American Academy of Political and Social Science*, 162 (1932): 241–272; Henry M. Wriston, *Executive Agents in American Foreign Relations*, Baltimore, 1929; H. K. Norton, *Foreign Office Organization*, Philadelphia, 1929; Algernon Cecil, "The Foreign Office" in Sir A. Ward and G. P. Gooch, *The Cambridge History of British Foreign Policy, 1783–1919*,

In general, the expansion of the means of contact multiplies the number of representations of social objects to which people are subjected, and reduces the time lag between the occurrence of an event and its symbolic redefinition. This brings into active dialectical interplay an enlarged spatial and ideological configuration. An important point brought out by Malcolm M. Willey and Stuart A. Rice is that expanding communication may increase local contacts more than distance contacts. Thus there is a greater reported increase in local than in nonlocal mail.

> As each agency lengthens the radius and increases the frequency of contact at a distance, it also makes possible an increased frequency of local contacts. Where is the change relatively greatest? The balance between these cannot be stated. On the one hand are the forces seeming to make for standardization, and on the other, those perhaps tending to enhance localisms. The two processes may proceed together; in externals there may be a cultural leveling, while inwardly old traditions, attitudes, and beliefs may gain reinforcement through mutual interaction. Overt likeness does not guarantee subjective similarity.[17]

The initial effect of expanding secondary contact may be to increase the danger to peace in world affairs, since insecurity reactions are easily aroused when new adjustments are required, and numerous local interests can profit by propagating insecurity. The adjustment crises arising from primary contact are generalized for the rest of the population through secondary means of contact. Nationals involved in difficulties abroad (primary contact) may have their situation communicated in exciting terms to all who are identified with the national symbol. The reiteration of the common symbol of identification is a means of rallying potential allies cheaply to the support of the demands made in primary situations. Since those in secondary relation to the situation have a poorly developed ego organization (knowledge) with reference to it, they may react to alleged slights to their personality in elementary fashion. All the insecurities arising from the changes in the division of labor inci-

---

Vol. 3, Chap. 3, Cambridge, England, 1923; R. W. Rowan, *Spy and Counter-spy*, New York, 1928; my articles on "Censorship" and "Propaganda" in the *Encyclopaedia of the Social Sciences*. See the forthcoming annotated bibliography on propaganda and promotional activity edited by Harold D. Lasswell, Ralph D. Casey, and Bruce L. Smith for the Social Science Research Council to be published by the University of Minnesota Press.

17. *Recent Social Trends*, "Communication," p. 217, Vol. 1, New York, 1933.

dent to the expansion of contact are heightened by the symbolisms circulated about the secondary environment. The local "we" symbols and the symbols of collective demand and expectation are so frequently circulated in favorable forms that the chances are good that they will be introjected by the personalities exposed to them. Insecurities are thus provisionally alleviated, as they are evoked, by symbolic redefinition.

The vested interest of the private press in circulating alarmist material is well known; it came candidly "out of their own mouths" when a former associate of Lord Northcliffe said in answer to the question, What sells a newspaper?

> The first answer is "war." War not only creates a supply of news but a demand for it. So deep rooted is the fascination in war and all things appertaining to it that . . . a paper has only to be able to put up on its placard "A Great Battle" for its sales to mount up.[18]

It was the Civil War of the seventeenth century in England which established the *Diurnal,* the campaigns of Marlborough at the beginning of the eighteenth century which created a demand for Buckley's *Daily Courant,* the Revolution in France and the succeeding wars and alarms which fed the press of the later eighteenth and early nineteenth century, the Crimean war which contributed so largely to the prosperity of the *Times* and led to the penny daily; and it was the Indian Mutiny, the Franco-Prussian War, the Egyptian and Eastern campaigns, and the Boer War which aided in the growth of the nineteenth century press.

Sensationalism is a vested interest of every specialist on human expression, since not only income but also deference depends upon "getting a rise out of" the public. Orators, actors, playwrights, essayists, and novelists are united in this common interest in eliciting wide immediate reactions from an audience. The "profits motive" adds to, but does not create, the sensationalism of media of communication.

The spread of literacy favored the substitution of national symbols for local symbols, but in the world perspective national symbols are another form of local symbol. Partly educated readers require relatively crude stimuli to arouse them, and the coming of hypersensationalism is an adaptation to this new audience and new market. In 1894 Alfred Harmsworth (later Lord Northcliffe) and Kennedy

18. Kennedy Jones, *Fleet Street and Downing Street,* p. 108, London, 1920.

Jones took over the *London Evening News and Post* with this announcement which was retained by the *Daily Mail* in 1898:

> Freed from fad and prejudice the *Evening News* will preach the gospel of loyalty to the Empire and faith in the combined efforts of the peoples united under the British flag.

The second day of the *Mail's* life saw a leader on Cecil Rhodes which began:

> The dogs of Little England bark at his heels as they did in other times at Clive and Warren Hastings. But the Empire of India remains, and the faults of the men who won that splendid inheritance for that country are forgotten.

Lord Salisbury's famous epigram that the *Daily Mail* was a sheet "written by office boys for office boys" is matched by the slurs at the "concierge" or janitor's press in France. But many of these contemptuous remarks about the "chauvinism of the masses" and the "excesses of sensational newspapers" are expressions of caste annoyance that the general public should presume to have an opinion of any kind about world affairs, which was so long the prerogative of the governing classes with their practical monopoly of higher erudition, travel, and diplomacy. The *Daily Mail* is a *Morning Post* in shirt sleeves; it is distinguishable from the latter in speech, if not in thought.

Expanding secondary contact intensifies many international situations by mobilizing many people very rapidly. Lord Lyons, the British Minister at Washington at the time of the Mason-Slidell incident, wrote later, "If there had been telegraphic communication, it would have been impossible to avert war."[19]

The long-run effect of expanding contact may reverse the initial results. New devices for the prevention of conflict may be developed as reactions against the heightened danger; but to generalize from this to the expectation of world unity is doubtful operation, as we shall presently have occasion to show. Thus far in the history of the world changing zones of conflict have both widened and restricted the area of peace. In recent times the spread of secondary means of contact has favored marketing and control interests wider than local but much narrower than the earth.

19. *Lord Lyons: A Record of British Diplomacy*, London, 1913.

Chapter X

POLITICS, PERSONALITY, AND CULTURE:
THE AMERICAN CASE

Political symbols and practices are so intimately intertwined with the larger array of symbols and practices in culture that it is necessary to extend the scope of political investigation to include the fundamental features of the culture setting. A culture pattern is any human act or artifact which is not prearranged in the inherited equipment of man. When we desire to stress the degree to which individuals differ from one another owing to experience with contrasting culture environments, we use words like "peasant," "aristocrat," "priest," "diplomat," "politician," and "bureaucrat." These terms refer to *social* types. When we want to emphasize the degree to which individual differences are assignable to inborn psychobiological traits, we create words like "eidetic" or "leptosomic."[1] It is becoming customary to speak of types of *temperament, character,* or, more loosely, of *personality* to indicate such differences. Careful comparison shows that most of the words refer to patterns which are complex results of the interaction of original nature and environing stimuli.

Politics is the study of the changing value hierarchy, the pyramids of safety, income, and deference. Some symbols embody definite demands or expectations or identifications, and may be called political symbols in the narrower sense of the word, without losing sight of the larger problem of discovering the actual significance which can be attached to them in redefining the value pyramid. Political symbols and practices in the narrower sense are in complex relation with all symbols and practices, and the scope of political research must include the analysis of significant connections of this kind. All significant patterns of personality and culture must ultimately be

1. The first term relates to the mechanism of visual perception (after-imaging); the latter to certain morphological and physiological traits. See E. R. Jaensch, *Eidetic Imagery,* New York and London, 1930; E. Kretschmer, *Physique and Character,* New York and London, 1925.

assessed in terms of their influence upon the pyramids of safety, income, and deference. The comparative study of cultures has been pursued by many methods.[2] One interesting method proceeds on the assumption that the highly specialized patterns in a culture are elaborations of the fundamental patterns of that culture; therefore the principal features

2. For historical and critical studies, see F. Schneersohn, "Zur Grundlegung einer Völker- und Massenpsychopathologie," *Ethos*, I (1925–26): 81–120; L. Schweiger, "Philosophie der Geschichte, Völkerpsychologie und Soziologie in ihre gegenseitigen Beziehungen," *Berner Studien zur Philosophie und ihre Geschichte*, Bern, 18 (1899): 1–78; A. Leicht, *Lazarus der Begründer der Völkerpsychologie*, Leipzig, 1904; Carlo Sganzini, *Die Fortschritte der Völkerpsychologie von Lazarus bis Wundt*, Bern, 1913. For general theories, see Lazarus and Steinthal, *Einleitende Gedanken ueber Völkerpsychologie als Einleitung zu einer Zeitschrift für Völkerpsychologie und Sprachwissenschaft*, 1850 (reprinted in Volume 17 of the *Zeitschrift*); Wilhelm Wundt, *Elemente der Völkerpsychologie*, Stuttgart, 1921; Gustav Adolph Lindner, *Ideen zur Psychologie der Gesellschaft, als Grundlage der Sozialwissenschaft*, Vienna, 1871; Gustave Le Bon, *Lois psychologique de l'évolution des peuples*, Paris, 1894; Aug. Matteuzzi, *Les facteurs de l'évolution des peuples*, Paris, 1900; P. de Rousiers, *L'élite dans la société moderne; son rôle*, Paris, 1914; Adolphe Coste, *L'expérience des peuples*, Paris, 1900; E. Hurwicz, *Die Seelen der Völker*, Gotha, 1920; W. Dilthey, *Der Aufbau der geschichtlichen Welt in den Geisteswissenschaften*, Berlin, 1910; Felix Krueger, *Ueber Entwicklungspsychologie*, Leipzig, 1915; L. Frobenius, *Paideuma, Umrisse einer Kultur und Seelenlehre*, Munich, 1921; Alfred Weber, "Prinzipielles zur Kultursoziologie," *Archiv für Sozialwissenschaft und Sozialpolitik* 47 (1921): 1–49; A. Fischer, "Psychologie der Gesellschaft," *Kafkas Handbuch der vergleichende Psychologie*, 2, 1922; Max Weber, *Wirtschaft und Gesellschaft*, Tübingen, 1922.

For the psychology of the simpler peoples, see F. Boas, *The Mind of Primitive Man*, New York, 1911; R. Thurnwald, "Psychologie des primitiven Menschen," *Kafkas Handbuch der vergleichende Psychologie*, 1, Munich, 1922; and the work of Lévy-Bruhl, K. Th. Preuss, Bronislaw Malinowski.

For group studies, see Alfred Fouillée, *Psychologie du peuple français*, Second Edition, Paris, 1898; *Esquisse psychologique des peuples européens*, Second Edition, Paris, 1903; Emile Boutmy, *Essai d'une psychologie politique du peuple anglas au XIXe siècle*, Paris, 1901; *Elements d'une psychologie politique du peuple anglais au XIXe siécle*, Paris, 1901; *Elements d'une psychologie politique du peuple américain*, Paris, 1920; J. Bardoux, *Essai d'une psychologie de l'Angleterre contemporaine*, Paris, 1906; S. de Madariaga, *Englishmen, Frenchmen, Spaniards*, New York, 1928; Richard Wilhelm, *The Soul of China*, New York, 1928, and *Chinesische Wirtschaftspsychologie*, Leipzig, 1930; Wilhelm Dibelius, *England*, New York, 1930; Ernst R. Curtius and Arnold Bergsträsser, *Frankreich*, Stuttgart, 2 vols., 1930; Karl A. Wittvogel, *Wirtschaft und Gesellschaft Chinas*, 1–, Leipzig, 1931–; Leonard S., and Virginia Woolf, *After the Deluge: A Study of Communal Psychology*, London, 1931.

of a given culture may be exposed by careful analysis of the specialized details. These highly specialized patterns are particularly amenable to rigorous study, as they have been objects of much scientific consideration. The recommended procedure is therefore to examine the philosophical, scientific, and esthetic manifestations of a particular case, and to compare each one with analogous formations elsewhere, thus exposing its significant characteristics.[3] The application of this method to the United States involved the selection of writings, in such a subject as philosophy, which were deemed "representative." These writings were then compared with the philosophic output in other cultures in order to show where assumptions are introduced without argument. William James waved aside with an impatient phrase the "absolute," and hurried forward to promulgate ethical rules which brought him into immediate contact with the problems of others without elaborating his underlying assumptions. Kant affords a striking contrast to this (Kant is taken as the typical German expression in philosophy), for he spent much space examining the nature of his fundamental assumptions. James is said to have sought to establish immediate contact with other personalities (possessing an "open ego"), while Kant was less concerned about outflowing contact (displaying a "closed ego"). America and Germany are thus contrasted as cultures with an open ego and a closed ego structure.

Leaving to one side the specific conclusion, and considering only the method, it may be doubted whether it can issue in trustworthy findings. Some specialized patterns of a culture may be counterexpressive of the strongest trends of the time, being reaction formations against the principal trends of the period. No criteria are stipulated for settling questions of this kind, and in their absence such a procedure is likely to lead to uncontrolled formalism. The view taken here is that culture comparisons are not demonstrably valid until they have been made in relation to the culture as a whole; and that the nature of the whole cannot be disclosed without using methods which show the role of the detailed culture patterns in the personalities who are shaped in relation to them.

The most intensive technique of observation now available is the prolonged (psychoanalytic) interview of sample individuals within a selected time-space configuration. Events are located along sample

3. Erich Voegelin, *Ueber die Form des amerikanischen Geistes,* Tübingen, 1928.

career lines by this means. The use of such *intensive* techniques must be supplemented by *extensive* procedures which order events within the context without considering their relation to many other events along the career line of the individuals involved. As previously emphasized, there is a productive relation between the correlative use of the intensive starting point and the extensive starting point; each significant detail which is disclosed in intensive personality research can be studied by extensive methods in order to ascertain its distribution.

The intensive psychoanalytical methods have drawn attention to the unsatisfactory nature of the material now collected by extensive procedures, about comparative culture. Psychoanalysts found that practices connected with the nursing and general care of the child in our culture led to certain consequences in the traits of the child; at once one searched for ethnological data about many cultures to see whether there was an obvious connection between child care and personality traits. (This does not imply that such simple associations are to be anticipated.) Scrutiny of our data about simpler societies disclosed mainly gaps in the treatment of subtle details of adult-to-child and child-to-child relations, with the result that recent field work among preliterate peoples has been greatly stimulated in an effort to supply the missing material.[4]

Even in our own western European area the nuances of culture interrelationships are inadequately studied and poorly reported. It is well known that English administrators possess certain patterns of speech and intonation which enable them to give commands in different parts of the world without giving offense. What is the precise process by means of which these patterns are transmitted to the growing child? When did these patterns become crystallized in the history of culture? Is there some peculiarity in the attitude of the English nurse maid toward the child which aids in creating the English adult style?[5]

Psychoanalytical methods have been unsystematically applied to diverse culture contexts thus far, and the records which have been produced leave much to be desired.[6] Indeed, it is probable that the

4. See my discussion of "Psychoanalyse und Sozioanalyse," *Imago*, 19 (1933): 377–383.

5. Fleeting references to these problems are occasionally found. On some details see G. J. Renier, *The English: Are They Human?*, Leipzig, 1932.

6. On the problem of records see Chapter 11 of my *Psychopathology and Politics*, Chicago, 1930.

full procedure cannot be used in some cultures, owing to certain formations in the culture itself.[7] The most elaborately executed analyses will continue to furnish the deepest insights into possible relationships, but there are many less prolonged methods which can display interesting relations within the limits of the procedures used. Thus it may be possible to secure enough intimate contact with selected people to procure dreams and some word association data over an extended period.[8] Various short methods are already in common use for the purpose of eliciting pertinent data, especially the life history method which has become very common among American sociologists.[9] The problem of comparing the results secured by these various procedures deserves extended attention.[10]

Valuable data may be procured by collecting technical as distinguished from intimate life stories. These technical or professional histories require some degree of intimacy with the contributor, but scarcely the exhaustive self-exposure of the psychoanalytic interview. We need to know how specialized functions have been performed in various situations around the world, how a hundred successful lawyers, civil servants, ambassadors, soldiers, journalists, business enterprisers, politicians have been able to "get by" in New York, Chicago, Tokyo, Shanghai, Moscow, Berlin, Paris, London, and elsewhere. We need the stories of a hundred unsuccessful professional people to correct the perspective of the successful cases.[11]

Various extensive methods of procedure can be perfected in order to supplement the data procured by relatively more intensive pro-

7. See Géza Róheim, "Psycho-analysis of Primitive Cultural Types," *International Journal of Psycho-analysis,* 13 (1932): 1–224; and my discussion of B. Malinowski's *Sex and Repression in Savage Society,* Analysis 34 in *Methods in Social Science: A Case Book,* Stuart A. Rice, Editor, Chicago, 1931.

8. This was done by Frederick Pierce, *Dreams and Personality,* New York and London, 1931. This book errs in assuming that its method of superficial association is a "test" of the prolonged association results secured by Freud; but such naïveté need not be associated with such investigations.

9. William I. Thomas, William Healy, and Paul Radin were pioneers in various fields.

10. The study of several forms of interviewing has made some progress. See W. V. Bingham and V. B. Moore, *How to Interview,* London and New York, 1931.

11. Much random material is at hand, but systematic work requires sustained field contact. For scattered references to biographies and autobiographies of administrators, see the several volumes of the *Studies in the Making of Citizens* edited by Charles E. Merriam. See also Graham Wallas, *Our Social Heritage,* New Haven, 1921.

cedures. Communities of various sizes, histories and structures should be selected around the world for comparative analysis, after the manner developed by the Lynds.[12] The distribution of reactions at selected intervals can be studied by sampling methods which require but brief contact with specific persons. Shock reactions to many words, acts, and representations can be used for the purpose of diagnosing the mores and countermores patterns. In general, the shock response indicates that the superego has been mobilized to preserve the repression of a prohibited act which has been stimulated. The distribution by social affiliation and by situation can be investigated by methods which range from diary note observation to more formal modes of procedure.[13]

As special students of politics, we require the systematic comparison of symbols from all cultures. The desirable collection would include all the vocabularies and connotations relating to policies, institutions, persons, and groups. The language of encomium and of opprobrium, and the language of identification, demand, and expectation would find a place in our comparative anthology. Available collections of political poetry, essay, and song adhere to no consistent principle in the selection of material, fluctuating between random esthetic preferences and half-hearted efforts at the choice of the "representative." Our hypothetical library of comparative politics would contain volumes for every culture executed on a common plan which would allow for the analysis of class and regional differences.

A more concrete idea of the problems involved can be conveyed by developing a preliminary sketch, fragmentary though it must necessarily be, of some of the political and cultural symbols and practices which are relevant to the analysis of the United States.

Let us assume that over the coming years the United States will live in a situation of increasing domestic and external insecurity. Existing political symbols and practices will be redefined as the community reacts to the strain. In very general terms it seems reasonable to predict that increasing insecurity will stimulate the invention and the diffusion of symbols of the kind which have been devised in western Europe where insecurities have been chronic. So far the United States has been relatively free from the play of the international and of the interclass balance of power, with the result that

12. Robert S. Lynd and Helen Merrill Lynd, *Middletown: A Study of Contemporary Culture*, New York, 1929.

13. The literature on attitude measurement has already been indicated.

the American political vocabulary shows striking deviations from the European pattern.[14]

The vocabulary of American public life is legal, ethical, and theological rather than analytical; and, where it is analytical, it is personal and partisan rather than impersonal. The propaganda of historical materialism in Europe gave currency to certain impersonal conceptions like the "class struggle." Constitutional documents, conventional morality, dogmatic theology were treated as secondary derivatives of the profit-making classes under the present system of production and distribution. All the older authority symbols were thus rendered suspect. Appeals to the majesty of the law or the pangs of conscience or the will of God in support of the established order were devalued. Was it not to be taken for granted that the judges, the moralists, and the theologians would automatically sanctify the position of the ruling economic dynasty whose bread they ate? The corrosive sublimate of historical materialism reduces all the traditional gods to puppets by exposing the wires which lead to the profit makers. The implacable march of modern technology, the impersonal demon of the pecuniary calculus, and the urge to maximize income over outlay are represented as hewing their way through inconvenient social institutions, shaping the role of the man of law or the man of God to fit their imperious necessities.

The insecurities arising from the domestic class struggle, which furnished the receptivities necessary for the spread of such analytical conceptions, were supplemented by the discipline imposed by the play of the external balance of power. The long fear of foreign invasion in France and Germany, the long struggle to have and to hold overseas possessions on the part of Great Britain and Holland, incessant preoccupation with the shifting potentialities of fighting effectiveness have kept the stern, impersonal realities of world politics steadily before the ruling élites. It is superfluous to spell out the theory of the balance of power in Paris or London or Berlin; it is, however, indispensable in Chicago, where the news in the press, the editorials in the papers, the skits in the comic strips, and the lectures of the

14. On some aspects of opinion in America, see Charlotte Lütkins, "Demokratie und öffentliche Meinung in den Vereinigten Staaten," pp. 190–206, *Soziologische Studien . . . Alfred Weber gewidmet,* Potsdam, 1930; André Siegfried, *America Comes Of Age,* New York, 1927; J. H. Denison, *Emotional Currents in American History,* New York, 1932. Useful data are in Charles O. Paullin, *Atlas of the Historical Geography of the United States,* New York, 1932. On the international position of the United States see Lucien Romier, *Qui sera maître? Europe ou Amérique?,* Paris, 1927.

week deal with war in sentimentalized terms which are poor in
specific context. The American college student who sees that King
Zog is reported to plan to remain at his capital rather than journey
to a watering-place registers next to nothing, but his European
contemporary instantly wonders if this report signifies that Zog is
trying to break away from Italian influence and curry favor with the
Yugoslavs and the French. The details of world news fall into some
order in the mind of the cultivated European since he has been
brought up to appraise the world scene from the angle of fighting
potentialities.

While it is true that America's relative isolation from the play of
the world and the class balance owes a great deal to geographical
isolation and to abounding economic opportunity, the parochial
character of American political symbolism is partly assignable to the
belated struggle over slavery. The problems arising from the institution of slavery on the plantation preoccupied Americans at the time
when modern industrial capitalism was making its bow on the world
stage. The struggle over the position of the slave distracted the
attention of Americans from the class implications of modern industrialism by creating a united front of employers and wage earners
against the plantation owner. The industrial north fought as citizens
and free men against the agrarian south and the identification symbols which were sanctified in this struggle included the manufacturer
and the wage earner as fighting partners and not as class antagonists.

The polemics of the slavery controversy were legalistic, ethical,
and theological. No one succeeded in injecting into the vocabulary
of the time a full-blown economic analysis of all social institutions,
laying bare the role of modern industrialism in driving a wedge
between capital and labor. The symbol of the proletariat or of the
bourgeoisie was eclipsed by language about plantation owners, free-
men, and slaves. Since to the northern factory worker the slave was
somebody who was black and Southern, the ringing call of the Communist Manifesto awoke but a feeble echo on this side of the water,
where factory hands were identified with their employers in a common crusade against the slave system.

The federal form of the American constitution put a premium on
constitutional argumentation, and the ever present problem of de-
termining the social institutions of new states which applied for
admission into the union played into the hands of constitutional
lawyers. Issues were argued in the language of conformity with
or deviation from a body of premises which were presumed to be

embodied in a short written document. These patterns of dialectic were familiar to a culture where Protestantism prevailed, and where pulpiteering consisted in arguing questions of private and public policy in terms of conformity with or deviation from the written Bible. The polemics of slavery were carried on in terms of the Constitution and the Bible; so all-embracing were these forms of language that the political vocabulary of the United States was enriched by no systematic work of social analysis. The entire dispute over slavery left no book that performed the role of intellectual orientation which has been played by *Das Kapital* in Europe. Almost the only legacy from the political past of the United States is the *Federalist*, which repeats the classical language about the rich and poor, but rises to no masterly heights of analysis of the peculiar formations of emergent capitalism. This new and portentous phenomenon thus remains verbally "uncontrolled."

Hence during the years when modern civilization in Europe was coming to grips with the momentous changes in its technique of production, and forming a vocabulary capable of designating the new world generated by these innovations, the United States was absorbed in polemics over an anachronistic relic of an earlier method of production.

It is worthy of passing remark that those who were interested in developing political and economic radicalism in America showed no special aptitude in resymbolizing socialism into a dynamic and compelling vocabulary for Americans. Socialists were expected to use alien words which were practically devoid of meaning in the American setting; "bourgeois," "class," "capitalism," "middle class," "*rentier*," "proletarian." Words like "socialism" or "communism" were reiterated in a community where words like "individual," "equality of opportunity," "free competition," and "free initiative" were potent symbols. At the very least socialism could have become "organized individualism."

Radicals talked about "exploitation" without making due allowance for the American outlook toward money-getting as a gamble, a sporting proposition, a risk, where some fellows are shrewd and lucky. Americans still have a sporting attitude toward economic activity and feel contemptuous of anyone who whines when he loses. There is a fundamental admiration for the "big shots," and a sneaking recognition that the "captains of industry" are slightly swollen lieutenants, corporals, and privates. Americans have the enterpriser's attitude toward money and not the peasant's attitude;

money is a scoring device and not a hoard in a sock. The expansion of personality possible in the new world generates a respect for unlimited possibilities and for bigness; Americans wince when they are accused of attacking big business "just because it is big." A phrase like "unfair competition" was a very sound one, since it made it possible to attack the big by making bigness a sign of unfairness. Since Americans have the individualistic enterpriser's psychology, the language which wins loyal support for political demands of a collective nature must be phrased in language which is acceptable to this psychology. So if the radical demands in America had been named something besides "socialism" and if they had been argued in terms of an American "joint-stock company" giving every citizen a "national dividend" and a "guaranteed income to all who work," substantive American policy might have been rather more collectivist than it is today.

If we were to offer the specifications for an American *Capital,* they would run somewhat as follows: (1) The title must be a slogan. The title *Capital* has become a diagnosis and by implication a pre-scription; for if capital is to blame for our plight, capital must be crushed. An example of what to avoid is V. Pareto's *Treatise on Sociology,* regardless of the brilliance of analysis. (2) The book must be thick. Thickness conveys authoritativeness and discourages read-ing by the masses who must revere the book as a symbol. (3) The book must be systematic and quantitative ("scientific"). The analytic pattern of thinking has now become so current in society that the volume must appear to possess imposing categories and sub-cate-gories. It must be studded with charts, graphs, tables, footnotes, and other impressive impedimenta of exactitude. (4) The vocabulary must be more than analytic—it must be ethical, legalistic (constitu-tional), technological, sporting, individualistic, nationalistic. (5) The selected "facts" must allude mainly to American experience. (6) The key words and the style must be invidious. Terms like "un-earned increment," "surplus value," "leisure class" can be handled with appropriate innuendo. (7) The volume as a whole should be ambiguous, obscure, and somewhat contradictory. This facilitates the redefinition of the book to serve the purposes of the self-selected revolutionary élite. (8) The style must be dull, in order to reduce the danger that the work will be extensively read or that the illusion of comprehension should sprout too widely and too readily without aid of centralized interpreters. (9) The prescription should

be activistic; join a specific organization, obey the revolutionary
élite, prepare for revolutionary acts![15]

One of the interesting contradictions in symbol formation is that
the bourgeoisie produced the intellectuals who developed socialism
in highly systematic style, but themselves dashed into political action
after the war with nothing more substantial than the speeches and
articles of Mussolini and Hitler to guide them. Hitler's *My Battle,*
the answer of the lesser bourgeoisie to Marx, is florid, personal,
rambling, and sentimental, in the manner which has been distinctive
of American political writing (though without the same legalism).
The lower bourgeoisie in America has been much more consistently
active in politics than it has been in Italy or Germany, where its
members rushed somewhat convulsively into the field of protest;
since contradictions have developed less explosively in America, receptivities are better organized for more pretentious works of
analysis. Abroad, the small bourgeoisie was utterly disillusioned
about the prospects of salvation by discussion, and submitted blindly
to the "leader." After the seizure of power, the systematizing intellectuals came back into their own to develop intellectualistic justifications of "anti-intellectualism."

Thus far the discontents which are generated within the American
social order have been successfully dissipated over the legalistic,
ethical, personal, and party symbols already at hand. The failure
of collective movements of protest to consolidate themselves more
rapidly is in part to be attributed to this plethora of symbols, and
to the distractions of attention which are fostered by the decentralized
practices of American government.

America's decentralized institutional life is itself an outcome of
past security; its present function is to keep questions about the
class struggle and the world balance of power subordinated to tech-
nicalities about the boundaries of local and central government, and
about the relative competence of public authorities. The governing
system discourages the discussion of issues in a national and world
perspective. The presidency goes to local administrators who have
no long record on national questions, which may be contrasted with
the situation in such a state as Great Britain, where the national
government is led and opposed by men who have been committing

15. The deeper psychological problems were referred to in the account previously given of the appeal value of Marxism. For ingenious comments on the
problem of presenting contentions, see Karl Otto Erdmann, *Die Kunst Recht zu
Behalten,* Fourth Edition, Leipzig, 1925.

themselves for years in the national legislature on questions of national policy. The effective executives of Great Britain (the Cabinet) are selected from those who have been before the public eye during national and imperial controversies for a generation. American presidential candidates are regularly recruited from among governors who must be pumped into national figures during the ballyhoo of the campaign. It is a positive disadvantage to have a career on national matters, since a record invites attack; senators are notoriously handicapped in competing with governors for the presidency. This premium on parochialism may produce able administrators and organizers, but it inevitably favors men who are inexperienced in national concerns.

The lack of integration between national and local government in American practice has permitted tendencies to find expression in American municipal politics which are very difficult for western Europeans to understand. With growing insecurity, centralization will be stimulated in fact and in form, and American municipal politics will lose the distinctive characteristics which are the result of years of comparative exemption from the play of the balance of power.[16]

In western Europe the relation between cities and the national area of organization is much more intimate than in the United States. The parochial areas which stand between the city and the nation are minimized, and urban affairs are more directly responsive to the nation's interpretation of its role in the international balance of power. Whether the mechanism of central control is the grant-in-aid (Great Britain) or the ministry of the interior (France, Italy), the effect is to create acquiescence for the modification of local affairs with reference to the international position of the state. The growth of socialism has strengthened the centralizing tendencies, either directly or indirectly, through provoking intervention from conservative elements through courts or administrative officers in suppressing

---

16. That external threats facilitate centralization is one of the most prevalent observations about politics. If the terms used are carefully defined the statement holds. There must be sufficient symbolic identification to permit a common threat to be recognized; otherwise an external change will not be construed as a "threat." For the extensive literature on the theme, see H. Spencer, *The Principles of Sociology;* W. G. Summer, *War and Other Essays,* New Haven, 1911; R. Pöhlmann, *Geschichte der sozialen Frage und des Sozialismus in der antiken Welt,* Third Edition, 2 vols., Munich, 1925; V. Pareto, Les systèmes socialistes, Paris, 1902–1903; G. E. G. Catlin, *A Study of the Principles of Politics,* New York, 1930.

local radicalism. The developments in the German Reich are especially notable since the World War.

It is to be anticipated that the growth of domestic and international insecurity will create the acquiescence necessary to bring about closer relations between national and local government in the United States. As the class struggle becomes more acute in the larger cities, the armed forces of the national government will be brought in, following precedents already established, and the consolidation of our governing structure will be expedited. In 1894 President Cleveland, against the protest of the Governor of Illinois, sent troops to Chicago, then the scene of a railway strike that blocked commerce and the mails. President Roosevelt prepared to use the army to open and operate coal mines in 1902. President Wilson intervened at Gary, Indiana, during the steel workers' strike of 1919. It is also on record that President Harding turned to the army in 1922 when a strike threatened to tie up the railroads.

It is to be expected that the diffusion of Marxist symbols and of centralized practices will be accompanied by the realigning of violence in the United States. Alongside the traditional generosity, moral sentimentality, bustle, and ballyhoo of American life is the shadier world of gang warfare, mountain feuds, race rioting, race lynching, industrial warfare, and civic corruption. No doubt the significant role of civil violence in the United States derives in part from the utility of violence in the historical struggles against the French, British, and Indians; since violence persists long after the colonization of the continent has been completed, there must be other factors which sustain it. Relative isolation from the play of the world balance of power has enabled the aggressiveness of the community to be directed against internal rather than external enemies; the specific character of civil violence is the result of the vicissitudes of a rigorous code of morals when exposed to threatening conditions.

A stringent code of behavior, once imbedded in the consciences of a rising generation, seeks to protect itself from disintegration by generating anxieties within the personalities which are tempted to defy it. The magnitude of the insecurities is in proportion to the seriousness of the threat, and the vigor of the methods used likewise depends upon the intensity of the conflict. One of the most potent and primitive methods by which the superego retains ascendancy over incompatible impulses is by savage repression, which results in turning some of the aggressive impulses of the self against other portions of the self which are to be held in check. Acute temptation

reactivates the earlier conflict at nearly full intensity, but the resulting tensions may be partially relieved by projecting the locus of the
threat away from the inner life and upon the environment. The
aggressions can thus be turned outward upon the world, and the
intrapsychic conflict mitigated.

A stringent superego is endangered negatively when the environment fails to provide the customary reenforcements, and positively
when the environment offers definite inducements to the violation of
the code. The rigor of the American conscience is the result of the
struggle of the early inhibiting structures to preserve themselves
against the positive and negative hazards of new geographical and
functional environments. During the early years of the country the
decisive role was played by new geographical environments. Men and
women from Europe and from the eastern seaboard moved in successive waves into new territory where they left all the conventional
props of correct behavior far behind them. Priest, policeman, neighbors, and friends were often entirely absent. Familiar faces and
familiar places no longer sustained the code of decency and propriety
so carefully ingrained during formative years. In this new geographical setting opportunities and provocations abounded which
seemed to set at naught the categorical imperatives of the earlier
code. Hunting and killing, stealing and squatting, violating the
holy days, and a hundred other ways of acting counter to the conscience seemed to offer security, income, and deference. The superego,
thus deprived of external supports when it was assailed by the lure
of tangible advantage, resorted to desperate measures to protect
itself. Ruthless, primitive, direct methods were employed on behalf
of the threatened order. Those who were most intimately tied to the
mores used arbitrary and even violent means of attacking others
whose conduct threatened the personality and the cultural formations
from which they derived livelihood and distinction. The bloody hap-
penings of recorded history in the Massachusetts Bay Colony reflect
the defensive struggles of those whose insecurities were aroused in the
new world. The westward expansion of the population was viewed
with alarm on the eastern seaboard by many men who believed that
only a gradual decline into savagery could ensue.[17]

Each westward zone was first on the exploratory and then on the
settlement, or covered-wagon, frontier. The first frontiersmen aban-

17. Details may be found in the colonial records, and in such standard
literary histories as V. L. Parrington, *Main Currents in American Thought*, 2
vols., New York, 1927, 1928.

doned the restraints of settled life, and fought, sneaked, or bargained their way through the Indian tribes. All the old forms of reverence for human life, of piety, of sexual reserve, were exposed to the acid test of survival utility, and often found wanting. It was the second frontier that brought the wives, schoolmarms (from New England), preachers, and lawyers into the picture; they were the ones who sought to restore and to preserve the remnants of the vanishing code. In this process the women played a dominating role because their economic value, owing to their scarcity, was high, and because the first frontier, removed from the old folks at home, had sentimentalized womanhood in song and story.[18]

The dissolution of restraints upon conduct on the geographical frontier was matched in the later stages of the nation's growth by what happened in connection with industrial expansion. Modern industrial capitalism creates new and unheard-of life situations for those caught up within it. The new divisions of labor present problems of adjustment for which no adequate precedent is available. Opportunities multiply for appeals to private advantage, since so many operations which the individual was once able to perform for himself now pass through intermediaries; and each relay is a nucleus of potentially distorting private motivations. As new functions emerge in an expanding society, they are indistinctly defined and inadequately supervised. Not infrequently they clash with older practices. Those who are immersed in the new would be definitely handicapped were they scrupulously to respect the methods by which formal redefinitions of usage are to be obtained, since general rule-making presupposes definite knowledge of what is wanted and leisure for the detached consideration of experience. The various acts performed in the urban environment are not fully visible to the bystander. Once your eye lights on the Indian who lies in wait behind a tree, you know you are being ambushed. But you may see a modern financier at his desk for hours a day for years and catch no clue to the nature of the security structure which he has set up to ambush investors.

The adaptive difficulties connected with the growth of modern industrial capitalism are by no means peculiar to the United States, and the insecurities generated by the new functional environment have been quite as prominent in Europe as in America. Some of the

18. Any collection of frontier ballads abounds in examples of this sentimentalization of women. For the last frontier, see John A. Lomax, *Cowboy Ballads and Other Frontier Ballads,* New York, 1911.

implications of capitalism have been allowed to disclose themselves more completely here, where many older social formations were missing as counterweights to its triumphal expansion; but it is the combination of tensions arising from stringent morality, threatened by the positive and negative aspects of new places and new functions, which have led to some additional developments peculiar to America.

Emotional fixation upon the unqualified reaffirmation of "principles" is one result of the anxieties generated by the threatened conscience.[19] This is evidenced by the social formation which has been so potent in American politics, and which may be called the theocratic habit of mind. By this is meant the attitude which assumes that it is natural for people to be made moral and kept moral by legislation. It is sought to enact into law a moral code of unusually stringent character, and to expect the law officers to coerce the population into living up to it. Prostitution, gambling, and drinking are not merely restricted; they are prohibited.

Experience shows that administrative demoralization is the result of the theocratic attitude in politics. To illegalize a market does not demolish demand; it necessitates the organization of the market by other than lawful means. Contracts must be enforced by privately hired "gorillas" instead of publicly hired soldiers or policemen.[20]

The theocratic habit of thought which is so deeply imbedded in American culture can work with rough and ready success in homogeneous communities where moral standards are not in dispute. The member of the family who fails to measure up is a "black sheep," a mental and physical "inferior," or a "lost soul." The organized might of the family and of the neighborhood can be mobilized against the offender. But the "black sheep" pattern is inapplicable to the complexity of the urban world. It remains true that some of those who violate the mores are unable or unwilling to bend themselves to their family code, and remain individual rebels. But a profoundly different problem arises. Tabulations show that those who perform so-called criminal acts are highly concentrated in certain districts within the city. Indeed, the acts which are named

19. For relevant exhibits, see John Chamberlain, *Farewell to Reform, Being a History of the Rise, Life, and Decay of the Progressive Mind in America,* New York, 1932.

20. See John Landesco's report on "Organized Crime in Chicago," Part 3 of the *Illinois Crime Survey,* Illinois Association for Criminal Justice, Chicago, 1929.

criminal or delinquent may not be the exceptional acts of black sheep but the statistical norm of a neighborhood.[21]

One result of the theocratic attitude is that what is ordinarily named the police problem in American cities is a terminological mistake. The people who expect the police department to function in metropolitan districts as it does in homogeneous small towns fail to give due weight to the fact that the moral consensus upon which police action depends has been lost. Without this moral consensus, police action ceases to be police action in the full sense of the word, and becomes military action, requiring for efficiency a will to ruthlessness which cannot, in fact, be mobilized in the situation. Those who support ineffective standards are in actual, though not in formal, league with all the influences which demoralize the administration of justice.

The tremendous emotional resistances which are encountered in adapting the formal enunciation of principles to the exigencies of the real world have apparently driven our crime problem to an impasse from which ordinary avenues of escape are blocked. Demand for certain goods and services cannot be abolished, nor the rigor of the code substantially mitigated, under present conditions; hence criminality can be reduced neither by changing the frequency of overt acts, nor by changing the definition of acts called criminal. The way out appears to be some drastic modification in the total situation which would transform gang war into class war or world war. Today the gang wars are intraclass wars among different categories of business enterprise.

By allowing larger conflicts to supersede smaller conflicts in response to rising waves of insecurity, civil violence in the United States may be realigned. Centralization of the government may be expected to muster enough strength by way of Washington to reduce the gangs, and also to pave the road for a diversion of the energies of conscience against class and foreign enemies, which may permit some liberalization of the domestic code in relation to abstinence and thrift.

In some respects the United States has fewer cultural shock absorbers than more stable civilizations. There is no ruling élite toward which deference attitudes are firmly organized, and which possesses the leisure, detachment, and technique best adapted to

21. Arrays of pertinent material have been developed at the instigation of Robert E. Park and E. W. Burgess. See Clifford Shaw, *Delinquency and Crime Areas in Chicago,* Chicago, 1929.

the smooth and confident management of human affairs. There is no bureaucracy with experience and prestige, nor is there a governing class evolved from surviving remnants of the feudal aristocracy. Prestige goes to the profiteers, who have made governing a rather blatant form of profiteering. Governing élites can be credited with detachment when the community respects the plurality of values which they represent and implement. There must be an unspoken consensus which enables the élite to coordinate the activities of the community with respect to common goals. Such a consensus has been alien to the United States where the pursuit of profits has been the principal mode of personality expression. No integrated style of living has found root in this country, where every question from the cradle to cremation is subject to debate or change without notice. The atomizing processes of pioneering and industrialization have demolished all order except surviving residues of ancient codes and febrile acquiescence in transient expediencies.

One of the cultural assets of the United States in softening the asperities of the class struggle is the fraternal code developed on the frontier. The utilitarianism of the frontier dissolved the code of manners evolved by the European aristocracy to preserve their ascendancy. The democratization of manners resulted in those "man to man" forms of social intercourse which are so potent in reducing hostility against anybody who gets rich and stays a "good fellow." This relative universalization of deference claims has tended to nullify the consequences of a steep pyramid of wealth distribution.[22]

No doubt the extraversion of personality in the United States has been favorable to the development of methods of mass manipulation. Complicated and indirect responses to stimuli are more characteristic of introverted personalities than of extraverted types. How the abounding economic resources of the continent fostered the activistic propensities of the individual is clear; but psychopathological research has begun to disclose additional sources of extraversion in our culture. Evidence is accumulating that mental disorders are quite differently distributed from one civilization to another, and that each culture tends to produce characteristic tensions within the personalities subjected to it. The abundance of schizophrenia, a disorder of adolescence, in the United States suggests that the problem of becoming adult is much complicated by some of the adaptive

22. See my article on "Fraternizing" in the *Encyclopaedia of the Social Sciences*. In general on the democratic influence of frontier living see F. J. Turner, *The Frontier in American History,* New York, 1920.

formations built up in early life. The stringent mores of conventional American culture not only impose sharp restraints on early sexual curiosity and experimentation, but adhere to an explicit and restricted code of adult sexuality. One consequence of life in America has been the partial dissolution of the family pattern in which the father ruled the home. The democratization of family life, with the resulting increase in the authority of the mother, has tended to obscure the sharp differentiation of masculine and feminine types. The prohibitions imposed by a strict superego are thus sanctioned by the mother directly. Although masculine and feminine functions are somewhat obscured in the democratized family, the heterosexual code of adulthood adheres to explicit distinctions. Since the emotional experiences of the child prepare him less adequately than in earlier times to conform to the code, a great burden of repression and adaptation is put on the child; hence we are justified in expecting a relatively large incidence of neurosis, psychosis, psychopathic personality formation, together with such crude efforts at adjustment as excessive alcoholism and sexual promiscuity. It is beginning to appear probable that the extreme extraversion of personality in the United States is a relatively crude effort at overcoming the anxieties connected with psychosexual development under the described conditions. The deference assigned to bustling busyness, to hyperintense salesmanship, and to manipulative activity in general derives in part from the underlying anxieties which may be partially stilled by activism.[23]

The upshot of the foregoing discussion is that increasing external and domestic insecurity will head the United States along the road of rigid centralization, revolutionary upheavals, and international war, unless the emotional tensions of the nation are handled with skill, luck, and persistence. A sound political psychiatry is of particular importance to the United States, if the recurring sources of insecurity within our culture have been rightly diagnosed.

Certain groups have large stakes in the growth of an American statesmanship adequate to the smooth adjustment of human relations. The Ku Klux Klan's expansion at the end of the World War revealed the precarious position of important minorities in our population where they live away from the principal metropolitan centers.

23. The consequences of the "maternal superego" will not be traced further in this place. If our analysis is correct, we should expect the new Russia to favor the extraversion of personality, since the fusion of masculine and feminine patterns is actively fostered. Some additional implications of the present point will appear when the small bourgeoisie is sketched in the next chapter.

Both Jews and Catholics are eligible targets for mass animosities during periods of economic adversity and international uncertainty, and the leaders of these groups would be well advised to take with entire seriousness the most unpleasant implications of what happened in 1919 and 1920. If the United States escapes Fascism, in the sense of mass movements of violent protest, this will be a matter of able management in a situation where the same ends can be obtained at less cost. If the United States does not resort to vigorous Fascism, it will be because organized labor is so weak that drastic measures are not essential to weaken its hold on economic life. Organized labor is weak in such major industries as steel, automobiles, packing; it is badly disintegrated in the coal fields, where West Virginia has grown at the expense of the central competitive area; it is conservative in the railroad brotherhoods. If the national government seems to give labor an advanced position with respect to wages, hours, and collective bargaining, serious contradictions may be expected to develop at once. Strike efforts will be made to enforce the paper terms of any concession, and the officials will gravitate toward the use of compulsion in enforcing arbitration. By striking, labor will appear to be the disturber of the peace, and small business and farming groups will react with fear of radicalism, which will be stimulated by the growth of some revolutionary action among disillusioned labor elements, and the "red label" propaganda of the big financial and big business groups. Despite all the demagogic successes of William Jennings Bryan, Theodore Roosevelt, and Woodrow Wilson in appealing to disaffected small business and farming elements, these middle income groups have been left with no common symbol of identification, no clear symbols of demand, and no symbol of hopeful expectation. If the Americans of middle income can be brought to self-consciousness in the demand for the ruthless use of the income tax to eliminate incomes above a modest figure, the problems arising from the inequitable distribution of wealth will be less acute. If they can also be brought to demand the separation of the deposit from the investing function by the elimination of commercial banking, some progress may be made toward the stabilization of economic development. (This also assumes a successful demand for a non-inflationary monetary policy by the government.) The problem of adequate leadership in American life is to stimulate effective class-consciousness among the middle income groups.[24]

24. See also A. N. Holcombe, *The New Party Politics*, New York, 1933; Julian Gomperz, "Zur Soziologie des amerikanischen Parteiensystems," *Zeitschrift für Socialforschung*, 1 (1932): 278–310.

Unrestrained by the obvious fact of relative weakness in fighting effectiveness (as are the National Socialists of Germany), the American élite will be strongly impelled to escape from internal difficulties by expansionism in Latin America and in the Pacific.

In these trying times to speak of political psychiatry does not imply the treatment of individual cases by psychotherapy, however rewarding this would be in many instances. The main application of the psychiatric method to politics is in devising expedients of mass management by means of significant symbols which induce the harmless discharge of collective insecurities, or abolish some of the recurring sources of stress in the patterns of institutional life. By the intensive study of representative persons, suggestions can be secured about the deeper meaning of symbols and practices whose general distribution by region and class can be studied by extensive methods. The material and ideological ties of the United States with the political development of the world as a whole imply that this task of analysis cannot be handled in terms of national isolation with reasonable hope of success.

Part IV

CONTROL

Chapter XI

IN QUEST OF A MYTH: THE PROBLEM
OF WORLD UNITY

The prerequisite of a stable order in the world is a universal body of symbols and practices sustaining an élite which propagates itself by peaceful methods and wields a monopoly of coercion which it is rarely necessary to apply to the uttermost. This means that the consensus on which order is based is necessarily nonrational; the world myth must be taken for granted by most of the population. The capacity of the generality of mankind to disembarrass themselves of the dominant legends of their early years is negligible, and if we pose the problem of unifying the world we must seek for the processes by which a nonrational consensus can be most expeditiously achieved. A sufficient concentration of motive around efficacious symbols must be elicited in order to inaugurate and to stabilize this adjustment. These symbols must have enough potentialities for the production of deference to permit an élite to recruit its successors with a very minimum of violence. The discovery of the symbols which in point of fact do elicit enough rearrangements of human reaction to inaugurate and to conventionalize a stable order is the essence of world legislation.[1] The discovery of the portentous symbol is an act of creative orientation toward an implicit total configuration. Insofar as the creative, or problem attitude, itself increases the probability of the appearance of such formative symbols, the creative attitude is to be cultivated by the self-appointed legislator. His task is to make himself, as it were, the maternity hospital for the delivery of the significant symbol. Insofar as the analytic attitude increases the probability of the occurrence of the directive symbol, the analytic attitude is to be cultivated. Insofar as rich experience with men or

1. See E. Jordan, *Theory of Legislation: An Essay on the Dynamics of Public Mind,* Indianapolis, 1930. The fundamental conceptions of Professor Jordan's system of jurisprudence are stated in his *Forms of Individuality,* Indianapolis, 1927.

materials contributes to the growth of a creative person, such diversities of autobiographical contact will be cultivated. Experience has sufficiently indicated the qualified capriciousness of creativeness. Men in their efforts to copy those whom they regard as creative have seized upon diverse details, setting great store upon "knowledge," "technique," "method," "love of truth," "exactitude," "gift of observation," or, when they are genuinely tired of trying to express other reactions than admiration, speaking of "genius." Libraries, universities, research institutes are institutionalized guesses about the conditions of creativeness; how bad these guesses have often been is indicated by the warfare between universities and truth.

The form so far used in stating the conditions of world unity stresses the importance of the world myth and neglects by implication the world material level. We allude here to the possibility that ideological uniformity depends upon material uniformity, and that the principal problem of spreading a world myth may be how to standardize the world material environment. This is no contradiction of the language used before in relation to world unity; however, it brings into the foreground the possibility that the emphasis upon an organizing symbol understresses the gigantic material aspects of the task. We have already shown in the discussion of imperialism how new universal symbols were initially bound to some parochial place, and how dialectical processes blocked their consummation. Suppose, however, that we ignore our previous analysis for the moment and pursue the problem of world unity along somewhat different lines. The demands discussed before were impositional in character, justifying the release of violence in the name of democracy or proletarianism. If we explore other ideological possibilities, the problem may be redefined.

Americans who think about the problem of unifying the world tend to follow the precedent set in their own history. But as Americans were united in seceding from a common obstacle and a common threat from outside, the American precedent has little value for the unification of the world, since we cannot unify the earth by seceding from a larger unity. Great Britain and the Indians were the group enemies in those days;[2] but we cannot organize against the Communists without sharpening the lines of conflict which are already drawn. André Maurois has seen the salvation of the world in a common threat from the moon,[3] but this passes responsibility for the

2. See my comments on "Der amerikanische Präzedenzfall und das Problem der politischen Einigung der Welt," *Amerika-Post*, Hamburg, 4 (1932): 21–28.

3. *The Next Chapter: The War against the Moon*, London, 1927.

future to the astrophysicists who are supposed to find ways and means of interplanetary contact. And it is too optimistic to assume that the earth would be united against the moon, since the minority bloc on the moon would probably combine with the majority bloc on earth, and the minority bloc on the earth would combine with the majority bloc on the moon to create an interplanetary balance of power in the customary pattern.

Insofar as the American precedent confirms the axiom that people do not unite, but unite *against* specific collective groups, it would seem to offer pale assurance to those who would unify mankind. Indeed, the pursuit of unity is itself an unrealized phantom of the human imagination. Large organized areas in recorded history have been sustained by threats from the periphery. The civilizations of the Nile or of the Tigris-Euphrates or of the Yellow River have been subject to invasion by less fortunately situated peoples; the outposts of the Roman state were aswarm with hostile tribes. A united world would be something new under the sun.

Possibly some other detail of the American precedent will prove more helpful in producing creative thought about the larger problem. It will be recalled that American historians who have reconstructed the story of America's achievement of "a more perfect union" have stressed the initiatives taken by minorities who were after definite economic advantages.[4] Those who owned bonds of the Confederation wanted a strong taxing authority to pay interest and to redeem the principal; merchants who were big enough to supply an interstate market desired to sweep away the tariff barriers; speculators in western land wanted a central government sufficiently strong to hold back the Indians and foster settlement.

Can we unify the world by multiplying the tangible inducements to unity? Can we multiply the bonds issued by international agencies, thus creating vested interests in the protection and consolidation of their position? Using the League of Nations as a case in point, we may stimulate our imaginations in order to discover opportunities for the bond issues. No doubt we could multiply League edifices, and erect on every continent subcontinental offices built in alabaster and furnished in gold. But such nonrevenue producing expenditures would so quickly reach a saturation point that nothing very epochal could be expected. Following the American precedent more closely, remembering how the "more perfect union" assumed the obligations of the Confederation, we might propose the pooling

4. See the classical work of Charles A. Beard, *Economic Interpretations of the Constitution,* New York, 1913.

of existing public debts of all governments, and the assumption of the whole obligation by the world authority, which would be given specific revenue sources.

The public debt stands for so many different things in various states that the difficulties of such a step are colossal. In one state the debt stands for the costs of war, in another for local public works. In one state the control of public finance means the control of a large proportion of the national income; elsewhere but a modest fraction. The losses and gains of such a consolidation as proposed would fall heavily here and indulgently there, and the cross currents generated in the process of calculating a defensible basis of action are easy to foresee and baffling to navigate. It is to be remembered that the partial consummation of pooling arrangements might in the long run hamper rather than help the larger aim of unity, since the strengthening of regional blocs in the world balance does not necessarily make for harmony in the balance as a whole.

May we not consider the development of chosen areas around the world by means of loans procured under central auspices (in return for control over revenue and some supervisory rights)? The mandated areas might be consolidated and administered under world control. The mandate principal might conceivably be applied to all colonies and areas where people of alien culture are found. By a rigid extension of this principle the United States would be asked to relinquish to world control the Philippines. Porto Rico, and possibly such states as South Carolina or Mississippi where much of the population is black. That such proposals are beyond the practicable is clear; indeed, the whole idea of a mandate is out of date in this day of ascendant nationalism. The Philippines would no longer be contented with trustees and conservators; they want self-control. The constant pressure exercised by the main mandated territories for admission into the present League of Nations indicates the strength of this nationalistic ideal.[5]

If such ambitious projects seem unduly encumbered with difficulty, we might hope quietly to extend the range of the Bank for International Settlements, drawing more operations within its province, integrating central banks of issue, and exercising continuous pressure on behalf of stable economic developments throughout the world. Insofar as banking operations are profitable, pressure is likely to be

5. On this complex of problems consult Ernest E. Hocking, *The Spirit of World Politics,* New York, 1932; A. de Kat Angelino, *Colonial Policy,* 2 vols., Chicago, 1931; Quincy Wright. *Mandates under the League of Nations,* Chicago, 1930.

effectively exercised to curtail the functions of the bank, and insofar as it is essentially restricted to some parochial group of states (like the Leagued States), it will foster regional alignments within the total world balance.[6]

Suppose we think of extending the existing health work of the world agency which we desire to promote. This means little financially unless control is gained of a product like insulin whose earnings could be capitalized in order to create the far flung network of investment interests which we desire for political reasons.

Shall we organize a world air corporation to control the air transport industry? The obstacle here obviously is that private interests are well entrenched, air lines are notoriously of strategic significance, and the chances of setting up a larger air fleet by our world agency are slim.[7] The same limitations apply when we speculate on the creation of world control of the iron and steel industry, the chemical industry, or any other major line of productive enterprise.[8] There are, of course, some operations which are chronically running under great disadvantages, and which might be unloaded on a public body. In this day of the bus, it might be possible to buy out street car franchises around the world at bargain figures. But the saddling of our international agency with obsolete industries would presently create more serious problems than it could dispose of.

Perhaps we can devise some direct means of creating a multitude of individual interests against war. We might consider the organization of a great international corporation to write individual insurance policies at low figures, the premiums to be conditional upon the abstention of the individual's government from participation in a disapproved act of violence. Individuals might be attracted by the very low rates made possible by the world-wide distribution of risk, and might be mobilized in a crisis to exert influence in favor of the policy recommended by the world agency. But since insurance is profitable it is scarcely probable that a world agency will be permitted to assume it.

6. See Eleanor Lansing Dulles, *The Bank for International Settlements at Work*, New York, 1933; Hans L. Schlüter, *Die Bank für internationalen Zahlungsausgleich*, Berlin, 1932; René Escaich, *La banque des règlements internationaux et l'économie internationale*, Paris, 1932.

7. See J. M. Spaight, *An International Air Force*, London, 1932; David Davis, *The Problem of the Twentieth Century*, New York, 1931.

8. Jean Louis Costa, *Le rôle économique des unions internationales de producteurs*, Paris, 1932; James Cooper Lawrence, *The World's Struggle with Rubber, 1905–1930*, New York, 1932; M. Olivier, *La politique du charbon, 1914–1921*, Paris, 1932; and special studies of oil and other commodities.

A vested interest might be created by legalizing the confiscation of private property abroad held by nationals of a state engaged in disapproved policies. No doubt such a penalty measure would moderate the policy of states previous to a crisis, and during the initial phases of crisis, but once a war starts, the certainty of confiscation unless victorious tends to prolong the struggle.

Special world funds may be created subject to forfeiture in case of disapproved official acts. Such funds may be built up from donations, but should have direct sources of public revenue (if any can be found which states are willing to relinquish).[9]

The result of the preceding analysis of the appeal to vested interests as a means to unity is to show the obstacles in the path of success, and to emphasize the danger that partial realizations of unity will operate against the larger ideal of unity.

Since the achievement of the consensus necessary for world union is a nonreflective process, it may be that little was to be expected in the first place from the study of how special interests might be successfully combined. It may be more profitable to consider which symbols should be selected for emotional incorporation into the personalities of enough persons to gain our end. Just how shall we choose our "we" symbol for the world? In English it is clumsy to speak of the "Earthians," although not of the "Martians," and it may be better to talk of "world" citizens rather than "earth" citizens. But it is out of the question to talk of the "worldians." If we consider "Mankind," "Humanity," "Men," "Human Beings," or "Cosmopolitans," unwelcome associations or grammatical difficulties appear.

Which map symbol should we propagate in the cause of unity? Our cartographical technique must be applied in search of the symbol best calculated to convey the sense of wholeness and of interrelatedness. The "mercator" projection which is still so widely used produces fantastic distortions the farther one moves away from the equator, and the various "orange peel" projections are alien to the eye, and convey disorganized impressions. There are related problems connected with the choice of world emblems, flags, songs, salutes, languages, edifices, and myths of victory and failure, of heroes and villains.[10]

9. See Evans Clark, Editor, *Boycotts and Peace*, New York, 1932.

10. The trait by trait analysis of nationalism which was utilized by Van Gennep in the first volume of his uncompleted *Traité* has valuable suggestions for the larger problem of world symbolism. The problem of language is handled in the report by Herbert N. Shenton, Edward Sapir, and Otto Jespersen, *Inter-*

The chances for a developing world identification are improved when world symbolisms are in active competition with existing parochial expressions. The power of the world symbols can be increased by reducing the incessant use of national terms in classifying activities. Athletic competition on an intercity basis rather than on an internation basis would be useful in breaking down the national label. It should be Chicago versus New York or Berlin rather than United States versus Germany. Intercity art exhibits, intercity university connections, intercity administrative arrangements can all undermine in some measure the potency of the nation. The imaginative redrawing of existing boundary lines to fit various rational purposes can add some plasticity to the existing arrangements.[11]

The search for symbols which are expressive of common aspirations around the world emphasizes the local character of each culture trait. Shall we use the slogan "World Equality of Income" and seek to equate the gifts of nature to the Pacific Islanders with the complex claims of the Western European worker for material and psychological income? Shall we speak of the "World Minimum" and expect active sentiments to crystallize about it? We might take advantage of the prestige of terms like "law" and sloganize the "World Legal Community." Perhaps it is appealing technique to deflate the pretensions of local groups by arguing that the world legal community is prior to and superior to municipal law. Theories of natural law have been useful verbiage historically in advancing a novelty in the name of plausible symbols, and a certain body of literature is already available for authoritative citation.[12]

The friends of harmony in world affairs have sought to develop a demand for peace by stressing the horrors of war. The term war itself is treacherously ambiguous. Having regard to the prolonged

---

national Communication, London, 1931. C. K. Ogden has a simplified English of 800 words which he is promoting as a world unifier. See his *Basic English*, New York, 1934.

11. See H. J. Laski, "The Problem of Administrative Areas," *Smith College Studies in History*, 4 (1918): No. 1; C. B. Fawcett, *The Provinces of England*, London, 1919, and the debates of the Constitutional Convention of 1919 at Weimar.

12. See Alfred Verdross, *Die Einheit des rechtlichen Weltbildes auf Grundlage der Völkerrechtsverfassung*, Tübingen, 1932; *Die Verfassung der Völkerrechtsgemeinschaft*, Vienna and Berlin, 1926. See Johannes Mattern, "Problems of Method in International Law: Alfred Verdross's "Concept of the Unity of the Legal Order on the Basis of the International Constitution," Analysis 6 of *Methods in Social Science: A Case Book*, Editor S. A. Rice, Chicago, 1931.

uncertainties connected with Japanese operations in Manchuria in 1931, it is perhaps appropriate to distinguish between "peaceful war" and "warlike war," the first being acts of violence whose legal christening is unclear. Since the friends of peace are desirous of changing the fact of organized violence rather than the nomenclature of international relations, the task is not to abolish war but to reduce violence.

Can we reduce violence by portraying the horrors of violence? Freud has made plain in his *Inhibition, Symptom, and Anxiety* that fear reactions show both an affective outburst and protective behavior. This pattern is stable whether the fear is aroused in the presence of dangers in the world outside, or whether it is precipitated by fear of a dangerous impulse which threatens to get beyond superego control. The first fear is "real fear" and the second is "neurotic fear." Not infrequently the protective reactions to "neurotic fear" provoke counterprotective reactions by others in the real world, thus supplementing the internally aroused fear by corroborative dangers in the environment.

The vivid presentation of the horrors of war appeals to the deepest drives of the personality toward explosive release in struggle. These impulses are sadistic and they secure partial gratification in the elaboration of the war fantasy itself, slipping by superego control on account of the pious horror with which the war fantasy is regarded. Concessions to the superego permit the indulgence of the id much as reforming zeal permits some reformers to approach and enjoy the contemplation of sexual and similar perversions. The destructive impulses of the person are not entirely gratified, but partially curbed, since the restrictive function of the superego is too strong to permit direct and full expression. This tension between the id and the superego reveals itself in the insecurity of the personality. In turn this insecurity may be partially relieved by projecting upon the outside world the danger from the inner impulses to destroy, treating the surroundings as constantly threatening. This adds the neurotic element to the real danger of violence in a world based on the assumption of violence. The person is prone to support defensive measures and hence to modify the real environment of others, in turn reacting upon his own environment and verifying the war danger. The postwar world is in many respects more militaristic than the world of 1914, despite the vehemence of verbal protests against armament. The denunciation of war is more common than ever, the portrayal of the horrors of war is more dramatic than ever, yet preparations for war exceed overt preparations for peace. Many personalities are relieved from their own unconscious pleasure in contemplating the carnage of war by the act of denouncing war, and their excitement spreads general insecurity reactions which can be taken advantage of by those desirous of promoting "legitimate defense."[13]

Constant preoccupation with war and with armament calls attention to the role of war and arms in world politics, and heightens the value put upon armament as a measure of collective prestige. The effort to regulate arms according to fixed categories has not only shown how impossible are efforts at rigorous measurement, but has fostered the use of the ratio as an index of national status; notoriously Japan and Italy have made the "category" issue one of national "honor."

The incessant repetition of the danger and horror of war strengthens the assumption of inevitability and to this extent preserves the expectation of violence. The symbol of a person or a group is relatively explicit. But war shades into many forms of violence, and violence tapers off to comprise many means of coercion which though effective are not bloody. Since the preservation of any world régime would require the threat and the use of violence, the problem is not to elicit categorical renunciation of coerciveness, but to create a situation in which its use is a coordinated part of a total system of policy.

The effort to attach sentiment to the symbols which support a specific procedure or agency for dealing with crises has so far led to dubious results. Energy has been expended on fostering loyalty to the League of Nations and to procedures of "Inquiry," "Mediation," or "Arbitration." It is important to remember that no procedure exists apart from an institutional order in which safety, income, and deference are distributed according to certain conventions. The League of Nations is composed of states whose inner structure reveals striking diversities, yet a majority of the states connected with the League are capitalistic powers who are unfriendly to the other association of states called the U.S.S.R. The ruling élites of the Leagued states are bound to protect the social patterns which enable them to stay on top of the heap; they are challenged inside their territories by proletarian socialism and outside by the U.S.S.R. If to strengthen the League is to strengthen capitalism during our historical epoch, and

13. See also Edward Glover, *War, Sadism and Pacifism*, London, 1933.

one regards capitalistic individualism as an anachronistic concession to human perversity, support of the League is an act of immorality. The support of procedures always occurs in a specific situation, and the support of procedures tends to preserve or to protect certain pyramids of safety, income, and deference, and to undermine others.

The approach to world politics which undertakes to sentimentalize procedures, or various parochial agencies, assumes that human beings ought to accept order rather than justice as a value. But men are led by phantoms of justice and repelled by sterile demands for order; the cry for justice is a cry for self-realization in a world of many values. Proletarian socialism demands material equality and portrays all history as converging toward a class-less society where all men are brothers and peace rules because justice has come. Utopias that move men are rich with the fruits of desire, and pacific as an incident to satiation. If Marx left his class-less society ambiguous in detail, he at least did not neglect to lay down the principle of justice which was alleged to guide it.

The efforts to achieve order as a value rather than justice promises nothing but disillusionment. Pacifism has developed no stirring mythology of ultimate justice, of maximal realization, to inflame the imaginations of mankind. Since there is no consensus on symbols of justice, the effort to proceed by glorifying a symbol of order distracts attention from the larger task of finding dreams of justice that can be exploited by self-appointed élites on behalf of a unified world order. All the constitutive myths of history have promised something besides pale peace to their devotees; democratic internationalism wiped out social barriers and opened the gates to more prestige and wealth for the bourgeoisie. Proletarian socialism would annihilate the social order that keeps some men rich and some men poor, directing its appeal to the factory hands and casuals and tenants who do not directly and obviously profit from "free competition."

The demand for world order rather than justice appeals to the style of thinking which was current in Europe during the rise of the bourgeoisie. Woodrow Wilson was the most significant recent spokesman of the ideal which glorified "Law" instead of glorifying "Justice," "Equality," "Socialization," and "Bread." Wilson was repeating the language of democratic internationalism which had helped the rising bourgeoisie to abolish inconvenient social formations, and to develop a competitive marketing game from which it profited. Wilson echoed the civilization of the last century; Lenin spoke for substantive justice in a changed world. Wilson was satisfied with formalities; Lenin went to the heart of the problem of establishing a uniform method of recruiting the élite in every country, sensing that without a consensus on symbols of justice, there can be no lasting peace.[14]

The development of a common cultural experience as a seed bed for the emergence of common symbols and practices has proceeded but a little way. There are few common objects which enter into the daily life of millions in the world, and there are even fewer symbols of a world order which compete for loyalty with parochial and functional names and emblems. The distribution of culture traits around the world is random in the extreme. Tipped matches, postage stamps, smoking tobacco all enter into the environment of millions; yet if one takes into account the interior of China or of Africa one is again reminded of the thinness of the contact among men. H. J. Laski was right in suggesting that a world postage stamp would be one of the few unifying symbols capable of entering into the lives of nearly all men everywhere.

The absorption of the individual in the symbols and practices of his restricted culture can be somewhat neutralized by various techniques which are capable of laborious diffusion. When we talk of Washington as the "father of his country," we may take occasion to observe that Lenin or Masaryk perform a similar function elsewhere. When we speak of the American Revolution, we may name other revolutions, such as the secession of the Swiss cantons from the control of the Hapsburgs. The habit of looking at every detail of the "we" symbol in terms of its representative character means that the we symbol is deprived of its utterly arbitrary uniqueness. The we symbol is a particular instance of general conditions which generate comparable results. This is the meaning of the scientific attitude, and the method of thinking just illustrated is that of functional equivalence. Continuous pedagogical emphasis upon the search for the valid comparison with each detail of the we symbol does not primarily depend upon materials, but upon the development of technique on the part of the teaching profession. Certainly the creation of common world perspectives can be greatly facilitated by the compilation of world histories. No doubt the charting of the spread of culture traits

14. For aspects of pacifism see Franz Kobler, Editor, *Gewalt u. Gewaltlosigkeit,* Zürich, 1928; Leo Gross, *Pazifismus und Imperialismus,* Leipzig, 1931; C. M. Case, *Non-violent Coercion,* New York and London, 1923; Max Hildebert Boehm, "Cosmopolitanism," *Encyclopaedia of the Social Sciences.*

like fire or the alphabet or the Christmas complex[15] creates a mental
set which assumes the complex and reciprocally influencing character
of world relations. No doubt theories of civilization like those of
Oswald Spengler in the *Decline of the West* widen the configuration
against which parochial details fall into tentative order. But such
material is dead unless it is brought to living expression in the whole
pedagogical and conversational environment, rigorously and incessantly chastening exclusive pretensions. But the incorporation of the
person into his own culture proceeds so constantly that counter-
therapy of this kind has but a modest chance of success in deflating
the quick investment of the we symbol with uncritical evaluations.[16]

As an illustration of the degree to which one may be entangled in
cultural presuppositions, it may be commented that the problem of
unification has been discussed as if it were mainly a matter of choosing an external person or group enemy. But why take it for granted
that the enemy must be a person or a group? May we not succeed in
finding nonhuman enemies against whom to organize the animosities
of mankind, and to create the situation appropriate to the growth of
identification reactions around a universal symbol? Do not the pathogenic micro-organisms extinguish more human lives every year than
die of war? Are they not the deadly enemy of man? We may dally
with the idea of mobilizing the vast resources of Hollywood in uniting the world against pathogenic bacteria, against "bugs." Imagine
conspirative bugs, large, slimy conspirative bugs, planning their
assaults upon the infant at the mother's breast, upon the maiden
and the athlete, upon the statesman and the scientist, upon the
toiler and the administrator. . . .

15. See Wilson G. Wallis, *Progress and Culture,* pp. 117ff., New York, 1930.
16. Among the recent works in education, see D. A. Prescott, *Education and
International Relations,* Cambridge, 1930; *La révision des manuels scolaires,*
International Institute for Intellectual Cooperation, Paris, 1932; Florence B.
Boeckel, *Between War and Peace,* New York, 1928; and the list of educational
organizations in J. E. Harley, *International Understanding,* Stanford, 1931. For
fundamental material on the growth of the idea of world organization, consult
Jacob Ter Meulen, *Der Gedanke der Internationalen Organisation in seiner
Entwicklung,* 2 vols., The Hague, 1917, 1929; A. C. F. Beales, *The History of Peace,*
New York, 1931; Fr. Meinecke, *Weltbürgertum und Nationalstaat,* Seventh
Edition, Munich, 1928. For a case report on world opinion, see Ludwig Wal-
decker, *Die Stellung der menschlichen Gesellschaft zum Völkerbund,* Berlin,
1931. On the historiographer's approach, see Ferdinand Schevill, "Voltaire, His-
torian of Civilization and Exponent of Rationalism," *Methods in Social Science,*
Analysis 29, S. A. Rice, Editor, Chicago, 1931.

It is thinkable that men will some day face a common disaster which is capable of uniting them in concerted efforts to survive. Suppose that science should presently discover that the germ plasm of every species loses its capacity to reproduce its pattern every ten millionth generation, and that mankind is confronted by this loss of structure unless treated by a special immunizing process developed by a small body of specialized investigators. In the presence of this common threat, those who had a monopoly of relief might exploit their position to unify mankind. But not necessarily so; the privileged may fall out among themselves. Those who are elevated to positions of great power may for the time being have few worlds to conquer, and those who are not able to externalize their aggressions along the accustomed lines may turn them against symbols closely connected with the personality, especially against one another.[17] Minority elements among the élite will seek to align wider elements of the community against the majority element, after the usual pattern of the balancing process, and the conflict will become generalized into revolutionary channels. The older élite by displaying weaknesses and perhaps by tempting the population with "bread and circuses" violates the ideal of leadership, releases the control of the superego upon anti-authoritarian acts, and legitimizes revolution. In this sense mass movements of revolution are fundamentalist drives to reinstate authoritative symbols which can be respected, and which no longer violate the patterns proper to rulership. Revolutions rise after intense stresses have been built up in personalities; they run their course by taking revenge on the symbols which betrayed them; and they end by bowing to new authorities with new symbols and new modes of perpetuating themselves.

Technological progress may advance with such imperious footsteps that it becomes practicable to reduce most of the human race to robots by infecting them with diseases which leave them competent to perform various routine tasks in a constant state of happy euphoria. Indeed, an Austrian physician some time ago proposed that if society could infect most of its members with silly dementia, most of the dirty work could be done by the happy dements. Of course the non-inoculated may continue to generate hostilities against one another, gradually reducing the survivors until, perhaps, but a single conscious being is left in full possession of his faculties, and he might

17. Administrative skill in relation to order was stressed by Brooks Adams, *The Theory of Social Revolutions,* New York, 1913.

become so resentful of the happy dements that he would at last inoculate himself and end the tale of man in a universal chuckle.

If we had complete ingenuity in applying our technical ability, we might remove the frictions of society by creating a situation in which everybody sits on top of some pyramid of deference. Somebody can be the champion card shark, glass sculptor, or tree sitter of all the world. The number of traits of the human body which can be matters of deference is practically inexhaustible, and the number of operations which can be accorded prestige is infinite.

Some patterns of behavior are relatively overrated at the present time in society, and the problem would be to devalue them. Administration, whether in business or government, is such an overrated operation. We might diminish the prestige of administration by attaching all sorts of negative symbols to such acts; but of course we should have to set one group of administrators busy devaluing the rest. No doubt we should stimulate the abandonment of the old ideal of making philosophers kings by debasing the ideal of kingship itself as a colossal impertinence, an unjustifiable narcissistic indulgence. From one point of view agitators and organizers who elicit deference reactions from their contemporaries are the scullery maids of all work who keep up an illusion of importance by shouting noisily over the back fences at one another. Looking after an enterprise of some sort is one of those things to be done without creating a disturbance; the enterprise is instrumental to private and intimate values, and has no business being an end in itself.

Such speculative solutions of our task of unity may be just as "practical" as the "practicable" ideas, if the practicable ideas fail, as they have failed so consistently in the past. But returning to more orthodox ruts of analysis, we may consider some of the problems connected with the spread of rival mythologies in the modern world. Catholicism, democratic internationalism, and communism are the chief ideologies in competition in the western world and in much of the extra-European world. Marxist symbolism has been expanding with all the vitality of a great constructive force in human history, and this diffusion has been traced in a previous chapter to certain advantages in its symbolic structure. Marxism outcompeted simple trade unionism, cooperation, and utopian socialism during the last century, and is today the most pretentious bidder for universal acceptance as the basis for a stable world order.

Some of the restrictions upon the spread of Marxism in the past and in the probable future have been discussed, but there remains an important problem. Marxism diffused reasonably well among wage earners, but failed to secure durable support among the rank and file of the middle classes. Capitalism has shown great capacity to multiply material configurations which separate the pure proletarian from the pure capitalist. The standardizing effects of capitalism have been neutralized by its diversifying tendencies. Contrasting material environments sustain ideological differences, and the middle classes are the social formations which display all the ideological nuances appropriate to the varied material matrices of modern industrialism.

The future of Marxism as the principal unifying myth may depend upon its capacity to win the middle classes. I say this without dogmatism, because it is possible that those revolutionary strategists are correct who say that owing to their accumulated timidities, the middle classes can be scared like sheep in a revolutionary crisis. From this point of view the task of revolution is to keep the revolutionary symbol ("communism") pure of entangling taints with words like "socialism" or "social democracy," and to develop a band of professional and active revolutionaries who can leap to the lead in the revolutionary crises which are inevitable as the fundamental conflicts in capitalistic society emerge. From this point of view middle class support, though not to be spurned, is not to be courted.

Some recent events have cast doubt upon the validity of this analysis. The middle classes of Italy and of Germany have not been sheep but lions; they or their sons have fought vigorously for Fascism against proletarianism. They have been materially "proletarianized," but they have swung to the symbols of nationalism and patriotism, furnishing the blood and much of the money for conservative movements directed against Russian Marxism. The middle classes have played active, positive roles, and it may therefore be more important than formerly assumed to win them for Marxism if Marxism is to win the world.

The activism of the middle classes is no wholly new phenomenon. Although it is not possible to demonstrate in absolute figures that the middle classes of Austria or of Germany were worse off at the turn of the century than they were before, it is understandable that their relative prestige had dwindled with the improved position of the organized wage earners and the expansion of the upper levels of the bourgeoisie. Since the declining position of the small bourgeoisie meant that claims for deference from the social environment were not gratified, the resulting resentments and insecurities modified the whole reactivity level of the class.

Denials of deference release tremendous hostilities against the environment, and the personalities involved remain insecure until they have worked out positive means of expressing themselves. Since the eclipse of the small bourgeoisie took place gradually, personality stresses were widely distributed; there was little of the frantic sense of urgency which arose during the crises of postwar inflation. But these insecurities were sufficient to create the receptivities favorable to various mass movements. In German Austria a strong anti-Jewish, pro-Germanic agitation fostered the political career of Lueger in Vienna, and many of the theories and tactics of this movement were later revived by Adolf Hitler who was intimately acquainted with it during his youth.[18]

The recrudescence of the anti-Jewish movement was a general phenomenon over Europe during the later years of the nineteenth century, and its stronghold was in the small bourgeois class, which was Christian, nationalistic, and patriotic. Hostilities generated by a declining role in society could be diverted from capitalism by stressing Jewish high finance, and from fellow nationals who toiled by stressing Jewish "agitators."[19]

The small bourgeoisie incorporates in clearest form the contradictions of capitalism. Each member of the class experiences in his own personality the insecurities which arise from the emphasis upon the rational, calculating function of the ego at the expense of the superego and the id. The social formation which is here taken to be typical of the lower bourgeoisie is the small shopkeeper who is married, has a small family, whose wife does the housework and possibly aids in the business. In order to etch a clear and serviceable picture, the numerous variations on the pattern to be found in different environments will not be described.[20]

18. Hitler speaks of it appreciatively in *Mein Kampf*, Munich, 1925, 1927.

19. In relation to Germany, see Paul Kosok, *Civic Training in Germany*, Chicago, 1933.

20. From the voluminous literature on the position of the middle classes, great and small, the following may be indicated: Theodor Geiger, *Die soziale Schichtung des deutschen Volkes*, Stuttgart, 1932; Werner Sombart, *Der Bourgeois*, Munich, 1920; Max Weber, *Gesammelte Aufsätze zur Religionssoziologie*, 3 vols., Tübingen, 1922 (Vol. 1 translated as *The Protestant Ethic and the Spirit of Capitalism*, London, 1930); R. H. Tawney, *Religion and the Rise of Capitalism*, London, 1926; S. Kracauer, *Die Angestellten*, Frankfurt, 1930; articles of recent years in *Die Tat;* Roberto Michels, *Probleme der Sozialphilosophie*, Leipzig, 1914; Bruno Archibald Fuchs, *Der Geist der bürgerlich-kapitalistischen Gesellschaft*, Munich, 1914; B. Groethuysen, *Origines de l'esprit*

The economic situation necessary for the small bourgeois is one which arouses his expectation of rising in the value hierarchy by means of planned individual effort. It is this which strengthens the role of the ego, necessitating the readaptation of impulses with continuous reference to their serviceability in achieving definite conscious goals.

One of the activities which is consciously fostered is work, which is regularity in the performance of nonspecifically sexual acts through which claims are established on society for safety, income, and deference.[21]

Thrift is the cautious spending and careful accumulation of money, and obviously involves the deferment of gratification. Through thrift, surpluses are accumulated to expand the income producing equipment by enlarging the enterprise.

Respectability is conformity to the mores on public occasions. Conformity is important to the shopkeeper who must cater to the prejudices of the community to expand trade. In some measure the shopkeeper is a public figure who occupies the focus of attention of many people. The censorship of his impulses in the interest of profit is imposed by the competitive dependence of his position.

To the man who thinks, deception offers many advantages (within cautious limits). Sharp bargaining and pretense are useful tools in business. Indeed, there is some foundation for the popular prejudice that clever men are crooks, since the keen person finds many ways of taking advantage of the credulity of his fellows. The exercise of the ego function in profitmaking puts a continuous strain on the super-

bourgeois en France, Paris, 1927; Kurt Wiedenfeld, *Das persönliche im modernen Unternehmertum*, Leipzig, 1911; Felix Pinner (Frank Fassland), *Deutsche Wirtschaftsführer*, Charlottenburg, 1925; F. W. Taussig, *Inventors and Moneymakers*, New York, 1915, F. W. Taussig and C. S. Joslyn, *American Business Leaders*, New York, 1932; Helen R. Wright, "Captains of Industry," *Encyclopedia of the Social Sciences*.

On the use of psychoanalysis in connection with the problem in hand, I have profited from the examination of a manuscript on Fascism by Dr. Wilhelm Reich, psychoanalyst, of Berlin, published as *Massenpsychologie des Faszismus*, Copenhagen, Prague, and Zürich, 1933. On methodological points my views are in many respects parallel to those of Erich Fromm, "Ueber Methode und Aufgabe einer analytischen Sozialpsychologie," *Zeitschrift für Sozialforschung*, 1 (1932): 28–54; *Die Entwicklung des Christusdogmas*, Vienna, 1931. A Marxist article hostile to psychoanalysis is W. Jurinetz, "Psychoanalyse und Marxismus," *Unter dem Banner des Marxismus*, 1 (1925): 90–133.

21. Exception should be made for prostitutes and dependent partners in loveless marriages.

ego,[22] since opportunities for forbidden fruit are continually discovered. The result is the generation of guilt feelings, directly
followed by certain consequences that will be traced presently.

Sexual abstinence is fostered by the advisability of caution about
contracting disease or missing work in the morning or spending too
much or shocking the cerberi and cerberae of the mores.

The direct indulgence of hostility toward the environment is pru-
dently avoided during business hours. "The customer is always
right." Even if insolent, sullen, quarrelsome, the customer means
purchasing power, and the seller learns "self-control."

Piety and moralism enable the individual to dispose of some of the
insecurities which arise in the continuous struggle for self-control
against wayward sexual, assertive, and mendacious impulses. Anxieties and guilt feelings can be exorcised by the solemn performance
of a ritual which projects the burden of guilt upon an external
symbol, and heightens the sense of importance in the whole cosmic
scheme. Aggressive morality consists in attacking manifestations in
the environment which constitute temptations to the inhibited life
of the individual. Self-protection by escape from a disturbing situation, or self-protection by driving away the disturbing features of a
situation, are means of preserving ego and superego control.

The life of cautious calculation in the primary world predisposes
the person to grandiosity in relation to secondary symbols. The inhibitions on aggressiveness facilitate the projecting of much animosity onto the outside world; the "Devil" or the "Jews" are treated
as conspirative enemies intent on undermining the righteous or the
loyal. The chastening of direct assertion also facilitates identification
with grandiose we symbols that live glamourously courageous and
successful careers. Such a movement for sentimentalized expansionism as that fostered by the Pan-German League in prewar Germany
gained a disproportionate share of its strength among small bourgeois storekeepers, clerks, and intellectuals.[23] The millennial dream
of the kingdom of God on earth is a fantasy of imperialistic success
which has appealed to the middle classes.

Since the small bourgeois business man hopes to rise, his gaze is
directed toward his "betters," and he tends to copy the externals of
the people who are further up the pyramid of income and deference
than he. The desire to be received (recognized) by those in better
positions meets with chronic rebuff, which is partly revenged by

22. See B. Kidd, *The Science of Power*, New York, 1918.
23. Mildred S. Wertheimer, *The Pan-German League*, New York, 1924.

snobbishness toward manual toilers. This process of withdrawal and of distinction from economic and social competitors increases the degree to which the small bourgeois group objectively differs from them. For purposes of display, the wife is sometimes kept from income-producing activities outside the home,[24] and hence she becomes preoccupied with impressing the environment by hypercleanliness, good cooking, successful child rearing, and many bits of technique from the upper classes.

Intimacy of contact is fostered among members of the family. The women are brought into constant touch with the children, working out their own frustrations (in the sexual and the public sphere) on the children, worrying about their food, health, masturbatory practices, and manners, and in general subjecting the children to over-interference. This favors the development of a maternal superego which is full of taboos great and small. Children are kept in the home so they will "amount to something" and avoid evil companions. The constant contact among members of the small family affords every opportunity to intensify the Oedipus situation. Rivalries are heightened among parents for the response of the children, and among the children for response from the parents. Parents oscillate between overindulgence and overdiscipline, tending to strengthen ambivalent emotional formations.

The frustrations imposed upon the child are used to motivate careerism. The libidinization of work is an alternative to the prohibited forms of libidinal expression, and the insecurities fostered in the child are constantly resymbolized around expressions like the "importance of getting ahead," and "amounting to something." The deprivations of the present are treated as necessary steps to the promised land of fame and success. Self-control and discipline are ways to power over others. The cult of self-control ("I am captain of my soul") is libidinized as an auxiliary to success. Those who can exercise self-control are distinctive people; they are the born rulers of the earth, for they shall ultimately inherit the earth. If one is not shiftless, lazy, weak, undisciplined, all things shall be added unto him. The symbol of the future is defined in the experience of the developing child to include great potentialities for wealth and deference; the child develops a claim on the future for indulgent consideration as a reward for suffering renunciations in the present. Faith is deeply implanted in the benevolent intention of the future to reward abstinence, work, thrift, and humility.

24. See Thorstein Veblen, *Theory of the Leisure Class*, New York, 1899.

An essential part of the outfit of the small bourgeois business man is enough language to handle human relations. Language is particularly important to him, because he needs it to out-argue his customers, and to master the verbal forms of acceptable social intercourse. The argumentative, persuasive role of language casts his speech in a dialectical pattern. Is not his commodity just as good as the brand mentioned by the customer? The utility of language as a tool of eliciting response creates great deference for language and for all who can use it well; hence there is provided an appreciative audience for small bourgeois intellectual types like the little lawyer, preacher, teacher, lecturer, and journalist. Dialectical displays are more keenly appreciated than linguistic performances which involve description or appreciation.

The foregoing analysis is sufficient to show why the crisis of adolescence is peculiarly intense in the small bourgeois family. The close emotional contact among the parents and the children in an atmosphere of constant discipline makes for the maximum of turbulence when maturing sexual and social processes culminate. The incessant supervision, the endless challenges to ambition and self-control, the stuffiness of the environment put the most severe stresses upon the growing potency of the youth who is passing through the quick changes bordering on adulthood.

So severe is the crisis of adolescence that we should expect to find many seriously damaged personalities among them. We should expect to find a relatively high incidence of forms of severe mental disorder fostered by emotional conflict.[25] We should expect to discover high incidence of the milder mental disturbances, such as hysteria, phobia, and obsession. We should expect to find that flights from home were frequent, escapes to the sea or the army, and we should expect very often to encounter such combinations of emancipation and self-punishment as excessive alcoholism, compulsive promiscuity, and other sexual perversions. Neurotic personality formations should be comparatively abundant, representing drastic ways of dealing with disturbing impulses, and chastening them to some semblance of social acceptability.

The verbal culture of the small bourgeois family favors the displacement of anti-authoritarian drives upon the remote social objects which are continually referred to in conversation, and stimulates the

25. Dr. Harry Stack Sullivan of New York City, the leading exponent of the role of functional factors in schizophrenia, has data corroborating this expectation.

recruitment of specialized verbalizers to fill professions like preaching, law, teaching, lecturing, and journalism. Linguistic dexterity is one of the skills which lends itself to the handling of many private insecurities, and the fact that it can easily be rendered socially acceptable means that the talkative professions become forms of self-therapy for small bourgeois children.

During the crisis of adolescence the restraints of the environment are so oppressive that the cult of activism appeals strongly to youth. This is expressed by romanticizing bold careers, or by dashing into exciting social movements. The prominence in social radicalism of run-away adolescents from bourgeois families is notorious, and has already been referred to in discussing the role of the intellectual worker in modern culture. The cult of the hero thrives as a means of gratifying deep emotional urges for submissiveness to a symbol of omniscience and omnipotence, and of restoring a relation to a personal symbol (the parent) which increasing reality critique has destroyed (omniscience is no longer imputed to the father).

When we consider the success of protest symbols in attracting the support of so many small bourgeois intellectuals, the movement toward the "right" on the part of the small bourgeoisie as a whole appears paradoxical. Certainly the schematic and dialectical use of language by Marx smacks much more of the middle classes from which Marx came than of the proletariat in whose name he spoke; the proletarians are essentially direct actionists and have a minimum of patience with the tortuosities of the intellectual. Insofar as the wage earners share the psychology of the small bourgeois they are not proletarian, and it is notorious how readily the small bourgeois pattern perpetuates and rejuvenates itself in the "labor movement." A little verbal radicalism and the individual lands a niche for himself in the party bureaucracy, or the city council, or the cooperative society, or the trade union, or the party paper, and cautiously adapts himself to preserving income and deference with a minimum of risk.

Is there any way to disintegrate the middle classes as a whole more readily for the benefit of the proletarian mythology which might unite mankind? Certainly the present practice of insulting and intimidating them has strengthened fascism. Is it worth while to show that the revolutionary state of the socialists is the only one where able organizers and technicians are given security and scope, the only society in which the road to reward for effort is open, where it cannot be shut off by the erratic malcoordination of the capitalist economy? Can the opprobrious epithet, "the bourgeoisie," be dropped or redefined, and can symbols be coined with which the desired persons can readily identify, and through which linkages can be established with the whole of proletarianism? Small bourgeois enterprisers demand symbols of deference for their abstinence, pacifism, and diligence in administration; their narcissism is incessantly and flagrantly assaulted by the verbalizers of the proletariat.

No doubt the most vulnerable flank of the bourgeoisie is the adolescent whose acute emotional crisis has been discussed. His sexual turbulence, his narcissistic frustrations, his lust for action can be rather readily capitalized by symbols of protest. The youth movements at the end of the last century expressed the restlessness of small bourgeois youths who were partially reflecting the insecurities which their parents had generated owing to the slow decline of their class prestige.[26]

The inhibitions on sexual curiosity in small bourgeois family life create vast receptivities toward sexual enlightenment, and this can be exploited in relation to proletarian symbols of social action.[27]

The preceding comments upon revolutionary propaganda strategy in relation to the reactive structure of the middle classes do not imply a definitive judgment on the matter. Further consideration may lead to the conclusion that the task of winning over the bourgeois groups, or even of neutralizing a substantial fraction of them, is insoluble. The success of several patriotic movements lends support to this view.[28]

Indeed, one may be led to reformulate the problem by examining the profound similarities between the trends of events in Russia, Italy, and Germany. Who gains by the centralized dictatorship

26. See Ernest H. Posse, *Die politischen Kampfbünde Deutschlands,* Second Edition, Chap. 1, Berlin, 1931.

27. Wilhelm Reich appears to be one of the few who are alert to the reconsideration of proletarian propaganda in the light of psychoanalytical findings. See his *Geschlechtsreife, Enthaltsamkeit, Ehemoral, Eine Kritik der bürgerlichen Sexualreform,* Vienna, 1930, and his book for youths called *Der sexuelle Kampf der Jugend,* Berlin, Vienna, Leipzig, 1932 (also translated into Russian for young Communists); also the *Zeitschrift für Politische Psychologie und Sexualökonomie,* Band 1 (1934), Verlag für Sexualpolitik, Copenhagen.

28. For sensitive psychological pictures of the "patriotic societies," see Vicki Baum, *Fehme,* Berlin, 1926; E. v. Salomon, *Die Geächteten* (by one involved in the Rathenau murder); for systematic details, E. J. Gumbel, *Verräter verfallen der Fehme!,* Berlin, 1929. On revolutionary propaganda-strategy, see especially Lenin, *What Is to Be Done?,* New York, 1928.

which is in transition toward a socialist state? The answer appears to be: the *skilled,* those who *sacrifice* to acquire technique. In the dictatorship and the socialist state (as distinguished from the hypothetical socialist *society*), differences in material reward are tolerated, although huge money incomes are no longer permitted to financiers, industrialists, merchants, and landlords.

This suggests that the socialist ideal is, in fact, the ideal of the lesser bourgeoisie, springing from resentment at the capitalistic distortion of the relation between *reward* and *sacrifice* exhibited in the rise of plutocracy. Sentimentally bound to the terminology of the French revolution, merging imperceptibly into the plutocracy, the lesser bourgeoisie has been notoriously deficient in self-consciousness. Some of its members, like Marx, who reacted against the plutocratic results of the first bourgeois revolution, frustrated in their efforts to arouse the middle class to united action, appealed to the "proletariat." But the true proletarian does not sacrifice to acquire a complex skill. The rallying symbol, the "proletariat," was an overgeneralization of the protest, exactly as the "rights of man" overgeneralized the protest of the most potent ultimate beneficiaries of the French revolution. The Russian élite is a skilled élite.

This second bourgeois revolution, conducted in the name of the proletariat, has for the time being eliminated the class struggle from Russia. The manual toilers of little skill have no prospects of united action. With the restoration of a more equitable relation between sacrifice (in the acquisition of skill) and reward, through the extinction of plutocracy and aristocracy, the class struggle is in abeyance; the struggle among different skill groups comes gradually to the front.

In Western Europe the tensions within the middle-class skill groups were heightened by the changes appearing in Russia. Goaded by disappointment, defeat, and impoverishment, alienated by the antinational and the insolent tactics of the direct spokesmen of the Russian revolution, the older middle-class elements cooperated with the plutocracy, and even the aristocracy, in obliterating the newer middle-class skill groups who were affiliated with the Russian proletarian symbols.

In the United States where the spokesmen of the Russian revolution are unimportant, and where the labor movement is less saturated with distinctive vocabulary, the older middle-income skill groups are less open to threat from the newer formations; hence there is less provocation to ally with the plutocracy. This creates a favorable opportunity for the attainment of self-consciousness ("Americans of Middle Income"), for the discovery of a definite program ("Effective National Income Tax"), and for the adoption of a justifying vocabulary (the moral superiority of sacrifice in acquiring socially useful skill, and hence reducing disproportions between reward and sacrifice).

As we examine the complex pattern of historic capitalism, and especially the bourgeoisie as a social formation, we are reminded of the possibility that we have to do with one of those ephemeral clusters which, though it expresses a host of local tendencies, is chiefly to be interpreted as manifestation of the simple dominant patterns of an epoch in civilization. Possibly all that we have treated as historic capitalism may exemplify the tendency toward *the externalization of fantasy* which has characterized our society since the later Middle Ages. The manipulation of natural power resources, the handling of men and machines according to pecuniary calculations, and the dispersion of control among many atomized entities are modern details of a complex division of activity which has been facilitated by the externalizing of fantasy.

There is nothing new in the play of fantasy for persons or civilizations. The fantasy life of the infant and child proceeds with a minimum of regard for the external reference of symbols. When the developing individual learns to distinguish rather clearly between symbols with and without external references, he is said to discipline the flood of inner fantasy by means of the continuous reference back and forth to the external which is called the reality principle.

In the culture that we know best the rearrangement of inner experience has become intimately connected with overt materializations. Each externalization may continue within the environment of the originator and of other as a continuing stimulus to attention and action. The remolding of the *environment* into multitudinous subdivisions vastly increases the possible foci of attention, thus redefining the *milieu* of those in each new matrix. The division of attention specializes the experiences of persons dealing with environment, initiating further rearrangements of environment, which in turn differentiate the foci of attention, and instigate further rearrangements of experience and then of environment. The whole labyrinth of subdivided activity which we call modern culture has thus grown up through the generations as a complex interplay between fantasies and externalizations. As fantasies are externalized, the symbols related to the environment are redefined in terms of expectations, demands, and identifications, and complex relations arise among these symbols as well as among the various external formations. With the specialization of the environment occurs the concurrent specialization of the psychological orientations interrelated with it; this implies growing complexity of technology, science, language, gesture, personality trait.

The dialectical relation between fantasy and environment has been much less intense in other cultures than our own. Our extraversion of fantasy may be contrasted with the introversion of fantasy in some oriental cultures. Possibly the future historian will be able to trace the subtle formation and the delicate elaboration of the western pattern, even discerning the critical moments when it began to diverge significantly from the lines of development in the eastern world.

One result of the externalizing of fantasy in our civilization has been discipline in the special pattern of thinking which we call analytical. The play of fantasy has been continually subordinated to the material world. The goal of fantasy has steadily become the forecasting of sequences in the material environment. The role of hypothesis is to prefigure reality, and speculative fantasy turns again and again to symbols which stand for routines in externality. If the individual thinker disdains the empirical reference, his expressions may be recast by others, who desire to observe "Nature" directly. The direct disciple of Nature may request the rearranger of very abstract symbols to direct him where to look, as when the modern experimentalist comes to the mathematical physicist for "tips." Sometimes the symbol arrangers have structures prepared in advance which serve the ends of the direct observers of circumscribed details of Nature. It will be recalled that the mathematicians elaborated non-Euclidean geometries before experimentalists recognized any need for them in furnishing clues in their quest for order in the material world. The prestige of the analytical pattern of thought is due to the receptivities which have been developed for any expedient which could furnish "leads" for the discovery of routines in nature which might be presently utilized in partially remodeling the environment.

An act of analysis is finished when terms are used to relate to configurations and the relations are corroborated. The symbol arranger at one moment in his autobiography states relations among terms which refer to configurations, and he may later in his autobiography so relate himself to a configuration that he regards this subsequent act of relation as forecast in the terms developed in his previous autobiographical episode. The theorist may himself refrain from corroborative observation, this function being performed by other specialists.

The cumulative deference paid to the analytical pattern in the western world is attributable to its success in furthering the incessant rearrangement of the environment. Fantasy has been made a slave of externality in order that externality might be mastered by fantasy; it is masochistic toward reality in the beginning in order that it may be sadistic toward reality in the end. Yet so universal has become this subserviency to reality that it may lose its capacity for creative mastery.

Indeed, one of the striking phases of modern culture in the west is the turning of the analytic pattern toward fantasy itself. So imperious is the analytic mode of thought that it has sought to locate the position of an act of fantasy in the larger configuration which includes all significant acts of previous and subsequent fantasy. Special modes of using the fantasy life have been devised to expedite this process by bringing relevant data to the focus of attention. This is the significance of the free-fantasy procedure of Freud. The fantasy relations are themselves embedded within physiological configurations whose structure it is also proposed to discern.

Any symbol configuration may be the point of departure for analytic procedures which locate its dynamic connection with the all-inclusive symbol series, and with the physiological, material, personal-cultural environment. By the use of free-fantasy methods, material may be brought to the focus of attention to disclose the partial components of the total activity in a given situation. The ordering of events requires the extensive exploration of the entire past of the person, and the provisional interpretation of these relations is continuously subject to revision in the light of the unfolding future.

The application of the analytic pattern to the self devalues the words which have been invested with mandatory significance in the history of the individual. He discerns the situations in which honorific terms like "nation," "justice," "truth" acquired their degree of influence over the verbal and nonverbal procedures by which he concentrates and removes his tensions. The various preferences with which the individual feels himself seized at a given time are not taken as simple mandates, but as points of departure for analysis to disclose various linkages with the total configuration. Preferences are the residues of impulses to act which are left after an analytic procedure, and they are subject to change without notice on further analysis, or further experience with the unfolding future. "Value" is the word we use to indicate that there are some impulses with which we associate our ego symbol at a given time; they are permanent to the degree that repeated analytic procedures yield similar results in developing situations.

The application of the analytic process to the "sacred ego" potentially arouses all of the insecurities of which the personality is capable. All of the external supports of the surrounding environment are devalued by the mere act of being placed in perspective, and the internalized environment (the superego formation) is steadily deprived of its categorical imperatives. The superego structure generates anxieties as the means of preserving its control, and of maintaining resistances against the expression of incompatible impulses. As a means of reducing these insecurities, the person may dash into the manipulation of the personal or material environment, or develop a number of compromise formations involving his own body (symptoms).

The profound effect of the analytic pattern in producing personal insecurity has been obscured thus far in western culture by the prominence of other sources of adjustive stress. The expanding subdivision of the environment has generated all sorts of difficulties, since novelty breeds uncertainty and precipitates conflicts of conscience. The new matrices created by technical innovation offer special foci of attention and new opportunities for the conscious pursuit of what are held to be values. Often the acts necessary to preserve or to extend claims to safety, income, and deference violate the categorical imperatives of the earlier and simpler social order which are implanted during infancy and childhood as the superego. The superego undertakes to preserve its hegemony with characteristic blindness, usually manifesting itself in self-punishing reactions. The new environments not only require new ego adjustments, but often fail to supply external reenforcements of the superego, leaving the conscience without support.

The difficulties which are inevitably connected with adjusting interpersonal relations in new and poorly understood environments are thus complicated by the existence of inner conflicts which generate insecurities. Insecure people are pitted over against one another under circumstances which foster the prompt reactivation of primitive modes of dealing with situations. Those persons who are best able to externalize their aggressions are the ones with the best chances of successful survival; but this externalizing must be done with the techniques best adapted to the situation. If the individual is in the competitive market, this means aggressiveness and skill in bargaining; if the individual is where the competitive market does not exist, this may mean aggressiveness and skill in killing. The requisite combination of assertiveness and technique is achieved by persons who succeed in "immoralizing" themselves insofar as necessary to achieve emancipation from old taboos upon the specific forms of action best adapted to survival in the changing world.

The breakdown of consensus on myth and practice in the western world is the subject of comment and usually of lament by students of culture. The emphasis upon the ego function in personality means that every detail of life is subject to modification in the interest of expediency. Capitalism puts the emphasis upon profitable expediency as the test, but fighting expediency remains particularly prominent in interstate affairs; fighting tests and profits tests are themselves inextricably connected with deference demands which cannot be readily measured by external standards.

Such harmony as exists in modern culture is based upon the expediencies dictated by the current evaluations of the environment and upon the legacies from precapitalistic culture. The competition among the "immoralized" for such tangible and honorific values as they demand has succeeded in maintaining some degree of local consensus. The symbols of nationalism have been potent substitutes for religion in harmonizing behavior within various areas, yet these are now challenged by proletarianism from within and from without.

The clashes of expedients, mores, and countermores, of ego, superego, and id are abundantly manifest in all that has been mentioned about modern culture. The spectacular consequences of the expansion of technology in generating insecurity have too often been stressed to the exclusion of the influence of the analytic pattern of thought. Since few persons can long endure the anxieties coincident to the incessant application of analysis to the "sacred ego," the analytic procedure strengthens activistic tendencies toward the environment. As the analytic process taps ever deeper sources of anxiety, the urge to flee into dogmatism, activism, and collectivism becomes intensified.

Yet the abolition of the analytic pattern is improbable, so deeply is it connected with modern civilization. Even the rejection of free inquiry, of science, of individualism, and the glorification of anti-intellectualism, of faith, of obedience, of leadership, of community cannot prevail against it. As long as we retain our technology, we retain the prototype capable of perpetuating the analytic habit of mind, and incapable of preventing its extension to the internal sequence of subjective events. The only sure and drastic cure would be the annihilation of the material environment which has been created and renewed through the discovery and the rearrangement of the routines of reality.

The partial application of the technique of analysis generates insecurities which may be reduced by the reaffirmation of the prevailing ideology, or by the affirmation of a new utopia. Hence the passivity of contemplation passes quickly to the activism of demands on reality. Those who specialize on contemplation may be sufficiently active to stimulate self-analysis in others, the effect of which is to generate contradictions to contemplation. Listeners or readers may introject, in some slight degree, the pattern of recurring self-scrutiny, but if they have been exposed to a culture which is well supplied with activistic ways of abolishing inner anxiety, the resulting insecurities are presently assuaged by new contacts with the environment.

Such contradictions between a little contemplation and a quick dash into reality were acutely exhibited during the stresses of the postwar years. It is of the utmost importance to distinguish carefully between mere autism and reflective thought. The heightened introspectionism of many personalities who have been deprived of deference or income is wholly autistic: moods run the gamut from despondency to ecstasy, and fantasies scale the heights of grandiosity or plumb the bogs of self-deprecation. Self-analysis involves the use of reflective thought in placing the self in relationship to other events, including the past of the subjective sequence, the physiological sequence, and the interpersonal sequence. Details which are available at the focus of waking attention must be constantly reconsidered in the light of the total context.

Much of the introspectionism of man is aggressively toned, and means that the destructive tendencies formerly externalized with reference to the environment are turned back against the primary self-symbol. The individual may make little progress in the direction of insight, in the contemplation of the self from all points of view, and in the integration of the several components of the reactive system into a serenely functioning totality. When the turning away from reality is neurotic rejection and not self-analysis, the individual may quickly return to revengeful contact with the world by way of the prompt acceptance of some set of readily accessible symbols and practices.

The self-preoccupation of many middle class personalities has had little to do with self-analysis. Introspectionism has often heightened the stresses within the personality system, and favored drastic resolution by way of patriotism or some program of utopianism. In some degree self-analysis as a technique is usually connected with self-attack, and the destructive components of the operation may become so intensified that escape into action seems an imperative alternative to suicide.[29]

Although the initial consequence of the analytic pattern of thought has been to reenforce activism in relation to environment, the final outcome may be passivity. Perhaps the steady application of the analytic pattern to the ego will steadily devalue the importance of the symbols with external reference and value the process of contemplating the symbols with internal reference, instituting in occidental culture the sustained introspectionism which is a distinguishing mark of some oriental cultures. Possibly the approaching phase in the dialectic of the material and the ideological involves renunciation of the material in favor of the ideological, owing to the application to the analysis of the ego of the ordering procedures developed in relation to the environment.[30]

Should the present externalizing of fantasy be reversed, there are no known limits to which the internalization of fantasy may reach. The locating of a given symbol in relation to its context means placing it in the postnatal life sequence, but this need not be the end of the quest. The prenatal history of the person occurred when he was

29. On some aspects of these matters, see the writer's "Psychology of Hitlerism," *Political Quarterly*, July–September, 1933.

30. This may be an alternative to the collapse of civilization owing to the anxieties generated by the growing burden of inhibition, adumbrated by Freud in *Civilization and Its Discontents*, New York, 1930. The depths from which our insecurities rise have but recently been tentatively plumbed in our culture. On the "anxiety problem," see the magistral works of Freud. The lead in applying some results of the study of the neuroses to world politics was taken by Miss C. E. Playne. An interesting appeal to his fellow doctors to cure war by individual treatment is Theodore Huzella, *L'individu dans la vie sociale en temps de paix et en temps de guerre, essai sur la sociologie médicale,* Paris, cir. 1925.

less "individualized" as a member of the species; indeed, he was closer to the prespecies history of biological development and to the prebiological phases of general evolution. The free-fantasy methods of Freud were used by him to render adult events clear in relation to the life sequence, and this, or various auxiliary techniques, may be applied in order to reactivate the earlier prenatal, prespecies, prebiological configurations just referred to.

If the result of the application of the analytic pattern to the ego is ultimately to devalue symbols of external reference, and to absorb the individual in autistic operations, the parallelism with the philosophy and practice of Buddha suggests itself. In a remarkable paper Franz Alexander compared Buddhistic training and psychoanalysis.[31] He observes that both Freud and Buddha emphasize the overcoming of affective resistance and of narcissism in order to facilitate the recollection instead of the repetition of the earlier reactions. But there are profound differences between Freud and Buddha, reflecting the "insurmountable" differences between Indian and European cultures.

Buddhistic absorption goes much deeper in the direction of regression, yet it must pay dearly for this depth. Through this it allows the entire outside world to pass into oblivion, conquers the self, but loses the world thereby. The objective of psychoanalysis is more pretentious, it strives to conquer the self without losing the world.

I see no reason for assuming that this culture contrast is insurmountable. The analytic pattern has been but recently extended to the ego in our civilization, and the early psychoanalysts were constrained to compromise with their earlier cultural conditionings by preserving activism toward the environment. There is no logical place to quit analyzing, nor is there a universal psychological limit to the process.

If our prognosis proves to be correct and a trend toward the internalizing of fantasy through the application of the analytic pattern to the ego develops, it will differ in some respects from Buddhism. The process will not be accompanied by the moralistic and preferential vocabulary of Buddha. It will use the objectivistic language of the West. Psychoanalysis was introduced by a physician in one of the principal centers of culture, who used a language which was

31. "Buddhistic Training as an Artificial Catatonia (or) The Biological Meaning of Psychic Occurrences," *The Psychoanalytic Review*, 13 (1931): 129–145. Originally read at Berlin at the Seventh Congress of the International Psycho-Analytical Association, September 25, 1922, and printed in *Imago*.

at least partially adapted to the scientific verbalisms in which our culture had come to prefer certain kinds of communications to be made. The material brought to the focus of attention during the free fantasy phases will be the object of analytical characterization during the phases of full waking attention.

Since the number of possible compromise formations between activism and passivism is prodigious, the net effect of the psycho-analytic approximation toward the Buddhistic pattern may be to favor the appearance of a provisional synthesis of eastern and western culture elements. The synthesis will not be by way of the ego thinker depicted by Bernard Shaw in *Back to Methuselah;* the thinker must have special technique at his command in order to bring to the focus of attention many of the data which are automatically excluded by the ordinary habits of directed thought.

We have reached a provisional stopping place in the configurative analysis of world politics and personal insecurity. Although the present study has been devoted to clarifying the standpoint rather than urging the validity of specific applications, the search for correct orientation in the continuum which includes the future as well as the past has led to some tentative findings about the social origins, special skills, psychobiological traits, subjective outlooks and distinguishing methods of emerging world élites.

The social origins of the élite which seized and retains power in Russia are non-plutocratic and non-aristocratic. The appearance of the latest pattern of world revolution has intensified the contradictions between the bourgeoisie and other social formations throughout the world, and within the bourgeoisie, between the middle-income groups and the plutocracy; but the principal long-run effect within semi-socialized states will probably be to shift the dialectic of development from the class struggle to the skill struggle.

Skills may be classified according to their connection with the handling of violence, propaganda, goods and services. Dictatorships afford ample scope for the talents of the élites of violence and propaganda. As the governmentalization of economic life abolishes free competition, skill in bargaining diminishes, but in a hierarchized society skill in acquiring privileges within the official hierarchy increases. To some extent this depends upon the verbal skills of the intellectual and semi-intellectual who systematize and popularize the premises alluded to by officials in guiding and justifying their conduct to themselves and others. The quantity of propaganda is not a function of dictatorship or democracy, but of the number of people to be coordinated in action, and of the material and ideological differences among them. If dictatorship is the façade behind which lie profound differences in the processes of production, such diverse material environments will preserve and foster differences in foci of attention and hence in ideology. If democracy is the official pattern of people living in simple material environments, contradictions will be unimportant (as in certain old democratic cantons of Switzerland). Pulsations of disaffection may always be expected to originate among the manual workers, but the contradictions generated in bringing them to effective mass expression are so overwhelming that the main locus of development will swing to the skill struggle, and away from the broader alignments of the class struggle. Intellectuals who ally themselves with medical, engineering, and similar groups will battle with intellectuals who are allied with other skill groups, bearing the brunt of the struggle within the hierarchized, partly socialized state.

Traits vary from élite to élite as a function of the contradictions, which are usually tacit, among personality types. In the long dialectic of history, the struggles among diverse psychobiological types have found expression behind the grand façades of the class struggle, and increasingly of the skill struggle. No doubt the future will witness the sharpening of the issue as the full meaning of what is involved in expressed in rallying symbols, demands, and expectations. The extraversion of personality in the United States and the Soviet Union has led to something like a war of extermination against the introverted types of reaction. The socialization of the child has been thought to require a minimum of private life, and a maximum of direct participation in the immediate activities of the group.

Closely connected with the struggle of personality types, though not coextensive with it, is the struggle between subjective outlooks which glorify either activism or passivism. Where great opportunities have existed for the molding of the environment, and where these opportunities have been vigorously seized, the subjective outlook of the élite has displayed the shallowness usually associated with extreme forms of extraversion. The pursuit of immediate distinction through the manipulation of men and materials suppresses the proclivities toward the self-scrutiny which may breed self-understanding. The introspectionism which appears is usually provoked by immediate rebuffs in reality, and represents rather an effort at self-aggression than at self-orientation. The acute anxieties which attend processes of self-analysis precipitate frantic rushes into reality; hence a little contemplation may breed its immediate contradiction. Our complex material environment is a residue of past externalizations of fantasy. The analytic pattern of thought which has been stereotyped in the process has recently been extended to the ego, eliciting profound cravings for certainty in activity. In the very long run, perhaps, passivism may overcome these immediate contradictions, since the analytic pattern of thought can perpetuate itself and threaten the ego with exposure so long as a complicated material environment endures.

Since changing methods of the élite depend upon the conditions of survival, the present tension between propagandistic and alternative means of power may be expected to inaugurate new departures. Modern technology complicated both the material and the symbolic environments; the cheapness of symbol manipulation, propaganda, prompted the disaffected elements in society to rely upon it to attack the prevailing principles of élite recruitment and élite justification. The threatened élites responded in kind, and the contradictions attributable to different material and symbolic formations were thereby intensified, maximizing insecurity and fostering the resolution of the major stresses by the use of other than propagandistic means of control.

Although dictatorships seek to exercise a monopoly of propaganda, they are constantly threatened by subversive propaganda, since symbol manipulation is elusive and cheap. In self-defense, they engage in the systematic invasion of privacy, searching even for the deviational child, whose propensity for developing a distinctive internal life is viewed with alarm.

Under constant provocation from counterpropaganda and from the diversifying potentialities of the human organism, dictatorships may be expected to retain and even to extend their reliance upon supplements to propaganda. If responses elicited by symbol management are unstable, physiological methods may be employed to add to their durability. The new age of physiology in politics may be expected to amplify the cruder dialectic of missiles and missives with the methods of sterilization and inoculation. Machiavelli, M. D., therefore, will become a more distinctive figure as contradictions sharpen and new knowledge is drawn into the struggle against dissent.

The statements which have been offered about the composition of the élite and their methods have been developed in connection with the application of two supplementary modes of analysis and attitudes of mind to the problem of correct self-orientation in the all-embracing continuum in which we find our unfolding way. Both developmental and equilibrium modes of analysis, and contemplative and manipulative attitudes of approach, are comprehended within the configurative method of political orientation. The provisional findings of the present will be constantly reconsidered in the light of new details about the past, and new emergents through the future.

Special attention has been given to the developmental hypothesis that our present is a transition between the last world revolution and that next one, between the emergence of the proletariat in the name of socialism and the appearance of new constellations formed as the skill struggle supersedes the class struggle. The latest revolution, like preceding world revolutions, has been thus far restricted by processes of geographical and functional differentiation, and by processes of partial incorporation. In some degree the equalizing, centralizing, and parochializing symbols and practices of the Russian pattern have been utilized elsewhere.

Considering all of the tendencies so far mentioned in terms of their localizing or universalizing consequences, the conclusion emerges that a united world remains remote and uncertain, and the unity, once attained by a process now unforeseeable, will be unstable. The most profound source of insecurity in our civilization is nascent in the processes connected with the externalization of fantasy, which has elaborated ever more numerous material differences which complicate the symbolic world as well.

The significance of insecurity levels is also brought out when political changes are conceived in equilibrium terms. Innovations in technology modify the life situation of people, rendering inappropriate many of their previous loyalties to symbols and practices; the resulting insecurities are available for discharge with reference to new symbols and practices. The many foci of attention increase the probability that numerous symbols of identification, demand, and expectation will be in prolonged rivalry with one another. By repeating symbols, intellectuals and semi-intellectuals can "bind" some of the labile energies which are available in a given situation, thus establishing claims to income and deference. Having a vested interest in repetition, they oppose those who offer incompatible symbols. The struggle over symbols abolishes superficial insecurities. Those which are generated by profound cultural and personality contradictions are not disposed of by these partial adaptations, and culminate explosively.

Finally, it may be said that the configurative analysis of the pyramids of safety, income, and deference discloses many processes whose complex interrelationships hinder the clear consummation of any one. The material-material, material-symbolic, symbolic-symbolic, symbolic-material aspects of change are interconnected. The thinker who uses the configurative analysis in order to find simple formulas for the past and future is mainly a propagandist interested in control. The analytic use of the method constantly devalues specific control objectives. The skepticism, pluralism, and passivism of the thinker are opposed to the dogmatism, simplicity, and activism of the propagandist, although there can be productive contacts between them, especially as the thinker clarifies the major probabilities of the future.

The configurative analysis may, however, be used by a thinker who is so organized that he is insistently impelled to associate himself with the attainment of a particular developmental possibility. Like Marx and Engels, he may be constrained to aid in the passage from capitalism to socialism. Or he may discern other dialectical processes in history which operate through longer historical epochs. He may be impressed by the struggle between biopsychic types for safety, income, and deference, and deploy some of his energy in support of representative samples of the types with which he prefers to be associated. He becomes a person capable of some self-determination in identification (affiliation).[32]

Those personalities who have been most sensitive in divining the diverse trends of culture, and exteriorizing them, have been recruited from zones of special insecurity within it. The most activistic symbols of protest were developed by a Jew (Marx) and the procedure most pregnant for the passivistic trends of our civilization was elaborated by a Jew (Freud). They were offspring of the bourgeoisie; they became professional intellectuals who displayed many of the characteristics typical of this social formation. Having dealt with their own insecurities by inventing symbols for the insecure, they rose to eminence as heroes of the insecure.

32. Albert Einstein's attitude toward the world illustrates a complex reaction: "I am a horse for single harness, not cut out for tandem or team work. I have never belonged wholeheartedly to country or state, to my circle of friends, or even to my own family. These ties have always been accompanied by a vague aloofness, and the wish to withdraw into myself increases with the years. . . . My passionate interest in social justice and social responsibility has always stood in curious contrast to a marked lack of desire for direct association with men and women." *The Forum*, October, 1930.

In our civilization the externalization of fantasy has created an environment which re-creates the analytic pattern of thought, which, when applied to the ego, precipitates insecurities usually assuaged by action. But the rearrangement of the environment at an accelerated rate as an escape from insecurity does not bring serenity, and possibly the broader sweep of historical development will pass through the present acute crises of activism to the devaluation of material rearrangements in favor of the internalization of fantasy.

Clearly, insofar as politics is the management of symbols and practices related to the shape and composition of the value patterns of society, politics can assume no static certainty; it can strive for dynamic techniques of navigating the tides of insecurity generated within the nature of man in culture.

INDEX

A

Abbott, Edith, 131*n.*
Abstinence, and middle income skill group, 182
Abundance, crises of, 109
Activism, and passivism as developmental processes, 210
  of youth of middle income skill group, 200
Activity area, defined, 8*n.*
  relation to attention and other areas, 141ff., 147
  and world unity, 93
Adams, Brooks, 93*n.*, 193*n.*
Adjudicating agencies, 139
Adler, Alfred, 78*n.*
Administration, British, 161
  over-rated, 194
  and theocratic attitudes in politics, 173
Adolescence, crises of, in middle income skill group, 200
  disorders of, in America, 175
Affects, displacement of, 30
Agencies, international, and contacts, 137ff.
Aggressiveness, in deprivation and indulgence, 116ff.
  of much introspection, 209
  passive, 78
  projection of, 54
  and provocative behavior, 80
Agitators, in mass movements, 121
Alcoholism, in America, 176
Alexander, Franz, 101*n.*, 211ff.
Aliens, attitudes of and toward, 125ff.
Allport, Floyd, 149*n.*
Almond, Gabriel, 121*n.*
Ambassador, as contact agent, 139
Ambiguity, of future reference sym-

bols, 102
  of terms of reference, 30
Ambivalence, toward other intimidated persons, 78
America (*see* United States)
Analysis, as a pattern of thought influencing insecurity level, 205ff.
  political, 3ff.
  symbols of, in Europe and America, 163
Andrews, Fannie Fern, 130*n.*
Anecdotal technique, in relation to some topics, 113ff.
  in reporting, 152
Angelino, A. de Kat, 184*n.*
Anonymous-one-to-many relationship, 150
Anthropology (*see* Cultural anthropology)
Anti-imperialistic nationalism, 75
Antitheses, in revolutionary situation, 108
Anxiety (*see* Insecurity)
Appeals (see *Symbols*)
Application of impersonal energy to production, a trait of capitalism, 94
Areas, of organization, of activity, of sentiment, of attention, 8*n.*
Aristocracy, characteristic demands, 112ff.
  relation to other classes, 86
  supplanted by bourgeoisie, 3
Armament, measuring of, 44ff.
  stocks, naval publicity and war scares, 66ff., 114
Army and Navy Journal, 68
Assertiveness (see *Aggressiveness*)
Attention (*see* Focus of)
Attention area, 141ff.
  measurement, 142ff.

[219]